THE OTHER CONCERTO

Also by Wendy Bardsley

ADULT POETRY
Amphitheatre
Steel Wings

CHILDREN'S POETRY
The Imaginator

ANTHOLOGIES
An Enduring Flame: The Brontë Story in Poetry and Photographs
Poetry in the Parks: The National Parks of England and Wales
in Poetry and Photographs

NON-FICTION
Introducing Information Technology

THE OTHER CONCERTO

Wendy Louise Bardsley

Smith
Settle

First published in 2002 by
Smith Settle Ltd
Ilkley Road
Otley
West Yorkshire
LS21 3JP

ISBN 1 85825 179 6

Set in Monotype Plantin

Designed, printed and bound by
SMITH SETTLE
Ilkley Road, Otley, West Yorkshire LS21 3JP

ACKNOWLEDGEMENTS

Thanks go to David Bergamini, *The Universe* (Time Inc, 1990), for information on the stars; Arnold Kellett, *Historic Knaresborough* (Smith Settle Ltd, 1991), for a colourful and inspiring tour of old Knaresborough; my friends and family for interest and support throughout the writing of the book; and finally Ken Smith for his cast-iron integrity and trust.

Love is a Many Splendoured Thing, words by Paul Francis, music by Sammy Fain © 1955 EMI Catalogue Partnership, EMI Miller Catalog Inc and EMI United Partnership Ltd, USA. Worldwide print rights controlled by Warner Bros Publications Inc/IMP Ltd. Reproduced by permission of International Music Publications Ltd. All rights reserved.

For AM

THE WATER'S EDGE

Daniel Ennersley watched the river, illuminated now by the floodlights from the great stone railway viaduct. A cloud of glassy insects skidded across its surface, humming strangely, almost like a distant searching music. He rested on the thin bench, stretching out his legs, aching from a ten-mile walk the previous day in the dales. Then he searched his pocket again for the note. He'd found it at his family home in Knaresborough, where he was now staying in North Yorkshire. The note was crisp and new, the paper clean and the writing clear, though it held a date in the left-hand corner that looked like 1812. Was it really as old as that? An astrophysicist, he'd been trying to fix a telescope in the attic roof. The note had fallen down with an old nest.

He stared at the words in the dim light of the walkway lamp: *'Meet me, my love, where the river bends at nine o'clock. You must come with me tonight! Yours forever, L.'* Romantic nonsense, he thought, though a steady and confident hand had written it. To a married woman perhaps? The writing was florid and ornate, and it seemed, full of feeling. Whoever he was, God help him, Daniel thought. Women? Women destroyed you. His thoughts returned for a moment to Bridget. He shrugged them off. He had made a vow to forget her. Bridget was over. She'd gone. Gone with Graham, her husband. Graham, though, would never have written a note like that. It wasn't love that Bridget wanted. She'd always gone on about justice, though Daniel had never quite understood what she meant. Justice was only a word. Most of the time it had little substance.

Anyhow, he had work to do. That would help. He was way behind with his writing. He folded the note and put it back in his pocket. Something made him want to preserve it. He wasn't sure what, but preserve it he would. At least for now.

I

A wind was up. He pulled his jacket closer about him and adjusted his collar. The weather was bitterly cold. He turned his eyes to the house.

The family home was a stone three-storey building, part of it cut from the rock, and high up. From the front it looked down on the woods and the river. The large grounds at the back led on to the high street, though they had few callers. The old place had a strange unearthly quality, as if filled with mystery. Around it cold light bent and twisted, erratic and irregular across the stone, whilst in the grounds, the oaks and yews moaned and whistled, sometimes even in summer.

Daniel Ennersley had travelled widely and at thirty-three was something of a name in the research world with eight outstanding papers and a highly successful book, *Restoring the Stars*, which had resulted in several TV appearances. One of them had included a mob of religious fanatics pelting him with bad eggs and berating him for what they called his 'lack of faith in God'.

'So you think you know what God is, do you?' he'd shouted, wiping the eggs from his face. 'Well, let me in on the secret!' He'd felt like Galileo and Copernicus in times past, persecuted for trying to tell the truth. 'Nothing's changed!' he'd yelled. 'There will always be people like you. You just won't listen!' And a group of reporters had seized on that, quoting him as if he were some patronising bastard who thought that science was the be-all and end-all of everything, treating him like a cold clod of scientific fact. An age of science, they said, had proved wanting. It was time to imagine again. And to feel. Daniel, they said was a man of stone. A man without a soul.

Bridget had been in the crowd that day. Her husband, a professor of physics, and leading the discussion, had apologised to Daniel, for what he called 'an appalling display of brutality'. Bridget had come to him quickly with a wet cloth, cleaning his face, her soft fingers gently touching his eyelids. It had happened immediately. Or so he had thought. Had he thought better, and longer, he'd have seen that Graham Reynolds had been putting up with his wife's affairs for years, and that her voluptuous charm left most men helpless if that was how she would have it.

Bridget had gone to New York, creeping out in the night, calling him first thing in the morning. A brief phone call. She'd gone with Graham. He'd had a promotion. She wanted to see if her marriage might work again. Not that it had worked before, according to her. After a whole year, she'd left him for her husband! Daniel had felt empty and angry. What with her — and the other thing ... he'd needed a change and had come to work for eighteen months in Yorkshire, sharing his time between Leeds and Cambridge universities with occasional visits to Jodrell Bank.

He shook his head and frowned at the night. He felt out of sorts with himself. He always did when he came home. At least until he adjusted. Despite wanting to see his father, he always felt uncomfortable in Knaresborough. They knew too much about him. He shrugged his shoulders. The scent of the attic clung to his leather jacket. A scent of the past. He could almost taste it. Being in there today was like going into another life. The life of his childhood. The musty room held few of his belongings now, but the ghosts of childhood lingered.

Elizabeth Ennersley, his mother, had been dead for twenty years. She annotated all she read and a sharp flood of tenderness had entered him as he saw again her handwriting in her books, and recalled the careful finesse with which she had done things. She had liked to paint in watercolours. After her death, Aunt Rachel, his father's sister, had taken most of her paintings to Wales thinking his father would probably sell up. Others were kept in a drawer in his father's bedroom or hung in the hall and lounge.

Reginald Ennersley was a general practitioner in Knaresborough, and at fifty-eight had aged prematurely. He hadn't sold the house. In fact he hadn't made any decisions at all. Once he was tall and strong. Now he seemed like a thin grey light finding its way through the Knaresborough streets on his day and night-time visits. Elizabeth Ennersley had died at just thirty-four years of age. She had even seemed healthy and energetic, he'd said, and it wasn't fair. Rheumatic fever, contracted in childhood, had at last caught up with her and a faulty heart valve had let her down one winter.

Reading her writing, Daniel had felt the wrench as he did as a boy, armouring himself with steel. He'd felt the loneliness of the boarding school, recalling how he could never settle and was always involved in fights. 'A boy of few words', his father had said. 'He tells you nothing.' But words were always thundering about in his head, sometimes they came too quickly. He was often confused and developed a reputation for being difficult. He supposed he was. Sometimes he wished he could be at peace with the world like the creatures down in the woods, or the stars so far away and free from anxiety. When young, his father had been dark like himself, but now his hair was white and thin. And whilst Daniel's features were square, his father's were thin and aquiline. His mother had been tall and fair and slender.

He gazed at the water before him. In the attic he'd felt his mother's presence. It hadn't happened like that before and the feeling had unnerved him. It wasn't a feeling he liked or knew how to deal with. When his father spoke of her night-time visits, Daniel had thought it a kind of coping. Now as his eyes searched out the yellow lights of the house he feared for the man's health. Nowadays his father scarcely ate or slept, and would often wander the house murmuring strangely.

He recalled how it was when his mother had died. How his father would sit staring at space, sometimes falling asleep in the chair, whilst he too fell asleep on the hearth rug, neither of them knowing a thing till the light crept in through the windows and the birds began their morning songs. Accompanying him on visits, he'd been amazed at how he could work. He talked calmly to people, acted a part, as if madness might be saved up for another time. Returning home, he went straight to his chair again and stared at space as before. It seemed it would never end. And it never had.

The lean shadow of the tall library reached to him over the water. Along this stretch the river curved. Was this where the lovers had met all that time ago? It was interesting to speculate. What had happened here, in this place? He hadn't meant

4

to come to the river tonight, and wasn't sure what had brought him. Leaving his father reading the newspaper, he'd made his way down the stone steps, passing a tiny waterway that gushed through a thin break in the rocks. Then he'd strolled along till he'd found the bench. He looked about, breathing in the evening scents, then glanced at his watch. It was eight-thirty.

A current of cool air swept across the water bringing a fast breeze whilst a thin grey mist cloaked the trees. Just then a couple approached arm in arm. The woman was tall with long dark hair, and turned while passing, meeting his eyes and smiling. The smile was knowing and meaningful. He did not think he knew her. A warm surge of feeling flooded him quickly. He did not want it. He did not want to be bothered with women. Not now. Not ever again. He bent his head, annoyed because he had looked at her and had found her attractive. The trouble with love, he told himself, was its animal strength. It seemed to have a relentless desire to devour you. A boy zipped by on a bicycle, ringing his bell. Within minutes the path was silent again. He watched the stars for a while, thinking. He was quite unprepared for what happened next.

From several yards away he heard a light limp slapping sound, like the sound of a fish hitting the river bank. It came again. And again. Locating it, he saw a blue mist gathering over the water, moving towards the edge. Curiously he waited for something to emerge from the reeds. Perhaps a river creature or bird.

Instead, to his amazement, two white hands lifted themselves through the skin of the river, gradually becoming arms, dripping with leaves and fronds. Next came a head, matted with long black hair, half covering the white face of a young woman. His ears were pounding with blood. His skin tingled. His hands perspired. He watched in disbelief as she took hold of the bank, her skin translucent in the moonlight, her mouth purple, her eyes half-closed. Lifting herself from the water and clothed in only a fine silk undergarment, she shuddered. The veins of her hands bulged with effort. She threw back her

5

head and opened her mouth as if going to speak. But nothing came. Her mouth dripped river weed and water. She stood for a moment perfectly still before him, gradually opening her eyes; dark black gems searing with pain that looked through and beyond him. Lifting a thin white arm, she pointed to the old library at the other side of the river, parting her lips. But all that came was the sound of a rippling sigh.

He rose shakily and moved towards her. Her wetness, the solid dead weight of her, thrilled him. This is a ghost! he thought. I am face to face with a ghost! He tried to pinch his hands, to rub them together. They would not do as he wanted. He was in a dream yet not in a dream. Where was his mind?

She pointed to the library again. A thin four-storey building, towering above the water. She gulped, trying to breathe the cold night air, slipping away with each attempt. Afraid she would vanish completely, taking with her some wonderful other-worldly experience, his and his alone, he called out: 'Please! Whoever you are, don't go!' though he heard nothing.

Finding himself at the water's edge, he drew back quickly. Already the woman was sinking into the folds of the river, her waist, her head, submerging.

Soon she had gone, and he stood on the bank for a while before turning back to the bench, where he sat trying to calm himself and order his thoughts. Just then he heard the sound of footsteps. The girl who had passed him earlier was coming back. This time alone.

LYDIA

The girl came up beside him, her hands deep in the pockets of her long black coat. She seemed to have hurried. He felt embarrassed, sitting there in the darkness. He didn't know what to say. He was still dazed after what he'd seen, wondering if he had dreamt it, though he knew he hadn't. The water before him seemed perfectly normal now. Might she too have seen the ghost? He turned to her slowly, bewildered.

'Hello', he said, trying to smile. He felt as if he was coming out of a long deep sleep. He rubbed his face. 'I'm feeling rather strange. You'll have to excuse me.'

His voice seemed loud. He was talking quickly. She stood in the dark by the light of the lamp looking at him in a perfectly calm manner. He wished he could feel as calm himself. He looked at her, trying to read her face, hoping she did not see how shaken he was.

She stood quietly. A half-smile played on her lips, though her eyes were serious. They glistened, moving quickly with concern. She still didn't speak. The river was still, the sky a deep and almost purple blue. A colour he hadn't seen before. A very unusual light. It dazzled him slightly.

'I saw you, from up there', she said, her voice strong and melodious. 'You seemed to be swaying. You were right at the edge of the water.'

'Swaying?' he said, rubbing his forehead. Had he been swaying? He probably had. He felt as if he must draw his voice from his throat, find his speech again, his thoughts, his feelings. It was almost as if he'd been in another place for a while, though he could not say how long. Wherever he'd been, it was somewhere outside of time. It was separate from anything else he'd ever known or felt. And yes, whilst it aroused him, it also alarmed him. How could he ever begin to understand it. He didn't think he could even find words to discuss it.

'I heard a sound at the water's edge', he said. 'I went to look. I've a bit of a headache ...' His body tingled, right to the tips of his fingers. Even now he doubted what he had seen. He doubted his own senses. The last leaves twittered like small birds in the trees about them.

'I usually keep something for headaches', she said thoughtfully, rummaging in a shoulder bag. She sat down beside him, searching it and tipping things on to the bench. She found a packet of tablets. 'Here, Paracetamol. Are you alright with that?' She burst two tablets through the wrap and handed them over. He put them on to his tongue and tried to swallow. He didn't have a headache at all, but they wouldn't do any harm. He would certainly have one later. 'Thanks', he murmured. 'I suppose I'm tired.' He blinked hard and looked at her. The tablets were bitter as they went down his throat. Nothing seemed real. Who could she be? Why was she here, sitting with him on the bench and offering him tablets for headaches he didn't have? Anyway, they would probably steady his nerves.

'It's a gorgeous evening', she said. Her skin shone in the moonlight. Her voice trembled a little. 'Chilly though.'

'Did I alarm you?' he asked, vaguely. 'I mean, behaving like that?' He rubbed his mouth with the palm of his hand. His lips felt cold. His tongue was tingling from what was left of the tablets.

'Yes, you did a bit', she said thoughtfully. 'The river is cold at night. I hardly wanted to rescue you. But I wouldn't have let you die.'

'Well, that's a relief', he said, sighing. What an odd conversation it was. He gazed at the water. At where he had seen the woman. The ghost. She had risen from there. Right there. He had seen her with his own eyes. A young woman's ghost, trying to make an appeal. What did she want? His knowledge of ghosts was scanty. He would never have thought to investigate them. He hadn't believed that ghosts existed before. The girl was silent. Almost familiar. Like someone he'd known for ages. She looked about her as if searching for something.

8

'I'm doing some writing', she said at last. 'Well, trying ...'

'Are you? Good', he said abstractedly. He didn't want to start up a conversation. His mind was whirling. He didn't think he'd make sense.

'I'm sorry', she said. 'I can see you're thinking.'

'Can you?' he laughed. 'Well, that's true. I'm up to my eyes in thinking.' He rubbed his face. 'Not that you'd want to know ...'

'I sit here sometimes, myself', she said, changing the subject. 'I bring my reading, or whatever it is I'm doing.'

'It's a strange place here by the library', he said. 'It's sort of hidden. The rocks and trees make a kind of canopy, don't they.' The rockface loomed above them huge and dark. The large trees swayed in the wind. 'Not that I've been here much. Well, not lately. I've been away.' He thought her brave to have come to him in the dark. The path by the river was lonely. Now it seemed it was also haunted. 'Is there something you've lost?' He saw she was glancing about.

'It's only a scarf. I bought it in Paris. I liked it though. We were sitting here earlier. It had been in my hand.'

'Better to look in daylight', he murmured, his eyes searching the bushes.

'Probably', she said. 'I expect its blown off. I'd like to find it though.'

He sniffed and breathed in deeply. He was warming up. She looked about five feet eight. Younger than him. Late twenties perhaps. Her features had a sculptured look that in the lamplight seemed almost polished. She went to a holly bush nearby, determined.

'Can I help you?' he called out, standing. He looked beneath the bench, running his hand over the gravel. So she'd sat here before then ... With the man she'd passed with earlier. Who could he be? Where had he gone? And why had he let her walk the river alone? Had the two of them stayed any longer, it might have been them who had witnessed the ghost instead. He wondered what this gently spoken girl would have thought of such a happening. The wind came in gusts along the path. Hordes of tiny pebbles scuttled into the river.

'No luck?' he said, seeing her searching the branches. He went to her and pulled back the boughs. 'There it is!' he said. Something was waving near the trunk. Something light and delicate. 'I think I can get it.'

She drew the foliage further back, their bodies touching in the small space. The moonlight shone on the silk. 'I hope I don't tear it', he laughed. 'Seeing it's such a treasure.'

'Watch your hands', she urged. 'The holly leaves are very sharp in November.'

He moved forward, venturing into the depths of the dark tree. 'Quite a battle!' he called. Drawing it out, the scarf appeared purple, though scarlet in the lamplight. Their fingers touched as he passed it over.

She examined it, then tied it in a loose knot round her neck. 'The thorns are like lances just now', she told him softly. 'I hope you weren't hurt.'

'They were quite ferocious', he said, smiling at her as she secured it. It was good she valued things. He liked it. 'I think I will fight another day', he said, rubbing his hands together. 'And will you be happy now?'

'So much fuss', she said, looking embarrassed. 'What must you think of me.'

He threw out his hands. 'If the scarf's important, then that's what matters. Simple as that. I mean, in the end, everything is relative isn't it.' The wind wailed in the trees. 'Anyway', he said. 'Holly for remembrance, eh?'

She searched his face. 'Yes, why not.'

His mind was in turmoil. He rubbed his forehead, gazing into the sky. Above the dark woods, black clouds rose behind the trees, striking the tops with a pink and violet light. The sound of the water swelling and splashing against the bank seemed quite benign. It was hard to believe what had happened earlier.

'I love it here', she said wistfully. 'Sometimes, in spring or summer, I swim.'

'What — in there?' He looked at the black water. The thought of the ghost chilled him. Then he thought of her. His eyes surveyed her quickly. He thought of her naked. He looked away. 'You swim in there? I can't say I've done it myself.'

'Oh, yes', she sighed. 'Whenever the weather's warm, I swim. That's when I'm here, of course.'

'So you live away?'

'This is where I was born', she said quietly. 'My mother lives in one of the cottages there.' She pointed. Just then it was hidden by trees and darkness. 'I'm living in Alderley Edge at the moment. I'm staying with mum for a while to do some work. She lives in the second house on Anderson Terrace.' She offered her hand. 'Lydia Ralphson — hi.'

Her hand was warm and soft. 'Daniel Ennersley', he said, lost to her now. So quickly lost.

'I think I know you', she said, searching his eyes.

He drew away, turning his head. Damn it! What did she know? 'Do you?' he laughed. 'Well, there's more folks knows Tom Fool ...' He wiped his face with his handkerchief. He was still perspiring. The ghost of the woman would not leave his mind. He wanted to think. To sit and let it register. He fixed his eyes on the water, watching the shadows. The girl gazed at the houses behind.

'Isn't that where you live?' she said. 'At Cliff House?' The night air settled, a thin film on her skin. It shone, flickering with light.

'I did', he said, confusedly, and wondering how she knew him. He could not recall her at all. He did not think he would ever have forgotten her face. 'I'm back from time to time. My father lives on his own. He's not so well. You will probably know him. Dad is a doctor round here.'

'Yes', she said. 'I do.'

He nodded slowly. Most people knew his father. He'd always worked in Knaresborough and was widely respected. Around them the air gave up its rich damp autumn scent, the cold of winter brooding in its cells, while the floodlights at the foot of the railway viaduct illuminated the huge grey stone, so that it too gleamed and quivered, holding its own with the cliffs.

'You seem to be worried', she said, returning her hands to her pockets. The air was cold.

He rubbed his face again, trying to wake himself up, drawing the clean night air into his lungs. His voice came deep and determined. He gazed at his palms. 'No, I'm fine. Really I am. I'm fine.' He had to be. He could never have said what he'd seen. She wouldn't believe him. He could scarcely believe it himself.

She sat quietly beside him, her legs crossed loosely, displaying a shapely calf inside a black ankle boot, small buckles on each side of the leather. They flashed in the moonlight. He brushed dead leaves and sticks from his corduroy trousers. She laughed. 'See how you've suffered.'

He thought of the man she'd been with earlier. Was the scarf a gift from him? A pulse of envy went through him. Looking down he saw that his hand was grazed. It was bleeding fast though it did not hurt.

She turned to him, watching as he rested his fingers against the wound. 'Let me help you', she said, going into her bag again and bringing out some tissues. He held one against the wound till the bleeding stopped.

'Look at the stones on the ground', she said. Beneath their feet, the floor glittered and shone like a mini universe. 'They look like stars.'

'I suppose they do', he said. His tone held a trace of amusement. 'Yes, you're right.'

They were silent a while.

'That's what I do, you know', he told her.

She crunched the gravel beneath the heel of her boot. 'What?' she asked.

'I watch the stars', he said. The blood seeped out through the tissue. He sighed tiredly. 'It's what I do for a living. I work as an astrophysicist. I've just come up from London. I'm working at Leeds University now and Cambridge. Now and then I'm at Jodrell Bank.'

'How long are you going to be here?' she asked. Her tone was urgent. It seemed to matter.

'Eighteen months, I should think', he told her. 'I'm writing up some work with a colleague. We've a paper to finish.'

'Your first?'

'My ninth', he laughed, shaking his head. 'Some of my work was done in Australia. The rest in London. I'm a bit of a workaholic. It's quite a scandal, really. They pay me for what

I'd do for nothing.' He was lucky, he knew. He loved his work.

'So you're quite a wizard at maths I expect', she said. 'Never my favourite subject.'

He didn't tell her his arms were covered in numbers, even then as they spoke. He always made notes on his arms. He'd done it from being a student. Sometimes his thoughts moved in so fast, if he didn't catch them he'd lose them. If his notepad wasn't handy, an arm would do. He was shaking slightly, searching still for his centre. 'And you?' he asked, raising his eyes.

She clasped her hands in her lap. The wind moaned high on the cliffs. Her voice was low. 'I'm researching castles. I'm trying to write a book.'

'Sounds great', he said, summoning up his strength. He felt strangely tired. Castles? He didn't know much about castles himself. 'I suppose you'll be looking at ours. I was often there as a boy.' He glanced up, at the old castle ruins, silhouetted against the sky, dark it seemed with solemn knowledge. Something stirred at the edge of the water. A little creature, thin and black, slid out from the reeds, making its way to somewhere else.

'There's plenty of folklore about', he said, playfully. 'Prisoners screaming from dungeons. Ghosts walking ...' He stopped at that. He would have to reformat his thinking. Ghosts did walk. Oh yes, they did.

'I can't stand dungeons', she said, hatefully. 'To think you can still see what the prisoners wrote on those walls. Imagine what it was like, waiting to die in there, scratching out an identity in that cold hard stone. How could they put a human being in there?' She was vehement.

He watched her, thoughtfully. 'Oh, I don't know', he drawled. 'Depends what they'd done.' His throat was dry, and he wasn't sure what he was saying. By way of changing the subject he pointed across the river: 'Have you been in the library there?'

'Of course', she said, throwing her hair behind her shoulders. He liked her manner. He liked her voice. He liked her a lot. 'Rosie, my brother's friend, takes care of it', she said. 'She's not really trained to look after a library. She does her best though. People say she's improved it since she's taken over. I can't say I'm in there much.' They were silent a while. 'I've a problem with inertia, you know', she sighed.

'Have you?' he said. He'd a problem with inertia himself at the moment. He had other problems too. His work. His father ...

'You know how it is', she continued. 'I just can't seem to get going. I will though. I will.' She nodded for certainty.

The old library was on the first floor of the tall building. The other floors were all blocked off. The librarian before, he remembered, had been an elderly lady who looked and moved like a cat. She had gone to Bristol now, his father said. A fiery young redhead had taken over. That was probably Rosie. She was building up a nice collection of music, he'd said. Apparently she'd thrown out a lot of books. His father had rescued some excellent ones from the bins.

'And so you know me', he said slowly. The thought bothered him. He frowned nervously.

Her mood was pensive. 'I never forgot you', she told him.

He laughed. 'That sounds ominous.' He felt embarrassed and anxious. 'What did I do?'

She spoke softly and told him how it had been. How she had been just eight years old, standing by the door of her mother's house in Anderson Terrace. How her mother had run from the house to his father's car, worried and fearful, talking quickly. Lydia's sick aunt, her mother's sister, upstairs in the bedroom, was dying. All around the weight of her illness had crowded the space. 'You must call me whenever you want', the doctor had said from his car. 'It won't be easy. A couple of days, I think. But call me whenever you like.' Her aunt had died that night.

'I saw a boy ...' she said, telling the story slowly and carefully, as if long overdue. Her voice was full of emotion. '... a boy with large dark eyes, in the back seat. A lonely boy. So very lonely ...' She turned to him, searching his face, and with quick intuition whispered, 'You didn't seem very happy.'

He glanced at her then away quickly. She frowned, knowing instinctively she had touched his soul. 'No', he said quietly. 'I wasn't.' They were silent a while. He spoke again. 'We had been bereaved. My mother had died just then. A terrible blow for dad and me. He found it hard to visit those who were dying. It always reminded him.'

Suddenly the outline of a heron crossed the sky before them. 'Look at that!' he cried. 'A heron crossing the moon!' From far away an angry shout came through the darkness. The bark of a dog. Laughter.

'Yes', he said, returning to what they were saying. 'A terrible time for us. And you too, obviously. I went to live with dad's sister in Wales for a while. Then there was boarding school again. Bloody awful it was. I'd sooner have any dungeon. I was always glad of the holidays.' They were silent again. 'Aunt Rachel's been great with dad', he sighed. 'He won't stop grieving. I wish he would, but he won't. He's draining away.'

She bit her lip anxiously. 'We always let the past torment us. We try not to, but we always do.'

Her body close disturbed him. He had reached out to her so easily, so naturally, he'd left her no reserve. A fish leapt up in the middle of the river. A sudden smack of skin. Silence. Church bells pealed across the trees.

'I'd better go', she said. 'They'll be wondering where I've got to.'

'Who will?' he asked, with strange authority.

'My mother and my brother. I said I wouldn't be long. That was ages ago. They'll think I'm lost.'

'The man ...' he said suddenly. 'The one you passed with earlier ...'

'James?' she said, tying a second knot into her scarf. She smiled, holding his gaze.

'James', he repeated slowly. 'I see.' He pressed his lips together. He'd ruined everything now. But the man might be a cousin. A friend. He wanted her to tell him more. He looked away and waited. The lights at the back of them in the small cottages flicked off one by one. Apart from the light of the lamp, the path was almost in darkness.

'James is my boyfriend', she said. The sentence as it left her throat was without life. He knocked it about in the air. 'You don't seem very pleased. Have you been with James for long?'

She threw out her hands. 'Ages.' The word seemed imprisoned, struggling, as if it might transform itself into something tangible, something that might escape. 'Yes, a long time ...'

He had taken a walk in the Tate that week. For a moment he thought her face like Leighton's *Leider ohne Worte*, overcome with sadness and longing, listening to the musical splash of the fountain and the song bird over her head. In seconds he thought of Rodin's marble, *The Kiss*, the lovers entwined in a passionate embrace.

She had been with James, she said, for six years. The time had dragged out harrowingly. They had bought a house in Alderley Edge. James was a singer and pianist at the Royal Northern College of Music in Manchester. He'd taken her to her mother's that night, then left for a tour. He'd be gone for several days. He was always away. Now she went away herself. They rarely spent time together. She spoke wearily.

Just then a youth of about seventeen came running towards them. He stopped, panting breathlessly. Tall and strongly built, with a wiry muscular frame, he wore blue jeans and a black T-shirt, standing flexing his nervous arms, the left of which displayed a fearsome cobra along its length. His hair was blonde and closely cropped. A gold dagger hung from his right ear, glinting in the night light. 'I came to find you', he panted. 'We didn't know where you were.' His voice was deep and sharp. It echoed around the rocks.

'This is my brother, Jeremy', she said. Standing and smiling she introduced them. 'Daniel got my scarf from the tree.' She stretched out her hand to him and he held it firmly. 'Perhaps I shall see you again, Lydia', he said softly.

'I hope so', she answered. 'I really hope so.' They went off into the darkness, climbing the path, leaving him on his own again by the water.

MYTHOLOGY

Lydia stepped from the shower and reached for a towel. She could hear her mother in the kitchen beneath walking about with quick determined movements, her shoes clicking across the stone tiles. Joking, because they were always eating take-aways from the Chinese restaurant on the high street, Jeremy had wound her up. Now he had set her off delivering wonderful wholesome food to the table all week and complaining if he wasn't there to eat it. What an ordeal! Jeremy would much rather eat at the boathouse with Rosie and come and go as he liked. He sat in the kitchen annexe now, brooding. It was only because he'd moaned about the price of two King Prawn Chow Mein. They'd gone up fifty pence. But he'd wound his mother up, and now he would have to wait until she wound herself down. Putting on her housecoat, Lydia went for her hair dryer in the lounge.

'I used to do all the cooking, once', her mother called, as if apologising. Apologies, apologies, thought Lydia frustratedly. Her mother apologised to people who came to the door if she didn't want their pegs and sponges. She apologised to people on the phone who tried to sell her things she did not need. Now, she banged about with her rolling pin. She hadn't made pastry for years. Why, Lydia thought, is she making pastry? The pies on the high street in Knaresborough were the best in the world.

'I even took a course in cake decoration once', she said nostalgically as Lydia came through to the kitchen. 'Roses. Trellis. You name it, I did it. I'd such a steady hand in those days.' In one clean sweep she lifted the pastry and filled a pie dish, cutting the edges with easy and confident skill. Lydia shook her head.

'Come on, mum', she said, putting an arm round her shoulder. 'Surely you don't think Jem was being serious? It was only a joke. Fifty pence means nothing to him. He wanted to pay for the meal. He wasn't getting at you. Anyway, you know he wasn't. You're trying to make a point, and quite honestly, you don't need to.' Lydia's face puckered with irritation. Jeremy didn't eat apple pies these days, he was mainly into savouries, and she was going away. A silence gathered about them. Lydia sat down, cupping her chin in her hands, her wet hair trailing about her. 'Where's that book?' she asked glancing about.

Eliza looked up, her eyes brightening. The very definite shades of anger subsided.

'You mean the one about Kendleton?'

Lydia nodded.

'Let me finish this work, and then I'll show you.' She filled the pie with chopped apples then rolled another sheet of pastry, putting it on the top and cutting the edges quickly. She called out over her shoulder, 'I think you'll like it!'

'Your pies are marvellous, mum,' Lydia called back from the lounge where she'd gone to find the hair-dryer.

'I mean the Kendleton Manor book!' her mother replied firmly. 'Not my pies!' Now she was getting serious. 'The photos are quite amazing. The photographer has been so clever.'

'He wouldn't need to be very clever really', said Lydia. 'Kendleton's a magical place. You could take a photo anywhere, it would always be dazzling.'

'A change for me, this is Lydia', her mother said proudly, coming through to her. 'I've not been involved with a book before.'

'It's what you ought to be doing, mum. Interesting and exciting work. It makes you feel good.' Lydia found the dryer and plugged it in.

'It certainly does', her mother said, her voice rising. The hair-dryer started to whir. Eliza went through. 'I have to be there by two', she said, reading the time on the clock. 'A party is coming from Kent. I'm showing them round.' Most of the time she worked in the restaurant. Lately though, she'd become a guide.

Eliza Ralphson was a handsome and decisive woman. Or that's what she liked to think. Her hair was short and bleached, and she normally put on lots of make-up, doing her eyes in a Cleopatra image with heavy mascara and long strokes of black eye-liner. It made her look cat-like and menacing. A kind of madness took itself out on her looks. It did not enter her being. Sometimes Lydia thought her mother's face was so heavily painted you couldn't see her features. Perhaps it was what she wanted, Lydia decided. Perhaps she was hiding.

And Eliza was single-minded too. She thought. She'd always been single-minded. She boasted it often. But being single-minded, of course, wasn't always right. If something got fixed in her head, then it might be her downfall. Any decision she made was a blinding ray of sunshine, everything else in the shade. And should the decision be wrong, then that was that. She could not change her mind. She sat down on an easy chair and adjusted a tiny animal slide in her hair. Lydia was reading the Kendleton book by the fire. 'Your father's home for Christmas', her mother said softly.

Lydia turned the page. 'I'm off soon, mum', she said. 'I was looking at this. It's most impressive.'

'I expect he'll be much the same', her mother murmured.

Lydia yawned. So her father was back for Christmas. So what? Nowadays they rarely knew where he was. Sometimes they'd get a postcard, a few carelessly scribbled words rushed out in a pub, thrown into the nearest postbox. Her mother would scan the postmark urgently as if she were sifting for gold. And it did not matter at all how long he'd been gone. He could always come back. Once he had brought a woman, much younger than Eliza, with short dark spiky hair and clay fruit dangling from her ear lobes. 'A harvest festival', Jeremy had said, and had gone about singing *Come Ye Thankful People Come* all the next day, angry that his mother could put up with it.

But their mother preferred to close her eyes to things she did not like. It was easier. And anyway, the woman was 'very pleasant' she said, 'so quiet and pretty.' Being pretty and keeping quiet, Jeremy said, was all his father could manage. Real folk jarred on his nerves. 'He has to be in control',

Jeremy said, pursing his lips in the defiant way he always did when he talked of his father. The 'friendship', as Ian Ralphson called it, went on for two years, then petered out. He quickly wearied of all his women. Few were as tolerant as Eliza. And no doubt the women found things to say that he did not like. Which wasn't hard, since the only voice he wanted to hear was his own. But Eliza ignored all that. She loved him. It was one of her decisions.

But Lydia suspected her mother had made the decision in more difficult times, when it wasn't possible to make a decision at all. Putting up with his tyranny was all she could do when the children were small. She had made the best of things. She'd coped. Ian Ralphson wanted things his own way, or all hell was let loose. And Eliza was terrified of hell. Lydia knew her mother would always make her father welcome whatever he did. Though they'd certainly fight. Not because her mother did anything wrong. But because it was impossible for her to do anything right. Inevitably, after each visit she had a black eye, Lydia and Jeremy sworn to secrecy, having to tell lies at school, and knowing all the while that people knew. It was an old, old story. One that made Lydia sick at heart. Yesterday she'd seen a postcard on the mantelpiece in her father's handwriting. She hadn't read it, but she knew what it said. He was coming home. And hell would have its way. But her mother would manage. She always did. She would cope. She'd learned it from her mother. From her grandmother. It was an art: The sick sad art of suffering. Lydia hated it.

She gazed from the window. Great icicles hung from the railway viaduct, gleaming and flashing colours so that it looked like a portal to Atlantis. Over the years her mother had changed. It was hard to remember now how she'd been before. Before the trying stopped. When Lydia was small, the rooms sang with her tender and hopeful songs: '*Love is a many splendoured thing. It's the April rose, that only grows in the early spring. Love is nature's way of giving, a reason to be living. The golden crown, that makes a man a king ...*' And her voice had swelled on that last note, reaching Lydia wherever she was in the house. Oh yes, her father was a king alright and the house was his castle. The trouble was, her mother was no queen. She was a servant. His servant. Ian Ralphson could never have taken a queen. But in make-believe she pretended it, which is why she worked at Kendleton. Lydia knew how her mother felt wandering those luxurious rooms.

Lydia had gone to university to study history. Studying history, she'd told herself, helped you get the present in perspective. But she knew deep down that knowledge like that was merely academic. When it came to real living, human beings functioned in ridiculous and self-defeating ways, drawing little from their honest understanding of the world. Emotions were the power behind the wheel. And fear was the greatest of all. Only by conquering fear did you find real love and happiness. And Lydia knew her mother was weak. She suspected she was also weak herself.

But Eliza hadn't always been weak. Lydia remembered how strong her mother had been in the old days. Then she had fought for her rights. Trifling little jostles. Or so she thought, until she received her first black eye. The mirror doesn't lie, and Eliza hadn't enquired of it for days, going around the house silently, Lydia and Jeremy spending most of the time at the homes of friends and coming back late in the evening.

And on it went. And on. Until their father had broken her down and there was no fight left in her. No more laughter. No more song. That was when she'd dyed her hair, and started to paint her face. At first, Lydia had thought of it as a kind of rebellion. Seeing her hair change from a soft brown to a stark canary yellow, Jeremy, just six years old, had climbed on her lap, sitting there for some fifteen minutes, his eyes tightly closed and still as stone. That day Lydia had been angrier than ever. And the anger had stayed, smouldering inside her, sometimes it seemed, burning her up. She could never have spoken of it to her mother. There was little freedom to talk. A bridge had spread between them that only certain words dared cross.

Eliza Ralphson had stopped listening to people ages ago, while in her stare a creature grew. It was Ian Ralphson's creature. Sometimes Lydia tried to catch it with her eyes. But it was fast away. Her mother was staring now at her father's postcard.

Lydia put down the Kendleton book. She would look at it later. She went upstairs to dress, and to check her things. She was going to France that day and felt uneasy.

Sitting quietly a moment on her bed, she gazed at the photographs on the dressing table. One of the pictures showed her father, tall and strong, his black hair shining with Brylcreem. He was laughing, her there beside him, small, in the grounds of Knareborough Castle, in the very spot, her mother said, where her grandmother had stood as a Girl Guide, years before, singing community songs for Warship Week. On the wall was a framed picture of Mother Shipton, Knaresborough's witch, brandishing her broomstick and sweeping Hitler off the top of the world, a crescent moon behind. And Lydia could hear, as if it were now, her mother's voice, urgent and strong, and strangely young, long since gone, left now in the castle ruins. She felt her father's arms swooping down, lifting her on to his shoulders and hurrying down the hillside, her mother laughing: 'Stop! Stop! You'll fall!'

In those days there had been no Jeremy. The birth of a son had brought about a change in her father. He'd wanted a boy, he said. He'd said it often. That was alright. At least in theory. He'd always wanted a boy. But when the boy came he'd scarcely noticed him. His loving was all and only in imagination, and as his imagination changed, his family became a burden, a rope, he said, around his neck. Sometimes he'd thrashed Jeremy for no more than dirty hands. And once he'd locked him in his bedroom for a whole day, refusing him food because he'd broken one of his toys. Lydia believed Jeremy had broken the toy on purpose. And weeks later, as they'd fished in the River Nidd, he told her so, saying he didn't care. He despised his father. He had no choice. Ian Ralphson would not let him love him. It was too invasive of his private space.

And Eliza had taken Jeremy all to herself, trying to be both father and mother. But Jeremy made her see the truth, saying things she would rather not hear. Things that made her call for Lydia to shut him up. That was when 'The wretch' came. Lydia had seen it growing in her mother's eyes. A dark shadow tiring her out.

And the departures started then, Ian Ralphson slamming the door of the cottage. At first taking his things, then bringing them back. Then going again. And returning. Until it became a way of life.

Jeremy hadn't seen much of his father as he was growing up. There were postcards. Maybe one a month at first. An odd letter. A phone call. And yet his spirit had grown strong. He was kinder than his father. More thoughtful. And he could be relied on when it came to things of the heart. But he made his own rules, changing them as he wanted, causing problems at school, and wherever he went. Though it seemed since he had left school he was better. He'd quietened down. His job at the boathouse gave him pleasure and identity.

The front door closed with a bang. Lydia looked out of the window. Jeremy was going to work. Sometimes he worked as waiter. Sometimes he painted the boats or gave rides. Once he had done a rescue. A little girl had fallen into 'The Styx', a place where the water coiled by the old library and the light stretched madly between the trees in uncanny lines. 'A dark infernal region', Richard the proprietor said, 'where tortured souls twisted and turned in the water.'

Watching him now as he went down the road, pulling on his jacket, Lydia recalled how she'd gone to watch that day, an anxious crowd on the bank, the child's clothes filling up with water. Jeremy had flung himself in, bringing the little girl out on his arm. The day of the summer solstice, some said that Cerberus, 'the three-headed guardian of death's dark portal', was seen that day, stalking the banks. All that could enchant the fiend was music. Some days the river boats filled with musicians, the river loud as an orchestra.

After brushing her hair, Lydia slipped into a white silk bra and panties, then pulled on a woollen dress, examining herself in the mirror. She had firm round breasts and a small waist, and looked good in dresses. She checked her suitcase, then typed some notes into her laptop. She'd rather not set off for France today. But she needed some information for her bibliography. She hadn't been able to get it from the internet or the libraries. She would have to go to Paris. Where was Daniel Ennersley now? What was he doing?

She took the scarf from where it hung on her mirror. Not a single snag. Running it through her fingers she found blood in one of the corners. Two small drops of Daniel Ennersley's blood. She took the scarf to her lips and closed her eyes. Did he ever get those flowers she left ... so long ago ...

She recalled that warm spring day when Daniel's father had come to the house, and she had seen him in the back of the car, so very lonely and lost. And she'd fastened him into her heart, going off into the woods for wild flowers, securing them with cotton, and taking them to Cliff House where she had left them at the foot of the garden. A silly childish gesture. But it shone now like a great white light. And Cliff House came to her again. That strange disturbing place of which her mother was so afraid.

High on the crag, the old, mysterious house stood on a plateau, a narrow path winding through the gardens, rampant with ferns and shrubs. Some days the house was lit. Others it stayed in darkness. The house seemed far away. And Lydia recalled the sound of the stream that day, trickling down the rocky path and teaming with minuscule frogs. At a place where the water fled through the gate she'd captured one in her hands, its bright green bounding legs shocked to stillness between her palms. Once she had seen a woman in the doorway wearing a dark blue coat, her fair hair blowing wild in the wind. She had never seen the boy again, but had seen Daniel discussing his work on television. And last night, by the river, she had known him instantly.

'So what do you think of the book?', her mother asked as she joined her again. Lydia praised it; the text was good and the photographs were excellent. Also the paper wasn't too glossy. Sometimes, Lydia said, it was hard to read the words on glossy paper. She must come to visit them, her mother said, Lydia hadn't been there for years. There'd been lots of improvements. 'Have you heard from James?' she asked suddenly. She put the book on the table, her back to Lydia. Lydia was silent.

Her mother turned. The smell of the pie baking in the oven came to them. The room filled with the scent of cloves and apples. 'Not that I want to pry or anything ...' said Eliza. She'd hoped Lydia and James would be be married soon. She was glad of James. In the past, he'd helped them to organise Jeremy. And if needs be, he could sort out Lydia, too. Especially when she got carried away with one of her grand ideas. Like the time she'd wanted to go to New Guinea to live with a tribe. There'd been such investigations. It reminded Eliza of when she'd been young herself and had wanted to go as a missionary to the Belgian Congo. And look what happened there.

'Jeremy hasn't fed his snakes', Eliza said, breaking the silence. The snakes. Now that was something else ...

Jeremy had had the snakes for four years. Alexander, the python, was three feet long; a huge heap skulking in the corner of the vivarium. At first there'd been rows about whether or not he should have them. He'd promised to see they were always fed and kept at the right temperature. That was important with snakes. He'd build an annexe, he said. He'd build it himself. No-one would know that the snakes were there, he promised. They wouldn't be any trouble. His father, alert in those days, and offering to help, had accompanied him to Knaresborough Pets and Aquatics on the high street, where they'd bought an American red-sided garter, a bright red stripe down its back. And a python. The python was less than a foot long then, but it had grown big over the years. Now it was huge; a curious lump of a thing that Jeremy had come to love. Occasionally Eliza looked in on the snakes. But she could never take to them. She hated the things they ate. She couldn't bear the screwed-up eyes and crinkled skin of the little chicks and rat pups Jeremy gave them to eat. She could understand the fruit and the dog and cat meat. But not those. Nor the great wide mouth opening to receive them whole, the sullen features, smooth and slick as a cunning

25

racketeer. Sometimes Jeremy would bring one out, holding it between his hands, its great length slithering and sliding between them, winding round his back, the seemingly anaesthetised head appearing again beneath his arm, the slanting eyes opening and closing indifferently, as if creature and boy were one.

They were tame as hamsters, he said. Perhaps they were if taken care of. But what now, when they were hungry. And it was cold, too. The temperature must be constantly kept at 75 degrees. It was colder than that in there. The annexe soon chilled. How did a python die? They didn't move much at the best of times. She opened the door of the annexe slowly, the heavy smell of bark chippings and maize cat litter entering her nostrils. Even the smell of the snakes disturbed her. The place seemed warm enough though. She glanced at the python's case. A purple heap slumped in a corner. She shuddered. The garter slithered about slowly in the next case winding itself around an oak branch Jeremy had sawn from a dead tree by the church. How silent they were. How would you know if the things were hungry?

Lydia came through. Her mother was dragging a sack from a corner, peering in. 'There's fruit in this', she said, her voice muffled. 'I suppose we could give them that.'

'I haven't a clue', said Lydia, looking bewildered. 'I don't know what he does. He doesn't leave them unfed though, mum. He'll soon be back.'

'What's going on?' Jeremy called from the door, seeing they were in the annexe and that his mother was fumbling in the fruit sack. 'Is something the matter?'

'You didn't feed the snakes before you went out', said Eliza. 'You were saying they'd missed a meal and you'd have to get them some food from the high street ...'

'And so I did', he said, bringing in a sack and lugging it through to the annexe. Eliza didn't ask what was in it. 'Missing an odd meal now and then won't kill them', he snapped. 'I've never asked you to feed the snakes. Why should I ask you now?' Eliza stood clasping her hands and frowning. 'I'm sorry', she said. 'I really am sorry. I didn't ...'

'Oh, mum, stop saying you're sorry!' Lydia cried. She sighed. The taxi would soon be arriving. She didn't want to fall out.

Jeremy thrust his hand in the fruit sack and drew out a large apple. 'So what did you think then?' he mumbled. 'That I'd let them starve. Is that what you thought?' He shook his head. 'When did I ever neglect them?'

Lydia watched. Something else was bothering him. It was more than the snakes. He broke apples in half with his hands, throwing them into the cases moodily. Then went to the python's case, drawing rat pups and baby chicks from the sack. Eliza went to take the pie from the oven. Lydia followed. Jeremy came out later.

'So you'll soon be off?' he said to Lydia. He sat down resting his head on the back of a chair and closed his eyes. Lydia buttoned her coat. 'Mind you don't lose that scarf again', he murmured, still with his eyes closed. 'There's a fierce wind out. I won't be giving rides today.' He got up and went to the annexe again to glance at the snakes, then came back. He kissed Lydia's cheek. 'Look after yourself', he whispered. Soon he was out of the door and down the road.

His mother sighed. He liked his work at the boathouse. She was glad of that. It helped to contain his energies. Lydia went for her flight bag upstairs, then returned. She checked she'd got her laptop computer and anything else she needed.

Eliza watched. She knew that James and Lydia had been having problems. She'd heard them arguing that week. Lydia had called him selfish. But he wasn't really selfish, Eliza reasoned. He'd always given her lots of time when she needed to talk about Jeremy, and would often repair things for her. He'd mended the iron last month, and had planed the back door when it had started to stick. She spoke slowly, hesitantly, 'James is bringing me one of those little transistors like the one you have in your kitchen. I'm looking forward to that. I can listen to Radio 3 when I'm dusting up at the manor.' As well as her other duties, sometimes she dusted the furniture in the main hall and the frames of the paintings that hung on the walls. 'I was telling Howard ...'

27

Lydia looked up. Her mother didn't mention Howard much. She looked embarrassed and went to the mirror, putting her hair in place. A lorry passed, spattering mud on the recently cleaned window ledge. Yesterday, a tractor had hung about all afternoon, covering the window with dirt and gravel.

They were silent a while. Lydia was deep in thought. 'You were ages getting your scarf', Eliza murmured. 'I don't know what James would have said, you going back like that on your own, and the river walk so lonely.'

'I was perfectly safe,' Lydia said quietly. 'And anyway, I wasn't alone.' She glanced at the clock. 'I didn't tell you all of it. There was someone I knew down there.' She moved her bags to the door then sat down waiting. Eliza stood by, her hands in the sleeves of her housecoat. She wasn't yet dressed and her face looked white and drawn. Lydia bit her lip. She wished her father would leave them alone. She wished he wouldn't keep coming back and making her mother hope. But what did she hope for? Another bout of drinking and shouting? Another black eye?

'So who was there?' her mother asked, determined to find out in the short time left.

Lydia checked her money. She did not look up. 'A man I knew. Or at least I'd known him once. I recognised him from years ago. We were doing some catching up.' She didn't want to remind her mother of Cliff House. A place she had always feared and avoided.

'Someone you knew?' her mother said, frowning. 'Someone from Knaresborough? You're not making sense. Do I know him myself?'

'Stop playing games, mum', said Lydia, sighing. 'Jeremy told you, didn't he? You know who it was.'

Her mother was silent. She sat down. 'Yes I suppose he did. Well, he gave a description. The rest I can put together.' She rose slowly and went to the mirror again. 'Look at my face. What a mess I look.'

Observing her, Lydia decided her mother needed some new clothes. She would bring her something back. A nice blouse and some long dark stockings. She would buy some of those for herself too. She knew a shop where the stockings were strong yet sheer at the same time. She'd never found anything like them in England. Her mother turned. 'I've seen him about', she said, her skin tightening. Her eyes were worried. 'People are talking.'

Lydia gave a glance of surprise. 'People? What, about Daniel? Why should they talk about him? Oh, you mean his research?' Her mother guarded her closely. Lydia hated the hawk-like mood.

'You wouldn't know of course', her mother said quietly. She rubbed her nose.

Lydia felt bewildered. What had she missed? It seemed her mother was hinting at something sinister. 'Is there something you want to tell me?' she asked. 'I've only a few minutes. Look, you mustn't send me off like this.' Lydia was angry.

Her mother searched her face, then held her gaze. Ought she to tell her now? After all this time. Lydia, she saw, was emotional. Without doubt, she cared for Daniel Ennersley. She would see him again. And soon.

'You're looking strange', said Lydia. 'I hope you're not going to be ill.' She put her head in her hands. 'Oh, mum, you'll have to come to terms with this. James and I are ...'

Eliza smiled sadly. 'I know. It's just that I wanted things to be good for you. I thought you might ...'

'What? Get married? Well, I'm glad we didn't. You don't know how glad I am. I can't see James marrying anybody. James is in love with himself. Can't you tell?' Lydia's face was pained. She breathed in deeply. 'But what's all this about Daniel? Come on, out with it mum, before I go!'

'It's just his work', Eliza decided, speaking slowly and trying to sound nonchalent.

'No, it isn't', said Lydia. 'I can tell it's something else. There's something you don't like.'

Her mother was silent a moment. She met Lydia's gaze. 'Well, it's ... it's just his research, really. He offends people. He dismisses God you know, he ...'

'But he doesn't', cried Lydia. 'I know that's what they say. But it isn't true. He talks about the universe and what is happening out there. It's marvellous what he knows. As far as God is concerned, what has he said to offend people with?' Lydia was vehement. 'Why must people make assumptions? You'd think we were in the dark ages. He's only saying religious beliefs might be something we've used to get by with. It's just an idea. We're supposed to have freedom of speech. He's a scientist.' Lydia covered her face with her hands. 'Journalists will make what they want of things', she said, her voice muffled. 'People so often believe what they read, not what's true!'

Her mother pressed her lips firmly together. What Lydia said now was what she had thought herself, when she'd read about what had happened in London. Lydia had been abroad. Eliza hadn't told her about all that. She wondered now if she ought to have told her then. To disclose it now seemed wrong, and almost vulgar. She hadn't expected he'd ever come back to Knaresborough. But now he had dared to return, and like the great dark bird he was, he'd alighted on Lydia. Daniel Ennersley wasn't just famous. He was also infamous. And a man with strange secrets. For something else, closer to home, was bothering Eliza. Something she'd have to tell Lydia about before she left. Something she'd wanted to tell her about for years, and would have to disclose, however foolish it sounded.

'He was working in London before', Lydia said, folding a thin pullover and putting it into her bag. 'He's living here for eighteen months with his father. He's doing some work at Leeds and Cambridge universities. Sometimes he goes to Jodrell Bank.'

'I see', said Eliza, looking relieved. Perhaps he might stay busily out of the way. 'I wouldn't have seen him as your type actually, Lydia'. She spoke slowly, running her hands through her hair.

'My type?' Lydia snapped, stunned by her mother's words. Her mother looked confused, untidy and not her normal self. She'd been worrying all night, Lydia knew, about the postcard. 'How do you know what type of friends I like?' She said painfully. 'Oh, mum. What do you want to argue for, when I'm going away?'

'I know your friends ...' Eliza went on, determined. 'I know what they're like. And they're not like him. He's strange. He was always peculiar.' Eliza's voice trembled slightly. Lydia wondered if she should call her visit to Paris off. Her mother didn't seem well.

'You didn't know him', her mother said flatly. 'When you were young, he was always away. They sent him off to boarding school. He was such a difficult child. Always in trouble.' She lowered her voice. 'They'd a strange family ...'

Eliza Ralphson coughed nervously. 'There's something I want to tell you. I *shall* tell you. And after that, you must do what you like. But listen.' Eliza sat down. Her voice was almost a whisper. 'It's the house', she said gravely. 'There's something about it.'

'Daniel's house?' said Lydia, wondering what it could be that made her mother so fearful, and why the room seemed suddenly cold.

Her mother began: 'A woman comes to the house, they say. She's young. I haven't seen her myself. Though others have. She has long dark hair, like yours. And all she wears is a thin silk slip, even in winter. They say she's dripping wet from the river, and shivering with cold.'

Lydia listened carefully. Her mother's eyes were distant, her skin white with emotion. Lydia leaned across and took hold of her hands. 'What does she want?' she asked, curious now and emotional.

'She wants to come in', said Eliza. 'She wants to come in from the cold.'

'Then why don't they open the door?'

'God knows why, my love', her mother murmured. 'She bangs hard enough. Hard enough to bring out the whole of the street.' She bent her head and gave a quick trembling sigh. 'I never thought I would tell you this. As if ... as if it were true.'

'But isn't it?' asked Lydia frowning.

31

Eliza looked up and locked her eyes, filled with tears, into Lydia's. 'Of course not. How can a story like that be true? The woman's a ghost!'

Lydia stared at the ceiling. *'A ghost?'* she whispered. She breathed in deeply. 'Surely you can't believe that?' She felt exhausted and gazed at her mother worriedly. How could she leave her now, like this, believing in ghosts, telling her things she ought have told her years ago? Why had she kept this story all to herself? Lydia felt lost and annoyed. So this was the secret. The reason her mother had pulled her past the house so quickly. Sometimes going the other way in the darkness. A ghost? Her mother was afraid of a ghost? 'But how is this connected with Daniel?' she asked.

'She comes whenever he's there', her mother said flatly. 'That's the trouble. It's almost as if he summons her.'

Lydia got up and paced the floor. 'It's nonsense, mum', she murmured. 'Don't you see?' They were silent a while. Lydia said: 'It's probably just a coincidence. If Daniel's home, then people will notice the house. They will see the ghost at the door. Or perhaps she comes to find him. Perhaps she needs him ...'

'See', her mother said softly. 'You believe it yourself.'

The taxi had stopped outside. Lydia picked up her bags and opened the door. 'Perhaps I should cancel my trip', she said. 'Shall I tell him to go?'

No, I'm fine', Eliza insisted, smiling. 'You mustn't take notice of me, Lydia. You're right. It's a lot of nonsense. I don't know why I've told you.'

'But you have', said Lydia looking downwards and feeling dejected.

'Well I'm sorry', her mother said softly. 'You'd better go, the man's waiting. But keep your distance, Lydia, if only for me.' Her voice was distant and strained. Lydia embraced her, then drew back. She spoke calmly. 'I can't mum. You don't know what you're asking.' Then she got in the taxi and left.

REVELATIONS

Dawn broke suddenly. Daniel Ennersley opened his eyes, recalling quickly what had gone on the evening before; the two beautiful women, one real, one imagined. Or was she? He did see the ghost! he told himself. He did! He needed to go to the river again. To the very same place where last night it had happened. All night long the image had haunted him; the cold, white face, the frail limbs, and the suffering eyes ... The eyes, he thought, would probably haunt him forever. He dressed quickly and went out.

He had never been to the river so early before. This time of day it seemed like a different place. The reeds were still and the white dawn spread itself like an icy film across the trees. He went to the bench where he'd sat the previous evening. Yes, it was here. This very spot. He gazed about him. Everywhere was silent. As he stood, the air around him grew warm, and an almost purple light clouded about him, changing from blue to purple by turns and finally settling to blue. He stood transfixed. Try as he would, he could not move. Something was happening. He did not understand it, yet he felt excited, waiting for what came next. He listened carefully. The sound of the water was crisp and metallic. The river birds seemed almost transparent, as if in a dream. And the season was summer, not autumn as it had been just seconds before, but full blown summer. The trees were heavy with blossom, their scents strong in the air.

Looking down at the floor, he found a line of linens laid out for bleaching. The cloth was coarse and thick. He tried to bend to touch them, but found he couldn't. They seemed to be out of his reach. All he could do was look at them and wonder. Further along the path a throng of people had gathered by Castle Mill, talking amongst themselves. They sounded angry. Their image was blurred but he could see that they were mainly women, poor and tired, their clothes ragged and their bodies bent. A tall man in a trilby hat was waving his fists arguing, the women converging on him fiercely. He looked in trouble. Everything swam it seemed in the bluish light. At its edges were half faces, and half limbs. Into the picture walked a clergyman wheeling a bicycle. He frowned and mumbled. The people turned and the sound of the voices fell as he joined them.

Daniel took a deep breath. He still couldn't move or speak. His hands were tingling again and he felt giddy. His palms were sweating. 'Who can these people be?' he asked himself deliriously. 'Why is it summer? I must wake up! I must force myself out of this dream!'

Suddenly brilliant sunlight cut through the sky. And within seconds the linens, the workers by Castle Mill, the clergyman and his bicycle and the summer scene, had gone. He was back in the white sunlight of autumn again, the trees chasing their busy shadows over the water.

He sat down thinking. Who could he tell about this? He couldn't just keep it all to himself. He had to have someone to talk to. His head ached from lack of sleep and confusion. His colleagues would never believe him. They'd probably laugh or discuss him behind his back and suggest he needed a clinic. His mind was a fog. And he longed to see Lydia again. Perhaps she would be at her mother's house on Anderson Terrace.

For some time he watched the water, then went up the high street to the grocers, who opened early. He needed some bread and coffee and thought the walk would clear his head. All the time, as he walked, he thought he was sleeping. Nothing around him seemed real.

'Well then, look who it is!' called Harold Brown as Daniel entered the shop. He took a loaf from a basket. 'Fancy that', said the grocer. 'We thought you'd gone to the moon.' Daniel handed the bread across and smiled. 'And give me some coffee, Harold. Some of that up there.' He pointed to one of the large jars on a shelf. Daniel hadn't been in his shop for years. He watched him work. He was just as always, flour-faced clean, like one of the muffins he baked in the back. Much of his old equipment was still there. He was still using the same antique scales and bacon slicer. The shop was wholesome and warm. The scent of coffee and cheeses and newly baked bread filled the small space.

'Haven't you been in Australia?' Harold called, over the sound of the grinder. A glorious aroma filled the air as Harold ground the beans and spooned them into a small white bag.

'That's right', said Daniel. 'Then London. I've been in Iowa too. But Australia mainly, in the Goobang Valley.'

'Peggy's back soon', said Harold. 'She's up at the Tea Gardens. Gets there early she does. She's to put on the heat you see. People won't sit outside, it's cold just now.'

Peggy, his wife, managed the Tea Gardens up at the castle and sold what she claimed as the best ice cream in Knaresborough. She also kept geese. If you sat in Peggy's gardens, you must be with the geese. Which didn't suit everybody. She always kept a basket of goose eggs on the ice cream cart. Sometimes Daniel's father would bring some home for breakfast.

'I can't stop', said Daniel. 'Just the loaf and coffee, Harold. I shall have to be off. Oh, give me one of those Edams there as well.'

Normally Daniel's father collected the bread, and maybe some custard pies. But lately he'd lost his appetite. Daniel thought some fresh bread and a good Edam might encourage him to eat. 'Give my regards to Peggy, won't you', he said, as Harold wrapped the loaf in soft white paper, twisting it at the corners and making a quick little movement with the side of his mouth as if he were cracking a nut.

'How long are you staying?' Harold asked him, passing the groceries.

'As long as it takes, I suppose', said Daniel.

'Can't say more than that', said Harold. Daniel laughed and walked off.

His mind was a-whirl. He knew he hadn't been dreaming. Though each experience had been alarming and unusual. What surprised him most was that he felt no fear. Thinking about it, fear, he decided, would have been quite normal under the circumstances. But he hadn't felt any fear at all. Only awe and excitement. And he'd been mainly curious. But what was it all about? He had found himself in a world where his academic knowledge was quite valueless. Not even his common sense could come to his aid. This was the world of revelation, a peculiar, vaporous world, that he could not fathom and had no means of interpreting. A world in which he was a mere beholder.

Or perhaps he wasn't. Perhaps he was more than that. The ghost from the river wanted something. That's what it was. She needed him. He felt very grand at the thought of that. Yes, he felt like a god might feel when receiving a prayer. But what if he did not see her again, and could not help her at all? He blinked hard. He needed to sleep but his mind was racing. He felt good too. Filled with a kind of purity. A sense of wholesomeness and holiness. He enjoyed the sensation. It made him feel less tense.

He looked about. Everything was normal now. So very ordinary. How many secret worlds were lost in the air? The air that looked so innocent and solitary. The shop windows dazzled with sunshine, though the day was chilly. As he walked, he could see the purple light again before him, turning turquoise and blue by turns near the old apothocary. There it stopped, wavering before the window. The place was as it had always been, the owners having upheld its history. But the reprographics building, where he sometimes made photocopies, seemed to have disappeared. There in its place stood an old man with a cart of fruit and vegetables, calling out to passers by to purchase his wares. Though it seemed no-one heard him.

And a woman stood by the apothecary window, looking in. Daniel stopped, and stared. He knew who she was. He gazed amazed. What was she doing here, on the Knaresborough street, by the old apothecary, and wearing nineteenth-century clothes? She looked so real. But she wasn't. She was no more real than the scene he found himself in. And a shiver of fear ran through him as he wondered if he would find his way out of this time that had so quickly engulfed him. Here was the ghost again, and so alive and well. But the same woman. The same beautiful face, yet more fleshed out and so much happier. She was dressed in a white lace blouse with puffed sleeves and a ruffled collar, a long black skirt and ankle boots. Yes, it was certainly her. He had no doubt of it. He knew those slender bones, that beautiful oval face, that chin. And the sensuous full mouth. Her hair was done up in slides and she wore a straw hat, for it was summer again and warm. He walked towards her. This time he would speak! He was almost by her! But as he came to her, he found she turned to him, walking into and through him. He did not feel her substance, but turned to see her walk into the blue light and slowly vanish. He remained quite still. For a moment or two he dared not move. People hurried about indifferently. Traffic went up and down the road. A small child stumbled with his mother beside him, picked himself up and walked on.

Twice now he had seen her. He knew he would see her again. But how could he reach her? He leaned on the wall of the apothocary. Finally gathering his nerves, he made his way up the high street again to the back of his house and scrambled over the gate. When he got back inside, he told himself, he would make himself some strong coffee. He would sit down, and he would think it through. But no. It was not to be. That day Daniel Ennersley would have no peace.

An unusual silence filled the house as he entered. From the open windows no sounds came from the street. The trees in the gardens were still. The grandfather clock by the kitchen door no longer ticked. After his mother had died, the clock had stopped and his father had left it alone. 'And so the day is quiet,' he murmured. I shall do some reading. The *Astronomer's Guide* had arrived, his monthly magazine. He would spend a quiet half hour with that. He made some coffee. But the silence persisted, dead and uncanny, as if all sound had stopped for good. Even the sound of him stirring his drink had gone. Trying to make some noise he rattled the cutlery drawer and tried to sing. But that didn't work either. The drawer was silent. His voice wouldn't come. He stood very still and breathed in deeply. His nerves were completely shattered. He took a drink from his coffee, the warm liquid soothing his throat. He had made it strong.

As he moved to the lounge, he stopped again, confused. Was this his father's house? It wasn't his father's furniture or carpets. The walls were bare and lifeless. He looked down. Instead of the carpet they'd layed together during a summer vacation, there were polished floors. He put his drink on a small table, but it wouldn't stand up. He caught it quickly, spilling the liquid a little, which bounced like beads to the ground. He was back again in the almost turquoise light. He put out his hand, seeing his bones and veins highlighted, his finger nails gleaming, damp and as if they were new. Putting his hand to his face, his skin was soft and warm. 'I am still the same!' he told himself with a sigh of relief. 'I am still here!' He blinked hard and stepped forward, trying to make his way inside the lounge. There the light grew stronger. It was now a deep turquoise. Dare he walk through it again? What would happen? His limbs felt heavy. He took a drink from the coffee and tried to bend down to put the mug on the floor, but it fell over, spilling its contents, which bounced again like beads on the shining floorboards.

Looking into the room, he now saw, not the oak table he knew and the easy chairs, piled high with books, but a different scene. Something he would never have thought of.

There in the centre, covered in white linen, stood a dark mahogany table, set with sparkling china and silver cutlery. A man and woman sat, one at each end, a crystal chandelier shimmering above them, alive with light. Daniel watched astonished. Though he could not see her face, the woman appeared to be young. The man wore dark clothing and seemed older than she was, with black hair and a thick moustache. His features were blurred. The woman's hair was long and black and done up in small curls and ringlets, held by a black rose hairslide, leaving her elegant white neck naked. Her head was bent.

Slowly and cautiously Daniel approached, moving through the blue light, moving around the couple, catching sight then of the woman's face as she lifted her head. He stopped confused. How could it be? He was looking at the ghost again, here in his father's house, his family home, the place where he had spent his childhood. So this is where she lives, he discerned suddenly. Or did. Here, in our house. And a great ache of responsibility entered him. No-one else, apart from his family, had ever resided at Cliff House. Seeing her now, so strong and healthy, he grieved for the poor woman who had risen out of the water the night before. The man's voice vibrated on the bare walls. 'You haven't been to church!' he shouted. The words shook the room, reverberating for some time before fading away.

'I know', she said quietly. But there was anger in it and a desire to say more.

'Why aren't you eating?' he shouted.

She sat very still, scarcely moving, clasping her hands in her lap. The man crammed food in his mouth and took long gulps of red wine. He pushed a plate of meats towards her. It skidded across the table so that she put out her hands quickly, some of the food falling on to her dress. She lifted it off with her fingers.

'You did not take the flowers to my mother's grave', he said coldly.

'I forgot.'

'Precisely, my dear. You forgot.'

'I'll do it tomorrow.'

He banged his fist on the table, gritting his teeth. 'Tomorrow is useless, woman! It's a week since I asked you. Now it is too late. I wanted them for her birthday.'

From beneath his dark eyelids, he glared, the bones of his face long and dense. He guarded her with a growl. 'You never do as I tell you. I'll be master here! I will!' He stood up, pacing the room. The fire burned furiously. He faced it with his back to her, rocking, then suddenly turned, pointing a finger. 'Don't you understand how important it was?' He waved his hand. 'Ah, you don't understand anything do you?' He turned away from her contemptuously.

She sighed. 'Of course I do. I've been helping the sick.' She looked small and far away. Bracing herself, she straightened one of her curls.

'Helping the sick!' he bawled, coming up close, his eyes flashing with anger. 'Helping the sick! You're impossible. But listen, you will get your just desserts, my dear.' He scowled hard. 'Oh, yes. Yes. You will be chastened!'

A howl of wind blasted against the shutters. He darted across, and with a thud dragged them together, turning on her again, eager for sport, returning to the table where he sat down pouring himself more wine. He leaned back, wiping his lips with a napkin, shaking his head and watching her beneath his eyelids, his face twisted with bitterness.

'I am very busy', she said, bending her head. 'There is much to do.' She got up, walking to the window, her dress stained with food, a wonderful gracefulness in her movements, though she was agitated and nervous. 'I do not think', she began. 'No, I know, I have done nothing wrong.' Her voice was scarcely audible. 'In my heart I have sought to do what's right.' Her voice was weak and thin.

'Right?' he bellowed. 'What do you know about right and wrong? You, my dear, are a wicked and evil creature. Oh you are. You are. You have admitted as much yourself.' He rubbed his nose and straightened his moustache.

She worked her fingers together, her eyes darting about.

'Sit down!' he shouted. 'For God's sake, woman, you are twitching about like a bird! Keep yourself still!'

'I don't want to', she said defiantly. 'I shall do as I like.'

The man's eyes opened widely. He laughed out loud. 'Sit down, I said! Or do you want me to make you? Here ...' He went across to her and pulled her on to the chair, returning then to his own. 'You know', he continued, slowly and leisurely. 'They have had to lock the font cover at the church so no-one can steal the holy water. People steal it you see, for witchcraft.'

'Witchcraft?' She looked up quickly, white and afraid. 'Why do you look at me like that? I have nothing to do with it.'

He leaned back smiling. 'And did I say you had? My dear, you are looking guilty.'

She bent her head.

'They will put you in the stocks you know, that's what they'll do.'

40

'Don't be stupid', she murmured.

He played with her like a cat with a mouse. Lifting her eyes, she said. 'The boy came to do the gardens. I gave him two pennies.'

The man chewed slowly, watching her and drinking.

She carried on, 'And do you know. They are only paying the women a halfpenny to carry the water uphill.'

He shook his head. 'The water cannot travel uphill alone.'

'No. And the wages are bad at the mill. I see them some-times, the workers, passing the house at dawn. They don't come back till dark. Their hours are far too long.' She fired him with words.

'Why are you telling me this?' he stormed. 'I've enough concerns of my own.'

Just then the sound of a horse and carriage came from the front of the house. He got up quickly, wiping his mouth and banging his napkin down on top of the table. 'And so you are summoned!' he shouted. He folded his arms. 'You embarrass me', he said, bending his head. 'We do not need her charity. Why do you let her patronise us like this? You do not want for anything. You have more than enough ...'

'She is good to me. And to others. Don't you see, we're friends. I have to have friends. She works so hard for the parish. Her food and clothing have saved many lives. Today, we must go to Halifax to visit a family. We must hurry.' She straightened her dress and her hair quickly.

'Yah!' he shouted, as she passed him. 'Get out of my sight!'

She reached for her gloves from a small table. Beside him, Daniel could hear her breathing anxiously. Her silk skirts rustled, and the sweet scents of saffron and sandalwood filled the air. He stretched his hand towards her, though his fingers slid through the turquoise light, and into nothing. As she passed him, going towards the front door, though cast with sadness, her eyes were alert and alive. Meeting his own, he saw that they were lit with tears.

MUSIC

Rosie sat at the library desk. Her cocker spaniel, Gabriel, slept by her feet, an ear twitching momentarily. 'You didn't hear me, did you?' said Jeremy, whispering behind her. The sun streamed in, lighting up her black leather trousers. 'Don't do that!' she cried, annoyed that he had approached her silently.

She turned, swinging her legs on the desk and crossing them. She didn't like it if Jeremy saw her working too hard. She liked to play cool. She rubbed her eyes and pushed the books she was mending to the edge of the table. 'I've finished with that lot', she mumbled. She blew a large bubble of gum, cracking it in the air. 'Enough to make you fall asleep in here. Gabriel could tell you.' She glanced at the dog, still napping.

'Peaceful though, Rose. Nothing like a bit of peace some-times.' He went across to the wildlife section and took out a book. He was looking for one on country parks. Rosie had taken a book herself from one of the shelves. He glanced across. 'Motorbikes? Are you buying one then?' Rosie had just come back from a year in China. Intending to stay, she had sold her bike to Jeremy. Now she wanted it back.

'I don't know', she drawled, running her fingers through her short red curls and blowing another bubble. 'I thought I might go away again ...'

'Oh', said Jeremy nonchalantly. He went to her and knelt down by the dog, stroking its head. 'For good?'

Rosie's skin tightened. 'I didn't come back for you, Jem, if that's what you're thinking. There were other things ...'

'I don't doubt it, Rose', said Jeremy sighing and getting up. He smiled tight-lipped, gazing at her. 'There's not much sense in buying a bike if you're not going to use it. Who will you sell it to this time?' It was a sore point, Rosie going away. He felt it like a cruel wind. 'Anyway, Rose, like I said, it's peaceful in here. Don't you enjoy the peace?' He thought of the way he felt himself, out on the river, alone in a boat. Sometimes he'd row for miles.

'Peace?' cried Rosie. She stood up quickly. 'Who wants peace? I want some fun, Jem. I want to be with the action.'

Jeremy frowned. 'There's nothing abroad that I'd want, Rose.'

She sighed dismissively. 'You've lived a sheltered life, Jem. There's more than you know out there.'

'Aye, I suppose there is, Rose. Not that I'd want it though.' His tone hardened.

'Peace is for old people', Rosie said sullenly.

They were silent a while. She turned to the window and gazed out. 'There isn't a scrap of peace at our place', she moaned. 'You can't even get a decent night's sleep. Wretched baby!'

Jeremy's eyes widened. 'Come on Rose, it's your little sister, that.'

Rosie went to her chair again and sat down. The dog leapt on to her lap and knocked a book on the floor. It fell apart. 'This dog will get me sacked!' she laughed. Her voice was loud and independent. Jeremy felt there was nothing left of him in it. He retrieved the book and examined it. It would have to go in the bin. 'Doesn't sound like a bad idea, if you ask me', he said. The dog lapped at Rosie's cheeks. Its large ears flapped on her face. 'What?' she said, abstractedly. 'Getting the sack', said Jeremy.

'I need some money, Jem. Lots of it.' She spoke flatly, seriously.

'What for?' he murmured leafing through another book. He had found two that he wanted. Rosie would have to stamp them out, then he'd take them home. He could see she was in a bad mood.

'What do I want money for?' she said exasperated. She shook her head.

He observed her a moment. Always so energetic. Always so intense. Always so Rosie. She would never relax. Nothing was ever exciting enough for Rosie. She'd only come back through lack of money. He knew that. She'd said so in her letter. It hurt and annoyed him that she did not want him and spoke so glibly about their friendship. To him it was more than a friendship. When she wasn't there, he imagined her, pretending she might be thinking about him, too, needing him as he needed her. He looked away. Since she'd been back, Rosie had worked hard. As well as her library work, she worked three evenings a week as a waitress in Harrogate. Her free ones she spent with him. Sometimes they'd go on the bike to York, or along the dark lanes where there were no lights, speeding along the roads in the darkness. Then, at such times, the whole wide world was his and nobody else's. 'It isn't money that makes you happy, Rose', he said quietly, breaking the silence. He couldn't do much for Rosie himself. His pay was low at the boathouse. But he liked his work. And he wanted more of it. He fancied a job in a country park. 'I'd like to work with animals ...' he said tentatively.

'What, in a zoo?' she said, loudly, as if recoiling. 'I can't stand zoos.'

'I wasn't thinking of that', he said. 'I mean natural places, like nature reserves ...'

'Animals are alright ...' sighed Rosie. 'I've enough with this one though. Gabriel's so demanding.' She cupped the dog's bony face in her hands. Its liquid eyes gleamed, darting about nervously. 'I'm just like Gabriel, you know. Look at him. He always thinks that something's going to happen. It doesn't though. It never does.' The dog leapt down, sitting beside Jeremy. 'Look at that', she grumbled, removing hairs from her clothes. 'What with him moulting and mum breast feeding, I'm going spare.'

He watched her removing the hairs from her jersey, one by one, precisely, delicately. She wasn't really thinking about the dog hairs. It was displacement activity. 'Displacement activity' he'd read, meant when you were doing something to cover up for something else. The baby was bothering Rosie, Jeremy knew. She was jealous of Susie. He watched as she went to a bookshelf, rearranging the books. People were always mixing them up. And she'd cut her hair. It was far too short. Long red

44

curls, Dragon's Fire, or a hot summer day in the dales ... that was Rosie's hair for him, not the short spiked hair she'd returned with. She sat down again. Gabriel licked her hand, then ran off into the kitchen where Rosie kept the cleaning things and made them drinks, and the dog had a basket. She followed and filled the kettle. 'I'd like a hand with that desk', she called. 'The one by the window. I need to take it to the storeroom. One of the legs is loose. I shall have to phone the council to come and get it.' A thin corridor led from the library to three small rooms. The storeroom was the third along. The desk was heavy, she couldn't lift it alone. It made a screeching sound as Jeremy pulled it. 'Not now', she said. 'Let's have a drink. We can do it later.'

'Fancy going to York tomorrow evening?' he asked, as they drank their coffee. It was one of her nights off. It was also Rosie's birthday. She was eighteen. 'There's a good Greek restaurant our Lydia knows. I can book a table.' Rosie was silent, thoughtful. 'That's if you want ...' he said awkwardly. He remembered there'd been a problem with his bike the day before. Perhaps he'd ask her about it. Rosie knew all about bikes. He'd often watched her tackling it with tools, her fingers thick with oil, her face too sometimes. He'd known Rosie Baltimore all his life. Last year, knowing she was coming back, he'd brought her a glass brooch in the shape of an owl. She wore it now on her jersey.

He put the two books on the desk, ready for stamping. The library hadn't got round to computers yet. Rosie still used a pad that had to be soaked in ink each weekend, and a heavy metal stamp she thumped on the books. She liked it, she said. Computers? Who needed them? And anyway, she'd heard from somewhere, you had to feed everything in, before you could even start. All those books ... Not on your life.

As she stamped them out someone came in, walking across leisurely. He picked up a book, then looked at them. His manner was easy and familiar. 'Hi there', he said, observing Jeremy first, then Rosie.

'Do you need any help?' asked Rosie, without looking. Her voice was alert, though there was little heart in it.

'Yes, perhaps i do', the man said, leafing through something he'd found. He sat down by her desk and looked at Jeremy, smiling. Jeremy leant against the wall, his books to his chest.

'What did you want?' asked Rosie. She still didn't look. Jeremy listened and watched.

'I'm not quite sure ...' said the man. He hadn't thought it out. He hadn't come in for books really. Seeing Jeremy leaving the boathouse, Daniel had followed him, waiting for him to come out. Having grown tired of waiting, he'd gone in instead. He wanted to know where Lydia was. He needed to see her. He looked about. This time the place seemed bigger. Now there was more light. Some of the bookcases had gone and there was more room. Now you could see the river and some of the trees. The smell of the place was less musty.

'Aren't you Lydia's brother?' he asked, offering his hand, and hoping he'd remember him from last night. By the river with Lydia, at the boathouse this morning, and now in the library, Jeremy seemed like three very different people.

'I hope so', said Jeremy, shaking his hand and eyeing Daniel cautiously. The men were about the same height. 'What can I do for you?'

Do for me, thought Daniel. Damn it! Was it really that obvious? Jeremy's manner was bold and sincere like his sister's. He wasn't for playing games. Daniel glanced at the girl in the swivel chair, her legs on the desk. The dog came through and whimpered. Rosie lifted it and stroked its head. Its eyes closed calmly. 'There now', she said. 'What's the bother?' She looked at Daniel. 'What were you looking for?'

'Just books', said Daniel, throwing out his arms.

'Well, there are some in here', said Rosie, blowing a bubble of gum. 'Not that they're up to much. There are bigger libraries of course ...You might find something in ...'

'Perhaps over there', Daniel murmured. He disappeared for a moment, behind a bookcase.

'I wouldn't go behind there!' Rosie called. 'That's where I keep the ghost stories!' She turned to Jeremy. 'Anyway, I'm off to New Zealand soon.'

Jeremy said, 'You don't know Daniel Ennersley, then?' Daniel came into view again with an old book. 'An expert on stars', said Jeremy. 'Isn't that right?' Daniel looked up and smiled. Jeremy said slowly: 'People know more than you think.' And added, 'Rosie's going abroad soon.'

'Am I?' said Rosie, frowning. 'Are you packing me off already?' She stroked the dog again, all the time chewing and blowing bubbles. 'I shall probably stay till spring.'

Jeremy rubbed his face. 'Well then, Rose. About this desk? I have to go back to the boathouse soon. What do you want me to do with it?' She took a key from a hook in the kitchen. The two of them moved the desk down the corridor into a small room. By the door in the gloomy light, her chin lifted determinedly, Rosie, Daniel thought, looked older, a stern no-nonsense woman. Formidable even.

Daniel glanced through the book, stopping at one of the pages and reading: *'For some time, after my sister's death, there was a peculiar feeling hanging about the house. I noticed another interesting fact; that the clothes she had worn, which I had kept, just as they were, in her wardrobe, were often moved about. And sometimes, it was as if the wardrobe had around it an invisible wall. I could not move towards the door. I could not even step within a foot of it. And on the Thursday of the week she died, I noticed a blue light emerging from the chair where I had last seen her alive. An almost turqoise light. And suddenly, I saw her again! My dear sister was there! I saw her again!'*

Just then his thoughts were interrupted by Rosie's dog, bounding around his feet excitedly, giving a series of sharp yelps. And as it did, the sound of music came to him, rising strangely about him and filling him with powerful surges of feeling. Struck with surprise, he listened hard. This was no ordinary sound. This was spectacular music! Music made for the heavens! Where did it come from? He could not place the composition. It seemed to be there in the room. Alive. More than alive. He listened as it rose and fell; ardent; tender; angry. He felt bewitched. The music, it seemed, was playing itself inside him, almost as if he himself were com-posing it.

But how could it be? He felt hot. He wiped his forehead with the back of his hand. Suddenly as fast as it came, it went. But for the sound of Rosie and Jeremy coming back down the corridor, all was silent. The dog was calm and resting.

Jeremy held some books he had found in the storeroom. They were mildewed and old, but seemed of interest. 'I got them for Lydia', he said. Rosie put the large key back on the hook.

'Did you hear any music?' Daniel asked, still feeling dazed. He searched their faces. 'You must have heard it ...'

'Music?' said Rosie, joining them.

'There was music in here', Daniel continued urgently. 'Wonderful music. Marvellous music ...' He sat down baffled.

'Can't say I heard it myself', said Rosie. She glanced at Jeremy. 'Me neither', he said, frowning. 'Was it outside?'

'No', said Daniel with certainty. 'It came from in here. This very room. It was here.'

Jeremy watched him curiously. The three of them were silent a while. Rosie looked through the window then came back. 'See what you're reading', she said, gazing at Daniel strangely. *The Supernatural World*. Phantom music? Well, no wonder.'

She stood for a moment frowning. 'Anything's possible here', she said, lowering her voice. 'I knew it the day I arrived. Sometimes, when I'm alone, you know, I hear footsteps.'

'You will', said Jeremy smiling. 'People are coming upstairs for books.'

'It isn't like that', Rosie said frustratedly. 'It's like .. Well, other footsteps ... They sound peculiar. Oh, I can't wait to see the back of it.'

'What, the baby?' said Jeremy, raising his eyebrows mischievously.

Rosie blushed. 'What's wrong with our baby?'

What isn't? thought Jeremy, recalling what she had said earlier. But he'd have to forget all that. That was how it was with Rosie. That was their relationship. 'So, are we going to York then tomorrow?' he asked, again.

'Alright', she said. 'I'll be ready at seven.' She stamped the books and Jeremy put them beneath his arm, preparing to leave.

48

Daniel took his book to the desk. It seemed like a good read. He didn't want to get books from work. The girls in the library would probably laugh. What a mess he was in. Not only was he seeing ghosts, he was also hearing music now that wasn't there. Taking a deep breath, he stood for a moment thoughtful. Something had alerted the dog undoubtedly. Had the dog heard the music too? He felt tired and drained. Perhaps he was in the first stage of a mental illness? Ought he to speak to his father? Something was happening to him. He couldn't dismiss it. The thing was all too real: the ghost who had climbed from the river, the people at Castle Mill, the ghost on the high street, and at Cliff House with her husband. And now this, this music. Half of the time he could not trust his senses and thought he was overworked, dreaming in daylight. But he knew it was more than that. It was all too enthralling.

'Do you think they'll be useful?', he asked, walking back to the boathouse. Jeremy held the books beneath his arm. 'They look like they're falling to pieces.'

'Lydia will know', he said confidently. 'I often pick something up if I think she'll like it.'

'Is Lydia home?' asked Daniel.

'She's gone to Paris', he said quietly. He kicked stones. 'She'll be back in a few days.'

'I expect she'll be tired.'

'Might be', he said vaguely.

'Will she be going to Alderley Edge?' Daniel went on, bombarding him with questions. I shall have to stop, he told himself. I must go home. 'I didn't manage to speak to you the other night. You must have thought ...'

Jeremy stopped suddenly. 'I didn't think anything', he said. He looked at Daniel sideways and shook his head. 'He'll be gone again soon. He's always going away.'

'Who?' asked Daniel, feigning innocence.

Jeremy pulled at his ear-ring.

Daniel laughed. Lydia's brother was leaps ahead. 'So where is he now?'

'I'm not quite sure, London, I think ... He's like my dad. He just goes off.' Jeremy narrowed his eyes and turned to him.

'It's because of our dad that she lets it happen. If it weren't for him ... A waste of space our dad. A waste of space.'

'And Rosie?' Daniel said, changing the subject. 'Is she your ...'

'My girlfriend?' Jeremy said flatly. 'No, she's not. She's Richard's daughter, the bloke who owns the boathouse. That's why she's here. She's just got back from China.' His voice was heavy with sadness.

Everywhere seemed suddenly busy. People came down the path. Horses passed. The river teamed with boats. They had almost reached the boathouse.

'So which is yours?' asked Daniel. He gazed at Anderson Terrace; a row of stone cottages visible through the trees.

Jeremy pointed. 'The one over there with the white windows.'

Daniel looked, seeing the small cosy house in the middle of a row, neatly painted white, the stones glistening through the dark trees. Perhaps he would call on her later, ask her out for a coffee. They might take a ride on a boat.

Jeremy said, 'It's a blue Polo. You'll see it outside. Knock at the house if you want.' As Daniel walked away, Jeremy called out: 'Doctor Ennersley?' Daniel turned. 'Next time you go to Jodrell Bank, will you give us a bell? I'd like to come with you.'

Daniel waved and smiled. Someone, it seemed, had been talking.

FORCES

Reginald Ennersley had begun to cough heavily. Every day he was losing strength. Daniel had persuaded him to spend some time with his sister in Wales, and that morning had taken him to the train. Aunt Rachel said she would meet him at the other end. That done, Daniel tried to relax and think.

Back in the house, he thought of Lydia again. He had to see her. First though, he must e-mail some letters then go for a newspaper. Gathering together his things, he went out.

That morning the house had felt strangely still, and once or twice it seemed as if the rooms shuddered faintly. Worst of all, as he had bent to fix his shoes, he could swear a hand had touched his shoulder. A gentle hand that was benign. Though other forces were not so kind. Stirring a pan of soup at lunch time, a wave of coldness had passed through him, and the pan had slid from the stove, falling, its contents scalding his bare feet. Bathing the skin, he'd thought that sinister forces might be at work and out to destroy him. His mind played tricks whichever room he went in.

Over the past few days, he'd expected, at every turn, to encounter some strange phenomena. He was ready for any-thing. So far, he had told his father nothing. He knew he believed in ghosts and would probably think it concerned his dead wife. The book he had got from the library said ghostly presences such as this were normally temporary. But what if they were malicious? Daniel chilled at the thought. Ghosts had been known to throw people downstairs, or even cause them to behave violently to others. He felt tired and listless, as though he were in a dream, and wondered in fact if he were entering a kind of dream-like state that he hadn't experienced before. But his logic dictated different. Thinking about the music in the library, he asked himself over and over again, Why was I the only one who heard it? The music was loud and would easily have reached Jeremy and Rosie. Questioning his sanity all the time made it hard to work. All the way to the station he had thought about telling his father, each time changing his mind. He doubted his own reasoning, and the greater part of his energies now, were taken up in deciding what to do. But most of all, he wanted to talk to Lydia again. He must try to find her. When he had bought a paper, he would go to Anderson Terrace and look for her car.

The day was clear, white light streaming in long straight lines through the trees, hitting the stone and bouncing into the water. The weather was cold, though the snow forecast all week had never arrived. He'd put on walking boots and cords and his leather jacket. Apart from the ducks at the water's edge, the river was still. As Anderson Terrace came into view he saw the blue Polo. And as he approached, Lydia came out of the door.

'Hello', he said. 'How was your visit to Paris?' She smiled back boldly.

'Useful,' she called. 'How nice to see you.' He stamped about awkwardly. 'Your hair's even darker in daylight', he laughed, suddenly feeling embarrassed. He wasn't sure what to say. He hadn't wanted to talk at all really. Only to see her.

'Anyway, I found what I wanted', she said, stopping and turning to him. She gazed at him with gentle directness. She was wearing a purple roll-neck sweater and jeans. Her beautiful ivory skin gleamed in the sunlight. 'I always take too much', she laughed, removing a box from her car boot. He offered to help, but she seemed to manage, entering the house then coming out, by turns. It was good to see her like this in daylight, to know where she was, not miles away in Paris, but here with him. She emptied the car boot, removing a string bag filled with oranges, then banged down the lid. Breaking the bag and holding it so they didn't fall out, she threw one across. He caught it fast. 'Try one!' she called entering the house again. He stood for a moment alone, peeling the orange. The skin was thick and came off easily. Inside, the flesh was rich and succulent. He tore off a segment and put it into his mouth. She closed the door and came to him. 'Here', he said, offering her a piece. They stood for a moment, eating, and wondering what to do next. They were both silent. 'Would you like to go for a coffee?' he asked finally. 'Nice idea', she said. They made their way to the boathouse.

A couple passed on horseback. Daniel glanced at the sky. 'Looks like snow', he said.

'I wouldn't mind going out riding, myself', said Lydia.

'I was always on horses in Wales', said Daniel, watching the riders. 'My aunt has a farm. I haven't been riding in ages.' The thought was tempting, if the weather stayed dry.

'Do you want me to organise something?' she said. 'I'd be glad of the company.' Her voice trailed off, embarrassed.

'That sounds good', he said, though he couldn't avoid the surprise in his voice at how forceful she was. How strong she had become, it seemed, since she'd been away. He knew she was very unhappy. They watched the riders, moving into the open country and out of view.

At the boathouse café they sat talking. She told him of her brother's developing interest in astronomy. How he'd ordered some books from the library. He told her about his father's illness and how it concerned him. How he had gone that day to Wales to stay for a while with his sister. He did not tell her the other things. He was waiting for something to happen. For a kind of sign. Hoping that soon it would all make sense. He would like to have told her though. Reality, it seemed, had ceased to exist. Truth, he'd decided, was only a fashion. There was no truth at all, there were just happenings. He told her about the telescope he'd fixed in the attic, and suggested her brother might like to see it sometime. 'Mind you, it can be a hit and miss affair', he said. The stars could be very elusive. He explained the problems. Days you were lucky, days you weren't. So much depended on weather, and the skill, of course, of the observer. Lydia talked about Jeremy's snakes and how he had come to have them. For a while they sat silent, watching the water. He thought he might tell her about the music. That seemed safe enough at least. He wanted to talk about that.

As he related it, she smiled, without any hint that it sounded incredulous. Though he thought it weird himself. 'And did you know the composer?' she asked.

For a moment he felt foolish. Ghostly music in libraries wasn't what you talked to a possible girlfriend about. But the music intrigued him and forced itself in his mind. 'I'm almost sure it was Beethoven', he said, hearing it over and over. 'I can't say I knew it, though. Which is strange, since dad has all his work. He's quite a fanatic.'

'And Rosie and Jem didn't hear it?' Lydia remarked.

He shook his head. 'That's the point you see. That's what I can't understand ...' He felt divided from her, talking like this. The strange experiences were pushing him further and further away from reality. He'd said enough. I shall lose her if I carry on, he thought. And for a moment he felt disturbed and unhappy. That was what the music did. It disturbed him. In it was a kind of yearning. A searching for something. A longing.

Two mallards were looking for scraps of food by their feet. It seemed their silky heads changed from green to blue and back again as they searched the floor. 'Beethoven must have been very grateful to Broadwood', said Daniel suddenly. 'The way he improved the piano.' He threw a crust to the mallards. 'Beethoven was merciless though, they say, when it came to instruments. He always wanted more than they could manage.'

'Perhaps he wanted more than the music could give', said Lydia. She looked downwards. 'Love is like that, I think. It can never be what we want.'

'Can't it', he said quickly, searching her eyes.

Jeremy came for their order. 'And about time, too', said Lydia. The café was busy that day, she'd watched him, dashing about, glancing across at them, letting her know she must wait her turn patiently. He stood now before her in black jeans and a white T-shirt, a green apron tied round his waist. The cobra gleamed on his arm, its long tongue wound round his wrist, its body thickly twisting around his muscles.

'Coffee?' she said, turning to Daniel. 'Whatever you want', he said. They ordered black coffees and fruit cake. The order came quickly. Lydia continued. 'So your dad's a Beethoven fan?' He sighed, wanting to talk about something else. Something less traumatic. 'My father and I have often enjoyed a concert together. — And good reading, too. Sometimes we'll read the same book, sharing it, and discussing it later.' He broke off then, laughing briefly, realising that what he was saying was very much in the past. Not now. Now the time he spent with his father was brief. 'We sound like lonely people, don't we?' he said sadly.

'We are all lonely', said Lydia. She braced herself and leaned back, her eyes flashing again. She was quick to regain her spirits.

As he thought of it, he realised how little his father listened to music now, or bothered to read a book. He'd manage the morning paper, but that was all. Most of the time he was at the surgery, or filling in forms when he came home. If he could find a spare moment, he generally went to sleep. Daniel recalled the last time they'd gone out together. It had been to *The Winter's Tale*, in London, his father's favourite Shakespeare play. The words of Antigonus, holding the child and talking about its dead mother, came to him strongly. His father knew them by heart, and often recited them. Daniel chilled at their significance and portent now:

> 'Come poor babe:
> I have heard, but not believed, the spirits o'the dead
> May walk again: if such thing be, thy mother
> Appear'd to me last night; for ne'er was dream
> So like waking. To me comes a creature,
> Sometimes her head on one side, some another;
> I never saw a vessel of like sorrow,
> So fill'd and so becoming; in pure white robes ...
> She melted into air. Affrighted much
> I did in time collect myself, and thought
> This was so, and no slumber ...'

'Are you cold?' asked Lydia. There was room inside the café, they were sat by the water. Around them people were laughing and talking. Daniel thought, 'I am on the edge of reality. A narrow, precipitious edge ...' He gazed at the sky.

'What do you look for?' she asked, following his gaze.

'The secrets of the spectrum, I suppose', he sighed. 'The ever-elusive light of the cosmos.'

'It's all so vast', she murmured. Jeremy came and filled their cups again.

'The riding?' she said, recalling their promise. 'Do you want me to fix a date?'

'You do the booking and I'll be there', he said.

'I could pick you up', she offered.

Daniel told her his car was kept in the garage normally, when he came home. He scarcely used it. He could do the driving though, if she wanted. The car could do with a spin. She wasn't sure which of the riding schools they'd go from, she said, there were quite a number. She'd phone and tell him. He looked up at Cliff House, looming, mysterious. The place looked hard to reach just then, going on and on as it did, climbing into the sky. It was far too big for his father to live in alone. This time, Daniel realised, it was going to be worse than ever to leave him.

'See', she said, pointing. 'There's a star! You can even see them in daylight!' The star shimmered above them. 'What do you see?' she asked. 'Through the telescope?'

'I'm not sure what I shall see through the one in my attic,' he smiled. 'I haven't tested it yet. But I'm hoping for great things. It's the best I could buy.' 'You must come and look through it sometime.'

'Tonight?' she ventured. 'Can I see it tonight? I've nothing to do this evening.'

'You can if you want', he laughed. The words came fast. 'But, like I've told you, sometimes you're lucky, and sometimes you're not.' He was certainly lucky now. Beside them, on the river bank, the two mallards had returned, sitting in the roots of an old tree. 'See you at eight?' he suggested. It was all so quick. They were making up, it seemed, for lost time. Lost years perhaps. He raised his eyes to the sky. Disastrous. But he'd light a fire. A glowing fire. And they'd be together. What did the weather matter. The stars could wait. He was in love.

LIGHTS

It rained. And it rained. Weather of the most wicked sort, plagued the cliffs and the streets, making it almost impossible to walk the craggy paths by the river. A purple light obscured the trees. Almost the lamplight even. Lydia reached for the phone and rang Daniel's number. The line was dead. Perhaps it was due to the rain. She didn't have his mobile number either. But she wanted so much to see him tonight whatever the weather.

The thought of the climb to the house worried her. The path was steep and craggy. The rocks would be slippery and dangerous. She thought for a while. She could always see him tomorrow. But tomorrow ...

She found her wellingtons and raincoat. If she went slowly and carefully, she ought to be safe. She would take her car to the little gate at the foot of the cliff, then find her way, cautiously through the rockery, up to the house.

Jeremy was out with Rosie. As they'd driven off on the bike, the weather had been quite mild, changing suddenly. The rain came down in torrents. The wind had come with it. Her mother had gone to a costume dance at the manor with Howard. She wouldn't be back till late. Lydia scribbled a note to say where she'd gone, and urged her not to worry, then put it beneath the transistor radio James had brought from his tour. For a while, buttoned inside her raincoat, she sat thinking.

Having made a flying visit home, before leaving again for Bonn, James had kept his promise and brought her mother the radio. He hoped that Lydia's visit to France had been successful, he'd said. He was having to rush, but he'd bought her some gloves he would give her later. The kind she had bought for herself in Italy once. 'Like a second skin.' Lydia didn't keep gloves for long. She always lost them. Umbrellas too went missing in minutes. Sometimes she'd spent hours inquiring of lost property offices. But it didn't matter now. Losing gloves and umbrellas was something she did. It was something that happened to her along with everything else. 'Tell her I love her', he'd said. 'She must always remember that.'

Lydia recalled the first time they'd met. James had been in *Tosca* at the Palace Theatre in Manchester. She'd gone with Sara, her friend, who was also a student at the Royal Northern College and played the violin. James was in his final year and the best young baritone, the papers said, in England. When they'd been introduced there'd been an instant attraction. His voice had filled the theatre that night. And also her heart. He was tall and blonde with a proud bearing and piercing blue eyes.

At first, she'd enjoyed his forcefulness and what she had thought his strength. But the truth was different. As truth often is. James was a bully. And over the years she had seen him for what he really was. But she loved him. Or at least she'd thought she did. She'd decided to love him, and didn't know how to stop. Loving James had become a kind of habit. And since she was a responsible sort of person, she'd felt responsible for loving him and thought she must make him happy. He had managed to make her feel responsible for his misery too and constantly plagued her with how depressed he got if she chose to complain.

That night on the stage. James had glowed. When free, his long hair curled on his shoulders. Most of the time it was tied back in a pony tail. Sometimes at Anderson Terrace, when it flowed down his shoulders, and he sang his beautiful songs, her mother would watch in awe. And Lydia too was lost to him then, she and her mother both entranced by his charm.

But the spell was soon broken. At least for Lydia. Just as the voice rose and the abuse poured out, so the love she had felt for him dribbled out of her heart.

Recalling that first night, she remembered his eyes as they had searched her face, and the way she had wanted him. 'So you are Lydia', he'd said softly. 'Sara has told me about you. But she didn't say how lovely you were. Now Sara wouldn't would she?'

That year her father had given them all a rough time, and Lydia had needed James. He had taken her hand to his lips and she'd been on fire. 'A charmer', Sara had said. 'You must watch him.' Philip had said so too. He borrowed money from Philip and rarely repaid him. Sara said she wouldn't wish James on her worst enemy. She'd ruined Lydia's life she said in one fell swoop.

Philip was tall and thin. He was also kind and caring, and a rare find. Sara loved him. Always reliable, he planned ahead and had bought a house in Harrogate, doing it up in his spare time so they could live together properly. They were getting married the following year. That night James and Philip had argued.

'Mineral water', Philip had said firmly, handing the drink to James. 'I asked for beer', said James, frowning and angry, and thrusting the water back at him so it spilled on the floor. Philip mopped it up with a napkin. 'You shouldn't be drinking alcohol', he'd said, under his breath. 'You're singing.'

'I know I was a little bit drunk last night', James grumbled. 'But ...'

Philip gave him a quick contemptuous glance. 'A little bit?' he said. He looked at Lydia. 'I was carrying him home on my back. The neighbours were given an excellent rendering of *Auf der Bruck* at something like two in the morning. God, it was awful!'

James gritted his teeth. 'For fuck's sake!' he said, slumping down on a chair. 'If a fellow can't have a drink.' He reached for his cigarettes. Little lights flicked on and off in Lydia's mind. But she took no notice. She'd made her decision, and that was that.

'You won't make the top', Philip had said, 'if this is what's going to happen. Every time there's a concert, you just get drunk.'

James had laughed out loud. 'The top? I'm bloody fantastic, man! I've made five discs already. What do you want?' He ran his tongue round his lips and winked at Lydia. James was a brilliant singer, drink or no drink. Singing was second nature to him, easy as breathing, he said, and he loved it.

At Alderley Edge in the cottage, he sang constantly, bombarding the walls with his practice, the neighbours peering in as they passed. And he didn't care what time of day he did it. He often sang after midnight. If he wanted to sing, he sang. And Lydia knew his songs by heart. Sometimes he would play the piano and call her in to accompany him, singing simple pieces. But Lydia was no singer, and James was always impatient. 'Raise your voice, Lydia', he'd shout. 'Louder! Louder! Oh, you're useless.' She didn't try, he said. But she couldn't sing. He wanted too much from her. He wanted things she could not give.

But there were other things he did not want, that she could have given. He did not want her love of art and history. He did not want her kindess. And it seemed he did not want her love. He only wanted her anger.

She had worn a black silk gown that first night, low cut, and her hair had been pinned up. Bending forward to pick up her bag, she had felt his lips on her neck. Later he'd taken the pins from her hair and they'd made passionate love. For a while, when first they'd been living together, she'd called Sara anxiously on the phone, telling her how he was, how tired she was and depressed. 'He'll kill you', Sara had warned. 'I've always thought it.' But trying to end the relationship had never been easy. He always got round her. James had clever tactics, like making her think she was worthless so she must turn to him. She would turn to him from her misery, misery that was caused by him in the first place. And so it went on, a continuous cycle of pain. Wasted, wasted, years.

But some of the time had been happy. There were photos to prove it. Just like the ones at home, on her mother's walls and dressing table. Lies. All lies. In its own tedious and painful way, only time had delivered the truth.

The barren sensation of emptiness filled her again as she sat thinking, listening to the rain on the windows, the wind trying the doors. She stacked the fire with logs and adjusted the guard. Then she opened the door and went to her car.

As she approached the rockery at Cliff House, looking up she saw that a small light burned in the porch, though the rest of the house was in darkness. Carpets of moss and sprawling ferns covered her way. The rain continued to pour and the moss was slippery. She trod carefully. The yellow light in the porch flickered, smooth and thin. The stony rocks at her feet gleamed with wetness. Just then the light went out, then on again quickly. It was further than she had thought. The path seemed endless. Her breath escaped in tiny clouds before her. Suddenly she was there.

Through the partially opened door she saw that an oil lamp swung from the roof. She shivered, pushing the door and calling. Nobody seemed to be there. She stepped inside. But for the light in the porch where she now stood the house was dark. At least she was out of the rain. But where was Daniel, and why were there no lights?

Suddenly, from the shadows, he emerged, opening the main door and carrying a lamp. 'Lydia', he said, surprised. 'I didn't expect you would come in this. You're soaked.' He drew her in. She ought to have come the other way, he said, by the gate on the high street, and chided himself for not having told her about it. The power had failed in the house. The lights and the phone line had gone. Emergency lighting, he said, at Cliff House, consisted of one oil lamp and several candles. That would change, he said, straight away; he would put such matters right.

'A bit of a black hole, eh?' he said. By the light of the lamp she saw that his feet were naked. 'I never wear shoes in the house', he said, seeing her looking. 'Socks neither, I'm afraid. A terrible habit.' She blinked the wet from her eyelids and shook herself, trying to remove her raincoat which was heavy with rain. 'I've a fuse here', he said, opening his palm. 'I was going to try it. Damn it Lydia, I'm sorry.'

Now she stood in the hall. She could feel the warmth of the house and began to remove her wellingtons. 'At least I made it', she laughed, her wellingtons making loud squashing sounds as she took them off. She didn't care. She was right where she wanted to be. He took them from her and poured the water outside. 'Next time you come', he called, 'you must come through the back gate. The approach is by the high street ... ' He paused. There he was, taking her all for granted. Thinking she'd come again.

She hung up her raincoat. At least her jeans and blouse were dry. She blew on her hands which were red with cold, then stamped her bare feet on the earthenware tiles. She sat down on a wooden stool in the hallway. 'I made it', she laughed, her teeth chattering slightly. 'I actually made it. Don't I deserve a prize?'

His jeans and shirt were filled with dust from the cellars. 'Look', he said, seeing she was safely seated, and putting his coat round her shoulders, 'wait here till I get back. I won't be long.'

Within minutes the house lit up. Bright light flooded the rooms. He took her hand. 'There's a fire in the lounge. I'll make you a hot drink.' He gave her a long and gentle look. 'It's good that you've come.'

The ceilings, she saw, were high, and the wainscoting along the hall caused their voices to vibrate through the long corridors and up the high stairway. Cobwebs swung from the ceiling, black and shivering with age. The walls of the hall held pictures of birds and animals. As they entered the lounge the heat from the fire met them, the flames charging the chimney and lighting the room. He went to the hearth rearranging the logs, sending the flames shuddering, stamping like wild horses. The television had come back on. It was showing *Solomon and Sheba*. The sound was turned off.

She knelt by the fire, enjoying its warmth. Books on medicine, astronomy, maths, music and literature filled the bookcases about her. A long shelf by the window contained compact discs and a player. Her attention focused on an old HMV record player, placed on a small oak table, a collection of 78s beside it. 'Does it still work?' she asked, observing it carefully. It looked clean and well cared for.

'Perfectly', he told her, coming over and bringing a towel for her hair which had stuck to her face with wetness. 'I must let you hear it sometime.' She rubbed her hair on the towel, then followed him to the table where he straightened his notes. She looked at what he was writing: '*The triffid nebula in*

Sagitarrius contains tiny dark spots called globules. These are thought by astronomers to be stars on the verge of being born.'

'How can a star be born?' she whispered. 'What an idea.'

'Maths', he said, turning to the TV. 'Look', he said quickly. 'I must switch this off. I wasn't watching it really. I never do. I sort of half watch it. Actually, you know, I'm quite a madman in here.'

'Don't put it off for me', she said, enjoying him near her, watching him as he moved about and thinking how dirty his feet were as he stood before her, soiled as they were from the cellars. 'That is, unless you want to.'

'It's a favourite film of mine', he said, 'I watch it a lot.' He piled more logs on the fire. 'I like to collect the epics. I can see it's something you know.' Lydia turned on the sound. 'An interesting story', she smiled. He took coffee mugs he'd used through to the kitchen then came back, clearing books from the surfaces and putting them back in the bookcase. The place was chaotic. They were silent a while. 'She shouldn't have done it, you see', he said, as they watched the film together: Sheba in all her splendour, the music throbbing, attendants, votaries dancing around a great stone pagan god. The black and white pictures flashed in the dim room, mingling with the fire light.

'You mean when she tempted Solomon?'

Daniel nodded slowly.

'Do you think he was helpless?' Lydia asked softly.

'Pretty much, Lydia. Pretty much.' He got down beside her, taking her hand. Her eyes, he saw, were filled with a childlike vulnerability. The drumming was heavy. The firelight danced on the walls. 'I must make you a drink', he said, getting up. 'Why don't you come through. It's a funny kitchen, though. A strange little window looks out on the rock face. Can't think why it's there really. All you can see is water and green slime.' Lydia turned off the film and followed him into the small room where they sat by a pine table.

The kitchen had two windows, one of them large, and the other tiny, and as he had said, looking out on the rock, just then in darkness. From the larger window, in daylight, he said, you could see the gardens and the gate to the high street. The room was warm and comfortable, a pair of his father's glasses lay by a book on the table. Lydia thought it might have been where he sat reading. Piles of newspapers littered the floor, pushed to the sides of the walls. Drawing a bag of fresh coffee out of a cupboard, he spooned some into the percolator.

'The window is open mostly', he said, seeing her looking out. 'We like to listen when the water runs down the cliff. But as you can see it's a little bit damp over there. Look how it's crumbling. I doubt it's serious, though, it's been like that for years.'

She was quiet, observing things. He brought out mugs and milk. Suddenly a phone rang out on the wall. He went across. Answering it, he seemed anxious and irritated, hiding his voice as he spoke in almost a whisper. 'What do you want?' he asked urgently. 'You mustn't keep phoning me here! How can I make it plain?' He turned to Lydia, with a strained exhausted look. 'I'm sorry. Look, I shall have to take this call next door. Do you mind?'

He went to the lounge. Returning after five minutes, he feigned an equanimity, though his eyes were troubled. Lydia poured the coffee while he sat, almost oblivious by the table.

'I shall have to be going after this', she said, seeing him preoccupied. It was getting late. She felt suddenly out of place, as if she should not be there. She would have to make her way to her car again somehow. Perhaps she would go by the back entrance and find her way round the houses. 'You've things to do', she said handing him coffee and drinking her own.

'Have I?' he said. He got up frowning, his throat tightening. 'I'm sorry about that. Listen, Lydia. If only you knew ...'

'I'd rather you didn't say', she told him, looking downwards. 'It's none of my business.'

'Oh, Lydia', he said, covering his face with his hands. 'It isn't mine either. Honestly.'

'I'd better go', she said. It seemed the evening had drained down a hole. They were both quite flat.

'You came to see the telescope ...' he said miserably. 'I've tried to prepare it. Please don't go. You must let me show you?' He took her hand and went to the stairs. 'It's quite a climb', he said. 'But it isn't as bad as the rockery, and at least it's dry.'

They went up slowly. 'I doubt there'll be much to see, but you never know. We might be lucky.'

As they climbed he hoped there would be no ghostly manifestations. He hadn't prepared her for that. He wasn't prepared himself. And anyway, what could he tell her? She could never have taken it seriously. But he felt as if others watched. Just as he observed the stars it occurred to him that he too might be observed by others. Perhaps there were different ways of looking at time, outside scientific knowledge. Modern science, he concluded, was only as good as its day. The human brain, he speculated, wasn't equipped for the truth. Not the real truth. He knew now that there were presences in Cliff House, and he did not doubt the existence of ghosts. But their unpredictability worried him. As he neared the attic door he wondered what they might find. Would there be someone there? Would she be frightened? What if Lydia fainted?

'Attics are always mysterious places', he laughed. 'Ours is no exception. I've thrown out lots of rubbish, though. The roof was packed with nests ...'

The atmosphere was strangely cold, and as he inserted the key he started, for he saw a shadow moving across the wall. It wasn't his own. It wasn't Lydia's. He watched anxiously, his heart pounding. Who could be with them now? He glanced at Lydia, innocent of all he knew, watching the cobwebs swinging about from the roof. His eyes followed the shadow to the second stairway. It moved quickly, and for a moment burst into blue light, and a woman wearing a red silk dress, her hair pinned up with a black rose hairslide came into view. She disappeared in an instant.

'What is it?' asked Lydia, seeing him leaning against the wall and looking emotional.

'I don't know', he whispered. 'I just don't know.'

The door swung open widely on to the small room. It was lit with moonlight. The attic ceiling sloped so that at one side you could only sit. At the far end a pile of books were stacked by the wall. On an old grey trunk Lydia saw some white slippers, shimmering with what looked like wetness, though it was the shine of silk. For the best light, Daniel must place the lamp at the end of the room. He bent his head and went across, putting it on a table and locating the telescope. Their shadows bent on the walls and ceiling, the room warm and cozy from the fire beneath.

'Come and try it', he said quietly, watching her make her way. Carefully she put her eye to the eyepiece. It felt cold and metallic. He told her how to look, and she tried what he said, though without success. After a while she gave up.

'Here, I'll show you again', he said, calmly. 'You have to adjust it.' The telescope wasn't functioning right and one of the parts was missing. He intended to phone the place he had bought it from tomorrow. It ought to have worked though, he said, normally. 'It isn't behaving', he laughed. 'Hopeless tonight, I think.' The evening seemed to be doomed, he thought. Nothing was going right.

Lydia though was absorbed and contented. She went to the old trunk and looked at the small silk shoes, taking them off the top and putting them down on the floor. They seemed to be almost new. 'What's in here?' she asked, fingering the padlock. 'Is there a key?'

He came to her. 'I don't know', he said looking at it curiously. Whatever the trunk contained, it had been there for years. He hadn't even thought about it till now. 'I expect my dad will have one.' He went to the telescope again and looked through. Nothing had changed. He took some accessories out of a small box and sorted them out on the floor. Lydia, he saw, was putting her feet in the silk slippers.

'Georgian, I think', he said. 'I don't know whose they were. They've always been there. They weren't my mother's though, I know that.' He realised then how for long periods the house had been forgotten. His life had been taken up with other things. Sometimes, he remembered sadly, he'd even

66

forgotten his father. 'You forget things', he said. 'I was often at school. And then I was with Aunt Rachel. I didn't come up to the attic much.'

'Is your father's sister married?' asked Lydia.

He struggled to get the telesecope right, trying out various fixtures. 'She was almost married', he said, calling over his shoulder. 'Some photographer called Geoffrey. A monster he was. He jilted her at the last minute. It set her back. She's never trusted men since then. Dad tried to help her though, going over and that, but it wasn't easy.' He stood for a moment, thoughtful. 'She did get stronger though. Came into her own, dad said.' He breathed in deeply, putting all the accessories back in their boxes.

'And what is she doing now?' Lydia asked, curiously. Aunt Rachel had had an important role in Daniel's life. She would like to know more about her.

'She runs a farm — with a team of helpers of course. Dad used to see her a lot. Not much now though. She'll be happy to see him this week.'

They were silent a while. 'Do you think there's life out there?' Lydia asked, watching him struggling to get the tele-scope right.

'Life?' he said abstractedly. 'The billion dollar question.' He sighed. 'I'd certainly like to think so. If there was, they'd probably have found us by now. The galaxy must be double the age of the solar system. If life's out there, it's had plenty of time to develop the skills to find us.' He shook his head. 'Nice idea though.'

Suddenly the telescope seemed to be working. The clouds had cleared. 'Come and look!' he cried, beckoning her. He was quite determined she'd see the stars that night, in all their glory. 'Hurry!' he cried. 'Quick!' She went to him and put her eye to the eye-piece again. Beside him, the smell of her hair was clean and earthy with rain. The scent of her filled him with longing. He took her hand, drawing her close, and found her lips with his own. Her mouth was warm and open. 'Lydia', he murmured. 'I want you.' She softened into him quickly. Standing back, she opened her blouse then slipped her jeans slowly from her. Her skin shone in the lamplight, her movements filled with a sense of determination. He was aching to hold her and eased himself from his clothes, drawing her down and finding her breasts, her shoulders, the fine pelt of her skin beneath his lips. His penis hardened. 'Lydia, Lydia. I want you.' For a moment they locked together still and silent, breathing hard and filled with a kind of wonder.

I can't', she said suddenly, and pulling away. 'Not yet.' 'Why not?' he cried, hurt and confused. 'What have I done?' He tightened his hold. 'Don't turn from me now. Not now.'

'It isn't you', she said, her voice shaking. 'You mustn't think that. It's me.' Somewhere deep inside her, Lydia was mourning. She was mourning for the loss of herself. The time she had wasted with James. The woman she had sacrificed to a false love.

He held her tightly. 'Tell me', he said softly, kissing her cheeks. 'Tell me, my love, what it is.'

'I can't', she said, her eyes filling with tears. 'I don't understand. I can't make love just yet.'

He covered her shoulders with kisses. After a pause he said: 'I do understand, my darling. I do. But Lydia, I shall have you. In time we shall have each other. We will, won't we.' He gazed at her, smiling tenderly. 'Let me hold you, my love, and comfort you.'

The room was silent. 'I've always wanted you', she whispered. 'All my life. Even before my life. But something's happened. Before I can love you properly, I must know who I am myself.'

'We must wait', he said softly. 'All we can do is wait.' And they lay together for some time before finally falling asleep.

TRANSLATIONS

'I've brought you some coffee', said Jeremy. It was almost lunchtime. He put it down on a low table by Lydia's bed. 'I'm off in a minute.' He sat down on the floor, his back to the wall. Lydia stirred under the bedclothes. 'I was wondering where you were last night', he said. 'You didn't come in till five o'clock this morning. And mum was only a few minutes earlier. I thought you'd both run off.'

Lydia sat up, plumping the pillow. She blinked hard, remembering the previous evening, recalling how Daniel had driven her back early that morning then walked home alone. Her watch on the table read ten-thirty. She should have been up. She'd a chapter to do in her book. 'I left a message', she said. 'I know what I'm doing, Jem.'

'You didn't say you'd be out all night', he said sullenly. His shoes were dirty. It looked like he'd been outside. They were silent a while. Lydia took a drink from her coffee and stared at the ceiling. Jeremy said, 'You don't really know him, Lydia. You should take it slowly.' He frowned. 'I've finished with all that star stuff now. I shan't be getting in touch.' He'd always been protective towards her. Especially since their father had left. Now, more so, since she was leaving James. He knew there was something bad about Daniel, though he didn't know what. His mother was keeping it back.

'He's a wonderful man, Jem', Lydia said, her voice pained. 'And I'm happy. I haven't been happy for ages.' Jeremy seemed preoccupied. 'You ought to be pleased', she said, her tone sharper than she wanted. No-one would stand in the way of her happiness now. Not even Jeremy. 'And anyway, what's the matter? You seem to be in a mood.'

He shook his head sadly. 'I'm all mixed up, and I can't think', he said. The morning was warm and the air had cleared of rain. 'But I'm glad you're safe. It was terrible weather.'

'And you were out in it too. I thought of you both on the bike.' Lydia watched him. She knew he hoped to get Rosie back now she'd come home. Though it didn't seem to be working.

He bent his head sighing, 'Yes, it was.' His hands, she saw, were covered in cement dust. He must have been doing some work outside before going to the boathouse. He'd come to her to talk. Not just about her but also about himself.

'I fixed that washpole and put some bricks in the wall at the back where the foxes came in', he said. Once awake, Jeremy rarely went back to sleep. He blew out exhaustedly. 'There's something wrong with my python. They know things those snakes.'

Watching him, as he curled on the floor, Lydia thought he looked like the python himself. 'So what's the problem?' she asked finally. 'Something's upset you.'

He stood up, leaning against the wall, his arms folded. Last night, he said, had been awful. They shouldn't have gone on the bike. There'd been a skid and Rosie had bruised her arm. 'And it's not just that ...' He spoke wearily. Lydia waited. 'She's changed.'

Lydia watched as he wound his arms about himself, something he did when lonely. 'People do', she said. 'She's grown up.'

He smiled sardonically, running his tongue round his lips. 'That's what she thinks.' He gazed ahead. It was almost a glare. 'She hasn't really though. Not really.' He threw out his hands and pulled little pieces of dried cement from his jersey. 'Maybe she has ...' He smiled strangely. It was almost a smile from his boyhood. It hurt her to see it. 'So what about you?' he asked. 'What's going on?'

She slipped beneath the bedclothes again, talking into the pillow. 'I'm happy, Jem. I never thought I could feel like this. It's amazing. You waste your life ... You go on wasting it.' She turned to him suddenly serious. 'You mustn't do it yourself, Jem. You must promise me that.'

He frowned and looked downwards. 'You've got no choice sometimes. Whatever happens happens.'

She gazed at the ceiling.

'You'll have to tell James', he said.

'Well, I'm not sure I shall', she said sleepily. 'I think we parted years ago. What is there to explain? I'm alive. And before I was dead. That's all there is to it.'

'Don't be morbid', he said, trying to smile. His sister's moods went up and down like this. Sometimes she would hide away for ages if something hurt her. Just like the voles by the river. But he liked her happy. It gave him strength. They drank their coffee and thought for a while, listening to their mother downstairs hoovering the lounge. 'James phoned while you were out', he said. 'It was after midnight. I told him you'd caught a cold. I said you were sleeping.'

'You could be right', she laughed, glad that he'd lied for her. 'I got saturated last night.'

He buried his head in his hands, filling his hair with grey cement from his fingers. 'I don't like lying, you know. He's going to call again. Today, I think.' He spoke quietly. The boy in him had almost gone, a man was emerging now, strong and decisive. A man who knew what he wanted.

'Sometimes you have to', Lydia said, disturbed by his words. 'I expect he was drunk.'

Jeremy nodded. 'Sooner or later you'll have to tell him. He takes you for granted.'

She put her hands to her face. Daniel's essence lingered. She could still feel his body against her own, its hardness and strength. If only the part of her life she had shared with James could fade away. Evaporate like water. Why must it block her thoughts like this?

'Well, you know how I rate him', said Jeremy. 'It's good riddance.' They were silent again for a while. The vacuum cleaner had stopped. Jeremy lowered his voice. 'You know how mum thinks though, don't you.'

'I'm not really bothered', said Lydia, stinging with anger. 'Mum can think what she wants. She's made up her mind, don't you see. Daniel's a demon. She'll summon up every wicked thought in her head to attack him with.'

'That's a bit strong, Lydia', frowned Jeremy. 'It's all about caring.'

'I wish that were true', said Lydia.

'Everything's changing', said Jeremy. 'Nothing's the same any more.'

'It's James who wears the sheep's clothing', continued Lydia. 'Not Daniel. I wish she would get her facts right.' She closed her eyes and thought for a while. How many pathways had she wandered inside her mind. And why had she feared them. It was right and good to ask questions. Questions about the way you lived. The way you thought. To find things out was important. Jeremy shuffled about, awkwardly. 'You still haven't told me what's bothering you', she said. 'Not properly.'

'Honesty counts, doesn't it?' he said, earnestly.

'Well', she smiled. 'I'm glad you told the lie for me.'

'Yes, but most of the time, it counts?'

'Probably yes. Of course.'

'Well, she isn't honest.'

'Who? Rosie?'

Jeremy nodded. 'When somebody doesn't tell you something important, then it's like a lie. Right?' He spoke solemnly. Not like his usual self.

'I suppose so', said Lydia curiously. She got out of bed and reached for her housecoat. 'Why don't you tell me what's happened.' Jeremy was a practical man. Unlike herself, who was always thinking, and didn't always act on what she thought, Jeremy got on with it. If he came to a block it confused and frustrated him. Solutions would not come to him from inside his head.

'It's a mess', he said miserably.

'What is?' Lydia asked concernedly.

'Rosie's thinking. It's all in a muddle. I doubt I shall see her again.'

Lydia gazed amazed. 'That can't be true. You'll see her tomorrow. She'll be at the boathouse for lunch, won't she?'

'No, not like that. You know.'

Lydia couldn't think what to say. Jeremy had wanted to marry Rosie since he was ten. He'd probably asked her already. That would have scared her off. Perhaps it had. He looked away, as if he might cry like a child. Lydia had never seen him cry.

He was solid as rock. Most of the time she'd done his crying for him.

'I didn't do anything wrong. It's all her.' His skin tightened with feeling. 'She doesn't love me. She told me.' He went to the window, leaning against the architrave. 'She was seeing this chef in China. They were working together. He's gone to New Zealand.' His voice was thin in the still air. 'I left her innocent, you know. I never touched her. I wouldn't.'

'You mean they were lovers?'

Jeremy's face creased for a moment in pain. 'Well anyway, a rotten night it was in every sense.'

'There'll be other girls', said Lydia. 'If she doesn't want you, she won't be right for you anyway. If you want someone's love, and it doesn't fit, then you can't blame them for that.'

Jeremy pressed his lips tightly together and nodded his head. 'So she's better off with the chef? Is that what you're saying?'

'I expect he's a better cook!' Lydia laughed.

'I'm glad you think it's funny', Jeremy said moodily. 'I don't.'

The tension in him made her feel desperate. As though she must let his blood. She wanted his indignation. 'You're stronger than you think, Jem', she said. 'If you really want her, I'm sure you can get her. But I don't think you do, you see.'

Just then their mother came in from the landing. 'You must marry James, yourself, mum', Jeremy said, fastening his coat. 'Our Lydia won't.' And he went out.

The phone rang out downstairs. Lydia went down. It was James from Bonn, as he'd promised.

'Lydia, where have you been?' he asked urgently. 'I've been trying to get you. Jeremy said you were ill.'

'That's right', said Lydia. 'I haven't been well. I caught a cold in France.'

'Did you, in France? That's strange.' His tone was cautious. 'Perhaps you're overdoing it, dashing about like you do. I've told you to take it easy.'

'I had to find something out. Anyway, I've got it now.'

73

'At least that's something', said James, moving on to say what he was doing in Bonn. 'The concerts have been a real hit. I'm coming again next year.' He was silent a moment. 'You know, Lydia', he said slowly. 'When you didn't phone me this week ... You normally do ... I thought ... I thought there was something wrong. There isn't is there? I mean, could there be something wrong? Is there something you aren't telling me?'

Lydia stayed silent. No, she thought, there is nothing wrong at all. Everything is quite right. 'No', she said. 'I don't think so.'

'When I'm away', he went on. 'I worry about you. And when you don't phone, I ... Did your mum like her radio?'

Lydia saw that she'd taken it into her room upstairs. 'She liked it a lot', she told him. James carried on, punctuating his talk with laughter, telling her all the things he'd done that week. Her mother looked in, taking clothes to the washer. Lydia looked away. James would probably tell that she'd come to the end of her tolerance for his travels. And her tolerance for him too. 'Lydia?' he asked, a worried tone in his voice. 'Lydia, are you listening?'

'Yes', she said, 'I'm listening.'

He went on, telling her what they'd done that day. How he was lodging with an ancestor of Beethoven's in Bonn. An old woman. How she had kept a letter of his in her sewing box. 'Her sewing box, Lydia. I ask you! It's like a family heirloom, handed down and finishing up in a sewing box!' His talk was fast and intense. Whatever it was he had found, he was very excited. 'I've got it though, you see. I took it. She's more concerned with the needle and thread in there. I doubt she'll even notice. She tells me he came to England once to see Broadwood. Can you believe it? I can't say I heard about that. The letter was sent from there.' Someone was calling him. 'Won't be a minute, Tricia!' he called back. 'We're all going out', he said. 'A bit of a break, you know. It's been a hell of a week.' He was lighting a cigarette. With a sudden cold resolve he said: 'She's not going to get it back. She can keep her needles and cottons, but not that.'

74

Lydia sniffed. James thought the world his birthright. Whatever he wanted, he took. He went on. 'I'm sure it's authentic. I rang Broadwoods in London. They don't know a thing. I shall have to do some detective work, I think.'

'A lot can happen in a hundred years', said Lydia. And she thought, A lot can happen in twenty-four hours too. Again they were silent.

'Are you missing me?' he asked, his tone strained and unusually anxious.

Lydia stared at her feet. She did not speak.

'I might fly over', he said, breaking the silence. 'Just for a day. I shall have to come back here though, we've another concert this week.' Lydia was still silent. 'Are you okay?' he said. She could tell he was getting annoyed. 'I feel as if something's happened.'

'I'm trying to sort things out', she said quietly.

'What sort of things', he asked suspiciously.

'My notes. That sort of thing.'

'I see.'

She could hear him smoking. He coughed. 'I love you, Lydia', he said. 'I really do.'

Still she was silent. She'd never been so unyielding. 'It's cold', she said. 'I think it might snow.'

'I'll bring the gloves', he told her.

'The gloves? Oh, yes, the gloves.'

'Well', he said hesitantly, 'I'd better be off, they'll be going without me.'

'Goodbye', she said.

'Lydia?' he said, in a tone she hadn't heard before. 'Lydia, I ...'

'Goodbye', she repeated, her throat tightening. She put down the phone and sat by the window thinking, till her mother's voice broke into her thoughts.

'The fire's gone out', said Eliza.

Lydia saw she had let it burn down. 'I was talking to James.'

'You mean he was talking to you', her mother murmured. She took some firelighters from a cupboard and found some paper, starting it up again.

'You shouldn't be listening in', Lydia said, angrily. 'You shouldn't.' Her mother turned slowly and sighed. She hadn't removed her make-up from the night before; mascara was smudged round her eyes. 'Was the dance a success?' asked Lydia. Lydia spoke of Howard now, quite openly. To do so was a great joy. Though her mother was always reticent. 'Did Howard tread on your toes?'

Her mother smiled. 'He's a marvellous dancer', she said, with a hint of laughter. Lydia liked it. 'I haven't had so much fun in years!'

'I'm glad', said Lydia. 'You need to have fun, it keeps you young.'

'Well, I'm not so young as that', Eliza laughed. 'It prevents you from growing old though, I'll certainly grant you that.'

Lydia saw that her mother blushed when she said it. She watched her cleaning the hearth. 'There's something I want to ask you', Lydia said awkwardly. Her mother got up and faced her. She looked troubled, almost as if she knew what Lydia would say.

'I'd like to move in', said Lydia. For a few moments her mother gazed out of the window, a distant look in her eye. She looked downwards. 'Permanently, you mean?'

'No. Just for six months. I can't live there at Alderley Edge any more. You know that.'

'So you want to come here?'

'I'd like to', said Lydia. It was almost a plea. 'Couldn't I just have my old room back for six months?' She felt lost and uncomfortable. 'I'm always coming and going.'

'But your furniture? What would you do with that?'

'I'll store it. Except for that mahogany dresser I bought in Harrogate.' She pointed to a space by the door. 'I thought I might put it there. All my important things are in it. My photographs and such.' Lydia was talking quickly. She closed her eyes and prayed.

'Looks like you've thought it all out', her mother said quietly, her forehead tightening. 'So you're leaving him then?' Does that mean ...?'

'Mum!' cried Lydia. 'I know my own mind. I know what I want. Please don't hurt me like this!' She got up, pacing the room.

'Stop it, Lydia! Stop it!' Eliza cried. She put her hands to her ears.

Lydia trembled slightly. There were words she wanted to say, but they would not come. They were buried deep inside her.

'Does he know?' her mother whispered, her hand to her mouth.

'No, he doesn't', said Lydia. 'And I shan't tell him. I shall simply just do it. He'll find out soon enough.'

'Oh, Lydia, that's too cruel', her mother said, her eyes wide with alarm. 'You can't just ...'

Lydia sat down and put her head in her hands. 'Why is he so important?' Her voice rose slowly. 'Why am I always less important than him?'

'That's not what I'm saying', her mother moaned, looking bewildered.

'That's just what you're saying', said Lydia. 'And that's just what you think.' This was more than a conversation. It was an awakening.

'But he loves you, Lydia', her mother whispered.

Lydia laughed. 'Love?' she cried. 'You call it love?' She looked at her mother, the pitiable woman she was. 'Well, of course he does, in his own way. But I don't want his way. I want mine. I want to be loved in the right way, mum, by the right person.'

Her mother shrugged. 'Love is love. You should take it for all it's worth. It's a rare find.'

'No', said Lydia. 'You should find out what it's worth. And then decide if you want it.'

Her mother gave her a withered look and sighed. She spoke slowly, the words raw and personal: 'You've been ages finding it out if you ask me.'

If only she could be the woman she was last night, Lydia thought, instead of this wretch her father had made her into. Last night she'd been young and vivacious, and happy again.

'And you think I should go on with it, do you?' said Lydia. 'A wrong becomes a right because you carry it on. As if time has a value, whatever is in it.'

Her mother took down the brass monkeys from the mantelpiece and rubbed them against her skirt. Speak no evil. Hear no evil. Think no evil. Their yellow heads shone in the sunlight.

'It doesn't you see', Lydia went on, determined. 'Unhappiness leads down the same road. It leads to disaster. Mistakes are mistakes right from the start. Days become weeks. Weeks become years. Years become lifetimes.'

'People can change', her mother mumbled, rubbing the monkeys harder and harder. Speak no evil. Hear no evil. See no evil.

'People. People. Who are these people, mother? These people are you and me. They are us. And only if you really try can you change things.'

Her mother drew a deep breath, her eyes wide with confusion. She gazed at space.

'If you'd rather I didn't stay, I'll go', said Lydia at last. She had come to the end of her energy. Even the house seemed tired, as if its walls had had enough of talk. Enough of people.

'Where will you go?' said Eliza.

'I could go to Sara's', sighed Lydia. She put her hands to her face.

'You can't go there', said her mother. 'Not Sara's. There's the baby now. And besides, you haven't been talking lately.'

'Oh, that's alright', said Lydia. 'We've just been busy. We don't bother phoning much. And Michael is hardly a baby, mum, he's four years old.'

'You can't be staying with Sara', mumbled her mother. She put the brass monkeys back on the mantelpiece, then warmed her hands on the fire. 'Oh, you do cause trouble, Lydia.'

'The trouble is mine, not yours', Lydia snapped. 'Anything that's troubling me is always a trouble for you! That's how it goes, you see.' Lydia's eyes were burning. She went to the window and gazed at the landscape, the cliffs she knew so well, the trees that led to the river. She knew the hidden paths she had trod as a child. This was her place. The place where she had grown up. This was the place she loved. 'You're far too frightened, mum', she said softly. 'You always panic. You've never let me take chances. Make some mistakes. My own mistakes, not yours.' She turned. 'You see, you make them anyway, even when you are trying not to.' She faced her now. 'I'm sick of suffering, mum. I want to be happy. I want some peace.'

'James has been good to me', her mother said, meekly. 'He put those shelves up there, and built the wall at the back.'

'The one that Jeremy's just repaired, you mean', said Lydia contemptuously. 'It was falling apart.' Lydia sat down. 'And I am falling apart too. But I'm not bricks and mortar, you see. I'm flesh and blood. You can't just mix a bowl of cement and put me together again. I'm human. There are things I need.' Her mouth quivered, her eyes were moist. 'There are things I want.'

Eliza Ralphson went to the fire again and stirred the logs. Her voice was low. 'This is horrible talk. I won't even listen.'

'I'm talking honestly, mum', Lydia said sternly. 'And it's good. It's real and honest. There hasn't been much honesty in here for years.'

'Lydia, you're my daughter. I love you. How can you talk like this to me, I'm your mother?' Lydia saw that her mother was shaking now. The bridge was crumbling. Her mother went on. 'We don't understand each other, Lydia, do we?' she said. 'Listening to you now, I don't think I know you at all.'

Lydia sighed and rubbed her face. 'I don't think you do. Not the real me. The proper Lydia. You only know the one you want me to be. But it isn't me, you see. And I know why you'd rather I didn't stay here. You think I don't, but I do. It's him isn't it?'

'The man's your father, Lydia', Eliza said quietly.

'You think he'll come back. But he won't. He'll never come back. He uses you. You just don't see it.'

'How can you say these things? It isn't right.'

'Right? He'll get your money, and go. That's what he'll do. The reason he doesn't want me here is because I know him. I

79

know him better than you do. He can do what he wants with you. But not with me.'

'Lydia!' her mother said firmly. 'You're talking about your father.'

Lydia got up and went to the window again, looking outside. 'He's a human being', she said quietly. 'He isn't God.'

'He loves me', Eliza whispered. 'He's always loved me.'

Lydia turned. Her face was creased with pain. 'He doesn't, mum. Not really. He uses you. He uses everyone.'

'Where's your respect?' her mother snapped, wiping her eyes.

'Respect must be earned', said Lydia. 'I curse him for what he's done to me. What he's done to us.'

'I've always tried to hold this family together', Eliza murmured. 'I've always stood firm. I've tried to love him.'

'And that's okay, is it?' laughed Lydia sardonically. 'You don't love him. You don't even like him. And what's more, he knows it. If he keeps you frightened he runs the show.' Lydia's voice fell low. 'I know, because it's happened to me with James.' She felt limp with emotion. The two woman sat now facing each other in the small room, the fire glowed red as if forgetting to flame.

'Well', said her mother finally. 'So this is how you see it, is it?'

'It's how it is. It's the truth', said Lydia. Her mother got up and walked about. She straightened her hair in the mirror. 'And what about Howard?' said Lydia, watching her.

Her mother was silent at first. 'So what about him?'

'He's not going to wait for ever.'

'What do you mean?'

'He might find somebody else.'

'Howard?'

'Yes.'

Eliza laughed briefly, embarrassed. 'Well, he isn't waiting for me if that's what you think.'

'Of course he is', said Lydia. She leaned her head on the back of the chair and spoke softly. 'We all have choices. They're hard, but we must make them. How can we know the future?' She sighed hard. They were silent a moment. 'Anyway, I'm off', she said getting up slowly and finding her coat.

'Where are you going?' her mother asked without looking.

Lydia spoke wearily. 'I'm not sure. Anywhere, I suppose.'

'What shall we do?' her mother cried. She got up and went to her, putting her head on her shoulder, and weeping. 'Lydia, Lydia, this is awful.'

'I don't know what you're going to do, mum. But I must find somewhere to live. Somewhere that isn't with James.'

Her mother gazed at her with a sudden new emotion. 'We could tidy up Jeremy's room, and make more space ... I could empty the wardrobe ...'

'Only six months', said Lydia, her throat tightening again. 'Till we've sold the house.'

'Bring what you need, and we'll take it from there', said Eliza. And they embraced silently like two new people.

Over the next few days, Daniel would be at a conference in London, strangely though, he had left no number for her to reach him on. She hoped he would phone, there was much to tell him now.

DISCOVERIES

The following day was mild. Lydia slipped on a light coat, and for the first time in days, shoes instead of boots. It was almost two o'clock. People were out on the river again. The boathouse teemed with children. Pointing her car to the main road, she made for Alderley Edge. She'd bring a few things. Only what was important for now. Houses sold better with furnishings. She'd get the other things later. But she wanted the small dresser. It was an antique, and a rare find from Harrogate. Inlaid mahogany, it was something she had bought for herself with her first earnings.

Though they were called cottages, the dwellings at Ingleton Place were large terraced houses with high ceilings and long wide windows, through which she and James had enjoyed extensive views of the surrounding countryside. The second they'd viewed, they'd bought it immediately. The gardens had been neglected by the previous owners, and that first spring they had set about planting shrubs and fruit trees, hoping to see them mature. They'd chosen curtains and carpets together, planning the furnishings just as they wanted, and building in a new bathroom and kitchen. And there were other plans they'd left on hold while he went away.

As the garden grew, and time went on, James went away more often, and the plans grew stale. On her own in the house, Lydia's love for the place dwindled. As she lost her love for James, she also lost her love for what they had bought together, as though the very things themselves had died. And she too began to leave the house, going away to do her research, until the place had become forgotten by both of them.

Today, the journey to Alderley Edge seemed somehow shorter. In no time at all she was there. Suddenly taken aback, she saw that smoke rose out of the chimney and James' Land Rover was parked by the gate. She knew he had said he might make a flying visit, but he hadn't said when. Her knuckles were white as she gripped the wheel of the car and she wondered if she should turn it round and return to Yorkshire. She'd rather not see him today. She drew up and stopped for a moment, thinking. The deed would have be done some time. Why not now.

Stepping out, she drew a deep breath and braced herself. The house seemed strangely smaller. The windows were dirty and the front garden rampant with weeds. She stood for a while watching the trees across the road. The beautiful sorbus waved its boughs like a cheerleader. The tree was a wonderful sight the whole year through. She would miss it.

Putting her key in the lock, she thought about what she would say. He'd be reading a book by the fire. He'd quietly say hello, like he always did, while she took off her coat. Then he would come to her. That would be the difficult part.

As she entered the hall a damp and musty smell met her. The air, moist with smoke from the newly made fire tasted faintly salt. The door at the end of the hall was slightly ajar. She could hear someone talking with James. It sounded like Sara. She moved in closer. Why was Sara at Alderley Edge? Was Philip there too, and Michael? Sara's voice was loud and angry. They were obviously arguing.

'You don't like being tied to anyone, do you?' she cried. Her tone was petulant. 'You never did.'

'So what if I don't?' said James. 'It's none of your business.'

Lydia could hear the metal caps he put on the heels of his shoes clicking across the floorboards. Standing there in the hall, she felt anxious and curious.

'Isn't it?' said Sara, her voice rising. She laughed sarcastically. 'You can't decide who you want. That's the problem. You want us both.'

Lydia closed her eyes. What was it all about? What was she hearing? From where she stood, through the slightly open doorway, she could just see them. Sara sat very still in an armchair. James stood near.

'Anyway', said Sara. 'You're making her ill.' She drew a quick breath. 'Oh, yes you are. Don't give me that sort of look. It's you who's at fault, not me. You're wasting her life.'

James gasped contemputuously. 'What do you know? She loves me. You don't know anything.'

They were silent a moment. 'And do you love her?' said Sara quietly. 'Tell me you do if you dare. Tell me!'

'You know all about that', he said drearily, his voice filled with hostility.

'Oh, I do. I do', said Sara. Her voice trembling with anger. 'I think I despise you.'

Lydia heard James striding about the room again. She could hear the sound of glasses clinking. James was pouring a drink.

'Don't do that', said Sara. 'You're always drinking. Your going off soon, and you're driving. What if you kill somebody?'

'Oh, shut up, Sara', he snapped. 'You do go on. At least Lydia doesn't go on like this.'

Lydia heard Sara whimper. It sounded as if she was crying. 'Well, perhaps she should', she said. 'She's too soft. She always has been. You walk all over her.'

'Can't say I've noticed', he said coolly. His voice held a note of amusement. He gave a quick low laugh.

'No. You wouldn't', she said.

James laughed again. 'She doesn't complain.' Almost a whisper he added, 'I ought to kick you out, you know. I don't know why I put up with you. Why are you here, anyway? I didn't invite you.'

'Oh look at you, pouring more whisky', she said. 'You just can't manage without it, can you. Where's the man in you, James.'

Lydia heard him sigh. 'I could give it up now if I wanted. But why should I? I like my drink.'

'You'll lose it, you know', sighed Sara. 'You'll lose the singing along with everything else.

'Everything else?' he said, amused and curious.

'Well, let's face it', said Sara. 'You've lost Lydia that's why you've hurried over like this. Something's happened hasn't it?'

84

Lydia drew back and leaned on the wall. The house throbbed with the sound of their voices. Normally passive and easy going, it wasn't like Sara to argue. When it came to poise and self-possession Sara was queen.

'Don't be ridiculous', laughed James. He clicked his fingers. 'I can have her like that if I want. Just like that.' He clicked them again. And again.

'You're impossible', said Sara, her voice muffled in her hands.

'Am I?' said James, 'Well, that's how I am. And don't try to say you aren't turned on by it.' He smiled casually.

'I loathe you.'

'Good', he said, leaning towards her and whispering. 'I know.'

Sara rose from the chair and went to the kitchen bringing a glass of water. She sat down sipping it. 'You'll be sorry', she said quietly. 'I'm telling you, James Bowden, you'll be sorry.'

'Are you threatening me?' he asked calmly. They were silent a moment. 'Look Sara', he said. 'I don't know why you're here. It was Philip I phoned, not you. I'm far too tired to be bothered with this.'

There was silence again. Sara spoke sharply. 'It's time she knew.' Her tone was determined.

'What?' James thundered, turning on her. He gave a low little laugh again. Silence followed. Lydia could hear him pouring another drink. 'You wouldn't dare', he murmured.

Sara shrugged. 'Wouldn't I just?' she said, beneath her breath. 'I know all about it, you know. The way you treat her. Lydia's told me. Oh yes, I know all about Lydia.'

James laughed again, loudly. 'She doesn't know all about you though. By God she doesn't.'

'I'm different', Sara said softly.

'You certainly are, Sara.' He gazed at her for a long moment.

'I'm serious, James', Sara returned. 'I'm going to tell her.'

'Lydia's not stupid', he said, biting his lip. 'She'll know what you're up to.'

'So what am I up to then?'

'You're trying to split us up. You know you are. But you won't, you see. I shall never leave her.'

Sara got up and walked about, her arms folded. She sat down again. 'What if she leaves you first?'

'She won't', he said assuredly. 'I've told you. She loves me. She's ...'

Lydia listened, waiting.

Sara sat blank faced. James spoke slowly, precisely. His voice was thin and controlled. 'She's in my power.'

Lydia could hear him lighting a cigarette.

'You're very certain of that', said Sara, her voice weakening. James laughed. 'Well', said Sara, 'I'm warning you. You'd be quite surprised.' She shivered. 'You really are spiteful, James. I don't believe I'm hearing this. I'm going to tell her, you know. I shall tell her everything.'

'Look Sara', said James, his tone softening. 'We've been through all this before.'

'And that makes it easier, does it?' Sara snapped. 'What about Michael? What about him?'

'Michael's alright, I've told you.'

'Is he? He doesn't know who his father is and he's four years old. And you think that's alright? And what about Philip? He thinks Michael's his. We can't go on like this.'

'I'll give you more money. You know I will. Whatever you want.'

'It's not like that. Can't you see. I can't live like this.' Sara was crying. 'What about me?' she wailed. 'Don't you care?'

Lydia leaned on the wall. It couldn't be true. Suddenly she felt sick. When had it happened? How had she been so blind? So naïve? She took a deep breath and clasped her hands tightly, trying to steady her nerves. Sara was talking again.

'You can't just ...' She wept hard.

'Listen', James said, coldly. 'What's done is done. We can't get away from that. But you wanted it too, remember. We promised we'd keep it quiet. No-one would know. So why are you fussing now?'

'James, please ...' Sara's voice had fallen to a pathetic whine. 'You said you loved me.'

There was silence again. For a moment he gazed at her. He breathed in deeply then blew out, for a brief few seconds kind. 'Oh, for God's sake, Sara. Look, don't cry. I thought I did. Honest, I did. You're making this very hard.'

'But it is hard', moaned Sara. 'Are you saying there's no hope? You can't do this. You can't. I've been through hell for you. It should never have happened. I know that now. But it did. You were the one who started it. It was you who kept phoning. You who kept coming to meet me at work. It was all you.'

He lifted her coat from the chair arm. 'You'd better be going', he murmured.

'But what about Michael?' she sobbed. 'He needs to know who his father is. And what about Philip? He's a good man ... Oh, we should have come clean with this before. We ought to have told them both.'

'I'm sorry, Sara. But ...'

'No, you're not', she said quickly. 'You don't care a bit. You never do. Anyway, I shall tell Philip today. From now on, I refuse to protect you. I couldn't care less what happens to me. It's all about Michael now.'

'I thought you loved me', he said. James had sat down now, his head in his hands.

'I do!' cried Sara. 'I mean ... I did.'

Outside in the hall, Lydia's mind swam with memories. The times he was late back after taking Sara home ... The times he'd been out singing in places he hadn't told her about ... Her heart pounded. Her best friend and her boyfriend. The classic tale, played out here in her own house. Or at least she had thought of it as her own house. Just then, even the smell of it disgusted her. Her keys fell out of her hand, clattering to the floor. James came out within seconds.

'Lydia!' he cried, pale and staring. He turned to Sara. Sara gave a peculiar, frightened look. 'Lydia', she said. 'Oh, Lydia. I'm so sorry.' She bent her head. Just then, Lydia felt like an intruder. She wanted to leave quickly. James stepped back and took a deep breath. 'Lydia. What can I say? I didn't hear you.'

87

'No', she said weakly, 'Apparently not. But I heard you.' She held his gaze. For a few moments, sickness welled up inside her. And yet there came with it a wonderful sense of freedom. He stood for a moment watching her, then looked away. He glanced at Sara and then at her, and then again at Sara. He was quite lost.

Her eyes moved slowly between them. Everything suddenly seemed reduced to nothing: their love, their hopes, the things they had done. It was all reduced to nothing. All her pretending had been for nothing, as pretending always is.

'Sara', said Lydia, going to sit by her, 'I can't believe this is happening.' Searching her eyes, a deep sadness engulfed her. We have all betrayed each other, Lydia thought. But more than that, we have all betrayed ourselves.

Sara looked downwards, holding a handkerchief tightly between her fingers. She sobbed quietly, her dark brown hair long and limp around her face, falling about her shoulders. 'Sara', said Lydia. 'It isn't important now.'

'I didn't mean it, Lydia', said Sara mournfully. 'You know I didn't.' Her face was damp from crying, and her make-up was running. Her eyes looked weary. James leant on the wall, smoking indifferently. 'You see, I haven't been well', said Sara. Her face looked long and thin, and Lydia saw she was no longer beautiful. Something had drained her beauty.

'And Michael?' said Lydia, trying to smile, though her heart still pounded. 'I haven't seen him for ages. He must have grown.'

'He's here', said Sara, lifting her head. 'He's upstairs.'

Lydia looked at the ceiling. So the child was there in the house. James's child. A flood of tenderness entered her. She was glad of it.

'I'm sorry, Lydia', James said, coming across. 'It was ages ago. It's over now.'

'Over?' Lydia whispered. 'There's a child upstairs. He's yours.'

'I thought you'd hate me', said Sara. 'You see, I could never get it to work with Philip. It's all my fault.' She wept again, drying her eyes with her fingers. 'He was such a good man before. I've ruined him now. He's given up all his music. He won't do anything now at all. He's lapsed into a depression.'

James shook his head and wiped his mouth with the back of his hand. He watched and frowned. 'God, Sara', he whispered. 'They should write you into the *Guinness Book of Records* for whining.'

'Damn you, James!' she shouted.

He poured himself more whisky, standing before them, his head thrown back. Nothing would budge him.

Sara's face twisted in pain. She pointed to James. 'He's destroyed me, Lydia.' She went to the mirror. 'Look at me, I was beautiful once. See how weary my face is.'

'Jesus Christ', moaned James, under his breath. He blew smoke into the air and shook his head. Just then a child came into the doorway.

'Mummy', said Michael, reaching for Sara. He was dressed in brown corduroys and a green jersey. He was clean and neat, though sleepy. He rubbed his eyes.

Sara went to him and lifted him, taking him to a chair and sitting him on her lap, combing his hair with her fingers. It was soft and white. And Lydia saw with a rush of wonder the child had James's features; the same nose and eager bright blue eyes. James sneezed hard. It was almost a shout. The little boy got down and went for a packet of tissues, taking one out and handing it to his father who blew his nose. The boy watched, familiar and wide-eyed, returning then to his mother. He sat nervous, pinching his arms and legs and wincing.

Sara took his hand and held it, whispering to James: 'I'm going to Sussex tomorrow to see my parents.' The child reached up and put his arms round her neck. 'I shall talk to Philip first though.' Her voice was calmer now.

'Do what you want', said James, stubbing out his cigarette. She watched him boldly, then buried her face in the child's shoulder. The child's eyes stayed on his father. He pinched himself again and again. Sara stopped him.

The room smelt stale. It smelt of whisky and cigarettes. It smelt of the past. A past that Lydia no longer wanted. One she must leave quickly.

'What will you do?' Sara said, turning to her.

'Me?' said Lydia, suddenly drawn from her thoughts. 'Oh, I don't know yet. I shall think of something. The house will be sold of course.'

James glanced at her sharply. He frowned. 'What are you saying?' he cried anxiously. 'You're not serious?'

Lydia gave him a quick incredulous look. 'Of course I am', she said quietly. How strange it was she could find such strength inside this pain. A strength that should have come to her before.

James moved over to touch her. 'You mean you're going to ...' He glanced at Sara angrily. 'Listen, Lydia, you mustn't take notice of her. She tells it all from her side. You must listen to mine ...' He went on, grasping Lydia's hand, clutching it tightly, putting it to his lips. 'Lydia, you can't do this. Not to me. I love you.'

'He does', said Sara. 'He does.'

Lydia sighed and glanced between them sadly. The child pinched himself again. Sara took hold of his hands. 'I don't know why he does it', she moaned. 'He always does it. He's covered in bruises.'

'I'd better be off', said Lydia, turning to James and removing her hand slowly. She held his gaze. 'We'll talk again, tomorrow. Not now. I shall come for some things.'

'I won't be here tomorrow', he said frowning. 'I'll be back in Bonn. I'm giving a concert. Lydia please ...'

Lydia gazed at space. 'All the same I shall come', she said dismissively. She looked at him again, and thought of the part of him she'd loved. A part that was now dead. 'Good luck', she said, turning to Sara and back to James. 'Good luck. All of you.' And without a backward glance, she left.

DISSONANCE

Lydia woke early, having had little sleep. What had happened the day before would not leave her mind. To think that James and Sara had deceived her all that time. Could there ever be those long and perfect days she hoped for? Could they really happen. She lay thoughtful for a while then went downstairs. Daniel hadn't phoned her from London yet and she still had no number to contact him on. It was almost five days. Perhaps he was back in Yorkshire? She made some toast and drank some black coffee. Her mother came down from her shower. Lydia saw she was livelier now and happier.

'You didn't bring anything back from the house', her mother said curiously. 'I thought that's why you went.'

Lydia was worried and preoccupied. 'The visit was useful', she murmured. 'I've sorted a few things out.' Lydia watched her preparing the fire, she was glad they'd talked. Now that the wreckage was cleared, a kind of euphoria had taken over. Her mother was full of ideas.

'I've thought of something', she said exictedly. 'What do you think of a string ensemble at the restuarant? While people are eating?'

'But musicians would have to be paid', Lydia replied, 'Can the manor afford it?'

'The manor has funds for that sort of thing', said Eliza. 'They wouldn't be able to pay them much. We could bargain though.'

Lydia had taken a tape measure from a box and was measuring the wall.

'Do you think it will fit?' said her mother, coming to hold the end of the tape. 'I can't remember how big it is.'

'It's only small', said Lydia. 'That's why I like it'. She gazed at her scattered papers. The dresser would help her organise herself. She could bring it later with Daniel. Perhaps he'd returned to Yorkshire now. Maybe she'd go and surprise him.

'I was wondering if Sara might help', Eliza said hopefully.

Lydia wound the tape back slowly. 'I doubt it, mum. Sara's busy these days. And anyway, she doesn't play music much. It's a thing of the past. I think she works at the Travel Bureau now.'

Her mother frowned. 'It seems such a waste.'

'But there's just no money in music', Lydia said. 'Its compact discs and tape recorders now. You can't get the work.' She hadn't said what had happened up at the house.

'You could always ask her', Eliza said.

Lydia told her she would, but she didn't think she'd be talking to Sara again. Their friendship was over.

Eliza was heart and soul in the manor now. And heart and soul in Howard too, thought Lydia. He shone in her mother's eyes.

'Some photos have come', said Eliza. 'I've put them there on the table. They've come from Rosie, I think.'

Lydia picked them up and looked. Rosie had managed to get them from an old historian in Knaresborough. Lydia examined them briefly, putting them back safely, and noting as she did that her mother had already brought out the best cutlery, just for their midday meal. 'I made lasagne', Eliza called from the kitchen. 'I know how you like it!' The fire blazed strongly. Something had changed direction. An old and weary waterway had changed its course. You could turn the waters, Lydia decided. You really could. But only with painful effort. The food steamed, wholesome and good as her mother served it, falling thick and delicious, on to their plates.

'You might like to browse through this when you've finished', Eliza said, handing her a thin volume from the window ledge. 'It's another book. This time it covers our paintings. We've so many paintings up at the manor now, we thought we should make a catalogue. We've changed things round in the main hall, and we've altered the gardens as well.'

Lydia remembered what Jeremy said about change. Everything seemed to be changing. Her mother had changed. Sara had changed. Would Daniel have changed too?

The thought chilled her. Where was Daniel now? She finished her food and looked at the paintings displayed in the book. Her mother brought some coffee. Lydia went through her notes again and thought about where she would put the photos Rosie had sent. Most of the pictures were black and white and mainly showing the castle. Some of them, though, were artist's drawings and paintings, one of them showing Sir Henry Slingsby, a colonel in the royal army being beheaded. A bloody image, all the worse, Lydia thought, in black and white. After lunch, her mother went up to the manor, leaving Lydia to do her work. It was reaching six o'clock. All afternoon she'd been moving photos from page to page. She still couldn't think where to put them. Why wasn't Daniel phoning? She rang his number. Still no-one answered. She put on her coat and got in her car. This time she'd approach the house from the high street.

As she entered the back gate, the gardens, desolate in the dusk, looked strangely mysterious and dark. She stood for a while, looking over the tall house, the first time she had seen it from the main road. Cliff House was a strange building, the front cut out of the rock, though the back was quite normal. There wasn't much room round the side. Only someone slim like herself could have slid through there to the front. Lydia doubted anyone ever did it. The grounds at the back were like a miniature wood. In the boughs of an old oak, she saw a tree house rocking, silhouetted against the darkening sky. A path of glistening white pebbles led to the back door, and a yellow light shone from the tiny kitchen window that looked out on to the cliff. It seemed like someone was in. But supposing it was Daniel's father. What would she say?

Before her the hard wood of the kitchen door shone strong and ancient, giving her the sense of continuity she needed then. She raised her eyes to the sky. How immense it was. The stars shone bright like rays of hope. Where did they end? The grounds were silent about her. She rapped on the door.

For a while she waited. She rapped again. No-one appeared to be in.

Making her way to the kitchen window she tried to see through, but it was too high up. She went to the thin space by the house that led to the front. Perhaps she could get through it. Everywhere was unusually still. The scraggy branch of a withered sapling snatched at her cheek and sent a quick pain down her face as she squeezed through the gap. Having got through, she found herself at the top of the rockery, before the porch. The place looked enormous from here. Below in the lamplight the river and walkway glittered. Reaching the door of the porch, she banged hard with her knuckles. Still nobody came.

Moving to the front of the house, from which a thin light came, she could hear the sound of music, droning out of an open window. Someone had started the record player. Who could it be? It was playing the *Blue Danube*. She stretched up to look. On her tiptoes she searched the room with her eyes, for it was dimly lit. She saw that a vigorous fire burned in the grate. The marble fireplace shone above it. Shadows danced on the walls.

And someone was dancing ... Who could be dancing, she wondered, at Cliff House? Cautiously she pressed her face to the glass, catching sight of the dancers again. As they came towards her, she saw that it was Daniel and a girl of about seventeen, with white hair. Daniel was in blue jeans, though the top of his body was naked. As they danced, their bodies glowed in the firelight, the girl's head resting leisurely on his chest, her long white hair flowing about her. Lydia saw she was small and slender, and wore a close-fitting dress that sparkled with sequins, flashing with each swirl of her body. Her skin shone, glowing white, her breasts partly exposed above the low neckline. Daniel held her close, pressing his hand into her bare back, their legs entwined, their eyes closed. Both of them were lost in the music.

Lydia leaned on the wall. Her mouth felt dry. Was it another betrayal? Who was the girl? Why was she here, at Cliff House?

Casting her eyes to the foot of the rockery and the path by the river, she wanted to run. But where would she run to?

Where would she go? The river went by indifferently. The trees moaned. She slumped beneath the window. Above her the black clouds blew the moon from sight, so that for a moment, apart from the light of the room hitting the garden's twisted vegetation, she sat in darkness. She was waiting. Waiting as she had done before. For what?

She listened for some time till the music stopped. Then, taking a deep breath, she drew herself up. The light in the room went out. She would make her way through the little space again, back to the high street. Then she would go home. Wherever that was. For the time being it would be her mother's house. Most things, Lydia decided, were for the time being.

As she passed the porch, she stopped, thoughtful. Here she was, running away from what was most important to her. Fleeing now from her love in case it hurt. She had to be strong, she told herself. Address her pain, not hide from it like her mother did, but face it straight on. She gathered her nerves and rubbed the ache from her face, rapping hard on the door. She waited for someone to come. Within minutes Daniel stood there.

For a moment, images of James and Sara went through her mind. Jeremy had said to take things slowly. Perhaps he was right. But how important was time? She'd lived with James for six years and yet she had never felt the surge of joy that this man gave her whenever she met his eyes and whenever he went through her mind.

He stood for a moment, looking surprised and strange. 'Lydia. You didn't say you were coming.' His voice collapsed in the air. He glanced inside and back, frowning and moistening his lips. 'I meant to phone you. I've had so many problems this week.' He sighed exhaustively. It had started to rain.

He still didn't ask her in. She stood silently, feeling small and diminished, not knowing what to do. He did not embrace her. He looked as if he'd forgotten her.

'Look, come on in', he said finally. She did not move. He stepped out from the porch and put out his hand. Something made her cold as stone. She searched his eyes warily.

'Lydia, come to the lounge', he said anxiously, trying to hold her. 'Please, my love, come in.' He shook his head and sighed.

Eventually she followed him down the hall. Then suddenly she turned to him with a look of fear, almost a look of terror. 'You didn't phone me', she said.

'I know', he said, adjusting the logs on the fire. 'Lydia, I thought of you constantly. You have no idea how it's been here recently.' He did not turn.

They were silent a while. The fire was noisy. The room was alive with shadows. A peculiar tension filled the air. 'Have you been phoning Cliff House?' he asked, taking his books from the chairs and putting them back in the cases. The room felt strangely empty as if all she had seen had been just her imagination.

'Nobody answered', she said. Her voice was low and trembling. She realised now that he must have been at home for some time. She braced herself. The graze on her face was hurting. She could feel the uncried tears stinging her eyes, the rage and anger boiling within her. 'Are you avoiding me?' she asked.

He did not speak at first. He went to her, trying to hold her again, but she cringed away.

Looking downwards, he said, 'Dad's been ill. I'm sorry I haven't called you. I wanted to, but ...'

Lydia's fists were clenched, her eyes guarded him now with deep suspicion.

'You've hurt your face', he said. He wanted to take her into his arms, but he feared she'd reject him. He could not tell her the truth. Not yet.

'It's nothing', she said, pressing her fingers against the wound. She sat by the fire, watching the flames, glancing up at him from time to time. Something lost and lonely shivered between them. Kneeling beside her, he put more logs on the fire, brought from the garden that day. They crackled and spat with wetness.

'You thought of me though ...', she said quietly.

He stood up quickly. 'Of course I did. Constantly.' He wrung his hands frowning. Before him by the fire, she seemed small and helpless. Squatting down beside her, he said: 'Lydia. How can I make you trust me?' The light gleamed on his naked chest. 'There are things I must tell you ...' Her eyes, he saw, were empty now of sparkle. He shook his head miserably, sighing and rubbing his face so that charcoal from the logs smeared his cheeks. He pushed his hair from his face. Catching his eyes in the firelight, she saw they were heavy with thought. 'It's difficult ...' he began. 'You see, I ...' He paced the room. What could he say? He didn't know where to begin. The ghosts? The girl? His life was in chaos. He could scarcely sort truth from fiction. He wanted so much to tell her. He would like to have told her it all. From start to finish. But not just yet. 'Strange things are happening to me', he said, searching her face.

She listened, waiting. Whatever he wanted to say, she hoped he would say it now. Let it be said and done, she thought, then she could breathe.

He sat for a moment thoughtful, his head in his hands. 'Why don't you let me bathe that wound', he said quietly. Both of them were silent a while. He went to the kitchen and came back with warm water and a swab of cotton wool. Lydia was pale and brooding. Being with her now, Daniel felt safe, and a sigh of relief escaped him as he took the warm swab to her face. 'Did you tell him?' he asked, gently.

She gazed ahead in confusion.

'James', he said. 'About us.' His tone was serious.

'No', she whispered, her eyes large and uncertain. 'Let's not talk about that.'

Daniel saw she still distrusted him. In time though, it would all come right, and he'd tell her everything. He'd tell her how the killing in London had damaged his life so badly. How he'd never really recovered. Wherever he went, there were those who eyed him suspiciously. The only witness to the death had been a girl, the one he had been dancing with just now. Lydia, it seemed, knew nothing. And that was good. He was glad of that. For a while at least he could rest in her innocence. Once she knew, he might lose her. The risk was too great. He would not tell her yet.

She went to the record player, picking up one of the records. 'The *Blue Danube*. Do you play it?' she asked quietly.

'Of course', he said. 'I play them all.' His tone was tense.

'But this one. Do you like it specially?'

'I suppose I do', he said awkwardly.

'Do you dance to it?' Lydia asked, hurt and jealous.

He did not answer. From behind her she heard him breathing hard. Speaking again of his father, he said. 'Dad isn't well. I wish he would rest.' Daniel sat down exhaustedly. Forever longing for his mother, his father disturbed him deeply. It was wrong to long for the dead like that. It was like an obsession. Yesterday, he had found him fully clothed, sleeping across the bed. Yet he managed to do his work. Each emergency, it seemed, brought fresh strength from his weary soul. But how long could it last. And now there was something else ... 'There's been a death', he said. Lydia listened carefully. 'A little girl. She was only two years old. It's affected him badly. You can't always diagnose correctly with children. One minute they're well, the next they will have a raging temperature. Most of the time he works from experience. This time it wasn't enough.' Daniel's tone was grave. 'The child got meningitis. They couldn't get her to hospital quickly enough and her parents have blamed my father. It's easy to judge in retrospect, of course. And now they're trying to sue him.'

Lydia watched him, gazing at space, his features drawn and concerned. 'What a terrible shock for the parents', said Lydia, softening towards him. 'And your father too. How is he now?'

'Sensitive as an eyeball', frowned Daniel, standing up. 'To say the least. Very difficult. He shouldn't be working really.' Coughing badly, his father had still gone off to work in the cold weather. Sometimes he thought his father did things to punish himself. He was so immersed in his sufferings.

'I shall have to go', said Lydia, getting up and reaching her coat. She buttoned it slowly, observing him. He watched her closely.

'Why so soon?' he whispered.

'I've things to do', she said, glancing about.

'I need you, Lydia', he said earnestly.

'Do you', she asked. 'Are you sure?' She moved to the door.

He followed her into the garden, its sweet scent after the rain greeting them. As he met her eyes, he saw they held a look of reserve. It cut him through.

'I'll call you sometime', she said.

'Sometime?' he repeated painfully. 'What do you mean, "Sometime"?' The word tormented him. He turned his face to the garden, the bark of the trees, wet with rain, shining in the evening light. It seemed just then the whole woodland listened.

'I saw her', Lydia said quietly.

An owl's cry broke the skin of his despair.

'I looked in the window and saw her.'

Daniel spoke quickly. His voice was hard and controlled, as if she might not listen. 'I shall tell you about her, soon. I promise. I shall tell you all of it. But please, my love, not now.'

Lydia gave him a strange forsaken look. She gazed at him coldly. The night air throbbed about them. 'Alright! Alright!' he cried suddenly. 'Go then if you must! Leave me! You know your way!' And he turned and went through the kitchen door, closing it hard behind him.

That night as he took his father's milk, he listened a moment outside the door of his own room. The girl slept soundly. Going back to the lounge he lay on the sofa, wondering why he had treated Lydia so badly. He would phone her tomorrow. Just now he felt spent. He closed his eyes and was very soon asleep.

VISIONS

Daniel's neck was hurting. He turned on the couch and woke in the darkness. Quickly he thought of Lydia and their strange conversation. That he had acted so out of character worried him. He seemed to be moving away from himself by the day. Now he could find no peace. The real and imaginary worlds of his mind were becoming confused. He rubbed his eyes and looked at the clock. It read 3 am.

Slowly as he gazed at the numbers, it seemed the whole room revolved around him then stopped. He shook his head. It happened again. And again. This time revolving quicker, till it spun and he found himself gripping the sofa nervously. And just as before, the blue light filled the room, turning to turquoise, till the spinning stopped finally and he found himself in the room he had been in before with the wooden floor and the glass chandelier clinking and tinkling above him. The vision focused and he saw the man again with the moustache, a child of about ten, thin with large bones, standing before him trembling. Her clothes were ragged and her feet were bare and soiled.

'Why do you come to me for money!' he shouted. 'You should tell your mother she should not be sending you begging.' He drew in on his cigar, blowing smoke at her. 'Just look at you, child. You dare to come to my house with feet like that. And don't start babbling, girl. I'll have none of your tantrums here!'

The child shivered, bending her head, her thin hands clasped behind.

'Look at me, girl!' he shouted. 'The devil knows who sired you.' Circling her and lifting a lock of her hair, he rasped, 'Livid with lice, of course. I might have guessed.' The girl's lips quivered. Turning as his wife approached, he straightened his moustache and brought out another cigar.

The woman smiled at the child, joining her and taking her hand. Glancing at him she said coldly, 'What is it bothers you about her?' Surveying the child warmly, she whispered, 'You must not fear him. He's worse if you do. Here. Stand close.' The child leaned into her skirts. 'Have you made your request?' she asked, looking down at the frightened eyes.

'Made her request!' her husband boomed. 'What request?' He drew in on the cigar and coughed, wheezing as he came forward, putting his face to the child's. Her cheeks were hollow, her skin pale, her bones stuck out at strange angles with little flesh on them. She was a sickly scrap of a thing.

'She's very hungry', the woman said.

'She's very ugly', the man laughed. 'As ugly as her soul!'

'She's a child', the woman said softly.

'Take her out!' he bawled. 'Children are evil. I do not want her in here.'

The woman faced him, stepping forward and flashing her eyes. 'I wanted her to come to you. To ask you kindly. Her family needs some money. We have to help them.'

The man stood back mocking her. 'Because I rescued you from the jaws of hell, you think I must rescue her! You would have me take the whole lot of you on wouldn't you!' His voice was smooth and contemptuous. He said, 'You, my dear, are lucky to be alive. Remember that. A heap of rags you were when I took you in. Just like this foundling here.'

The child held the woman's skirts fearfully.

'And get your feet washed, wastrel!'

'She hasn't time', the woman said angrily. 'And she isn't a foundling either. Nor a wastrel. Her mother works at the mill. They're poor. The child has to work.'

'Why can't her father support her?' the man cried. 'Why is he sending her here to me for money? A man should look after his own.'

The woman stood back proudly, glaring at him and white with rage. The child, standing on the cold floor, her dark black eyes gazing ahead, was a dither of dust in the room. The woman guarded her fiercely. She turned to her, speaking gently. 'Where is your father?'

The man laughed, angry at his wife's boldness. 'At least she has one then', he said, under his breath.

The woman knelt down beside her.

'Yah', the man cried. 'Your father, girl. She's asking about your father.'

'I don't have one', the child said, trembling. 'He fell downt' steps by Castle Mill an' broke 'is neck.' She told them she worked with her four sisters and two brothers. They had to support themselves. Her mother had been a pauper.

The woman adjusted her black rose hairslide, then bent down, putting her hands to the child's cheeks. 'Would you like me to wash your hair?' she asked.

'You must send her off!' the man thundered. He went about examining things and putting them back, mumbling and smoking.

'I shall wash her hair if I want', the woman said sharply. 'Why shouldn't I?'

'Because you will have them all here, woman. I've told you. We shall never see the back of them. She can wash her hair in the river.'

'The river is cold. She must wash it in hot water.' Taking the girl's arm the woman turned.

'That's right. Take her out', he said. 'And you too if you like. There are provisions for her in the parish. Now see her out.'

'First she must have a bath', the woman protested.

'Get out of here!' he shouted. He waved his hand in the air, sending them off.

Glancing at the child's forlorn face, the woman took her arm, leading her to the door, and pushing something into her hand. The girl thanked her profusely. 'Shush', she urged. 'Now don't breathe a word.'

After closing the door she took up her embroidery from a chair and sat down. The man smoked and grumbled. 'You are not listening to me are you?' he said.

'So why must I listen to you?' she answered coolly, her head thrown back. She was proud and defiant.

'I want you to tell me what's happening.'

She was silent. Her needle worked quickly.

'I want to know what's going on at the manor.' His voice reverberated on the cold walls of the room. 'You are making a fool of me!'

Still she was silent.

He carried on mumbling. Then in what seemed like manic anger, he said. 'You are seeing "him", aren't you? I know you are? Confess it woman!' He spoke through his teeth.

'Don't shout at me', she said quietly. Her breathing came in quick tremors. Her eyes flashed furiously.

'Who is he?' her husband asked hatefully, his back towards her, his eyes searching the ceiling. 'Where does he come from? He turned on her quickly. 'A loathsome shadow, I'm told. Dark as the devil!'

He sat down at the table, wheezing and shaking. 'You don't care how you disgrace me, do you. How can you do it? I've helped you so much.' His voice trembled with bitterness.

She stood up facing him boldly. 'I shall do what I want!'

He looked at her beneath his eyelids. Lowering his voice, he said, 'Well then, if that's how it is. You must go! I won't have you here a minute longer!' And he took her arm, dragging her over the floor.

'Don't', she cried. 'I shall tell somebody.'

'Tell who you like', he bawled. He pulled her along the hall towards the porch, struggling and fighting. She cursed him, screaming and protesting as he threw her out on the rockery. 'See how that finds you!' he shouted, banging the door behind her. 'Sorceress! Witch! To hell with you! To hell with you both!'

She thumped on the door in the rain, the sound echoing round the house. The rain drummed hard on the windows. Slowly the blue light faded and the house became silent. For a while Daniel sat perplexed, wondering what it all meant. Knowing he could not sleep again, he shook himself wide awake and went to make some coffee.

SORROW

Making a quick visit from the boathouse, Jeremy sat in the armchair drinking his favourite brew of sarsparilla, concocted at the back of the herbalists on the high street. Lydia was at the table working. It was mid-afternoon. In the lounge where they sat, Jeremy saw that Lydia's papers were placed in piles on the table, ready to go in the dresser coming from Alderley Edge. The brasses were shining and the carpets cleaned for Christmas. Lydia had bought a new red hearth rug for her mother. Something she'd wanted for some time. It made the house look warm and homely. They'd been to Wetherby earlier that week for curtains for Lydia's room; the others were old and shabby. Everything seemed to be fine. But Jeremy knew it wasn't. Something was wrong with Lydia.

His eyes ran over the white roses he'd bought for his mother's birthday the previous day, now in a vase on the table, recalling how she had often asked their father for them, though he'd never provided any. It hadn't been such a difficult thing to do, thought Jeremy, and worth it when he'd seen her pleasure. Lydia looked up from her work, staring at space.

'What's the matter?' he asked casually. 'I'm not going to go till you've told me.'

'I don't really know', said Lydia sighing. 'It's probably me.'

'You always blame yourself', said Jeremy. 'Just like I do.'

'I know what you mean about muddles now', she said, closing her eyes. 'I'm muddled myself.'

Outside the sky had clouded over. The light in the room had dulled. Jeremy switched on the light. Lydia tightened the knot she had done in her hair. It was falling down. She hadn't worn it like that since schooldays, Jeremy said. It made him think of when they were young and they'd all lived together just like now. Somehow it seemed that life was going backwards. How did it happen, he wondered? Must life go backwards, he reasoned, before it went forwards? As if it must pick things up and re-examine them to see how they were. He flexed his muscles. His arms were aching today.

The smell of hot fruit and spices permeated the air. Their mother was baking a Christmas cake. Away for the day at the manor, she'd set the timer on the oven. 'Nothing like modern technology', she'd laughed on her way out.

'I think I might try to get some sleep', said Lydia, rubbing her eyes. Things weren't fitting together. Her book wouldn't fall into place, and her life was a mess. Perhaps if she went to bed, something might work itself out. Over the past few days, sleep had eluded her. She stared ahead blankly. Having reached a peculiar impasse, she couldn't phone Daniel now. What if he said that he didn't want her? That he wanted the girl instead? She wasn't ready for that. But the tension made her anxious. She sensed that something important and different had happened between them, but she couldn't make out what it was. If he loves me, Lydia decided, then it's got to come right in the end. But she wasn't sure.

Jeremy leaned back in the chair. His skin was a clean brown tan, his eyes alive and alert, and his muscles constantly eager. It seemed he might live a thousand lives at once.

'I'd feel better if you told me what's happened', he said.

Lydia felt flushed and sleepy. 'I wouldn't know where to begin', she said, remembering the scene at Alderley Edge, and what had gone on at Daniel's. She felt the events of the last week were much too painful to speak of.

'Go on if you want', said Jeremy. 'Criticise all you like. I don't care. And I won't remember it after, not if you don't want me to. That's how it works with Rose.'

Lydia smiled and glanced at him curiously.

'James and Daniel, I mean', he said. 'They've let you down, I can tell. You shouldn't be worrying though, like this. You've a life to live, Lydia. Your getting like me with Rosie.' She could see he was struggling, searching for words that might help.

She moved about on the chair awkwardly. It wasn't true really. No-one had let her down. Well, not exactly. There was nothing she'd learned about James that she hadn't known before. That is, if she'd faced it. It was different though with Daniel. She'd thought he was honest. She did not think he'd betray her and still puzzled over it. Jeremy listened though, as she told him about what had happened at Alderley Edge with James and Sara, the way she was hurt by it all. It had been like uncovering a plot, she said. Just like a plot. Every move they had made had somehow involved her. It was almost as if her own bones hid themselves inside her now, ashamed.

'Well, I've always said it', said Jeremy. 'Good riddance. You're better off without him.' Lydia began to weep. 'And something's happened with Daniel too, I know', he said boldly. 'Why are you asking mum and me to tell him you're out?'

Lydia looked away and frowned. She'd rather not talk about that. 'I'm taking things a day at a time just now. I need to think.' She stood up and went to the kitchen to make some tea.

Jeremy hung about. 'I know what I said, Lydia, about taking things slowly', he called through, 'but I've changed my mind. Love has a speed of its own. You can't interfere.'

She came back with a mug of tea. He was standing, his jacket slung over his shoulder, ready to go to the boathouse. He looked tall and melancholy, his hand pressed down on the door handle, waiting to go. 'Rosie has such an imagination', he sighed. He stared at the ceiling.

Lydia looked at him surprised. 'Why, what's wrong?'

He gave her a half smile. 'Ghosts. She thinks there are ghosts in the library.' For a moment his features looked heavy with worry. 'It's hard to know what to say. She needs to be occupied. Properly occupied. She gets some funny ideas.'

Lydia listened carefully. She sat down.

'She thinks the library's haunted', said Jeremy, coming to what he had really wanted to tell her. Lydia could see he felt awkward. 'She's hearing things now. Each time I go it's a different story.' He jerked his arms. The cobra moved in his muscles. Lydia saw he was suffering again. Somehow or other Rosie dictated his moods. She'd be glad when she'd gone abroad. 'Phantom footsteps', said Jeremy. 'Up in the store-room, she says. But there's nobody there when she looks.' Jeremy looked weary. 'I think she should hand in her notice.

It's not like she wants to be there anyway.' He stood for a moment, thoughtful. 'I think it's probably mice. There's got to be hundreds in there.' He paused. 'It might be those books she's getting for Daniel.'

'What do you mean?' asked Lydia curiously.

Jeremy looked surprised. 'Books about ghosts and such. He reads them. Didn't you know?'

Lydia frowned. 'I can't say I did'. There were lots of things she didn't know; she'd begun to distrust her judgement.

'Well, that's what he reads', said Jeremy. 'You wonder why he should want them, being a scientist and that. But Rosie keeps on getting them for him. She gets them from other places. The thing is ... and it really bothers me this. Rosie reads them as well.'

'I wouldn't have thought that Rosie would read them either', said Lydia wondering. 'I can see why she thinks there are ghosts in the library now.

'She thinks there's a man in the storeroom', he said quickly. He couldn't believe that Rosie would think that the old storeroom with its mildewed contents could ever have housed a ghost 'And worse than that, she tells me he talks in German.'

Lydia smiled. 'Well, at least he might talk in English', she said. 'A German ghost? What would a German ghost be doing in there? Does Rosie know German?'

'A bit', said Jeremy, 'but she can't tell what he's saying.'

'How many times has she heard it?' asked Lydia.

'Enough to make her nervous', said Jeremy, though still not knowing how to take it. 'And Rosie's not easily nervous.' There was something in his tone, Lydia thought as he went out, that gave it significance. He'd have to find out what was happening, she knew. Either Rosie was having him on, or else she was ill. Even if Rosie believed it, Jeremy, she knew, would never accept that a ghost was haunting the storeroom.

THE CREST

Daniel's mind was livid with questions. If only they were questions, though, that he might have answered from books, or even consulted his colleagues about. But no. These were questions that had no answers at all. He felt lost and without strength. Why was he suddenly clairvoyant? It had never happened before. It wore him out thinking about it. Perhaps there was something he needed to do for the ghost. But what could it be? He wiped his forehead with the back of his hand. What nonsense it all seemed. He could hardly believe he was capable of such thinking. But there it was, flooding his mind. The poor creature who'd lifted herself from the water was very real. She existed somewhere, he knew. But how had she managed to reach him, now, yet not before? And what did she want? And he had to look after his father too. There was also his work ... He was so behind with all that. And Lydia ... Dear Lydia. He couldn't tell her all this. It was much too heavy. But he needed Lydia desperately, and she wasn't answering his phone calls. Perhaps he had lost her forever. He would leave her alone for a while and give her time. He felt wretched now and miserable. Having found the heart of his life it had slipped away.

On his way to Rosie's library to collect his books, he thought of what he had witnessed at Cliff House, the woman flung out in the rain by that brute of a man, and he filled with anger taking the library steps three at a time, till suddenly, whilst he was still engrossed in his thoughts, Rosie appeared at the top of the stairs with three volumes.

'I knew it was you', she said. 'I got them.' It was almost as if they were on a secret mission. Her voice was a whisper. 'You must bring them back in a month. I've stamped them out.' She eyed him strangely. 'Peculiar stuff, all that. I wouldn't have thought you'd read it.'

He searched her eyes, embarrassed. 'Oh, Rosie. What can I say?' He threw out his hands. 'There's something I have to find out. Everything isn't as easy as science would suggest. The answers aren't all in the stars, you know. Not all of them.' He took the books and sat down, turning the pages quickly. She watched him. 'There are things that can't be explained', he murmured. Rosie stared, overcome with wonder.

'You see', he continued, putting the books in a rucksack and fastening it up thoughtfully. 'It's all about energy. I'm trying to understand ...' He stood by the window watching her. Rosie seemed like one of his students eager to learn about the universe just then. He wished she were. He'd have had no problem with that. With due effort, one might understand some of that. But this ... This was different. 'I'm trying to fathom it out', he said sighing. 'I doubt if I shall though.'

'What?' asked Rosie. The dog was asleep beside her. Everything seemed peaceful enough in the libary today. But Rosie was biting her nails. Something she did when worried. Sitting on her swivel chair, she looked up apprehensively. 'I'm being haunted', she told him directly. 'I know it.'

'Are you?' he said suddenly intrigued. 'In what way?'

She played with her fingernails, frowning. 'I know what you're thinking', she murmured. 'It's true though.' She bent her head. 'It's lonely in here', she moaned. 'I know that, but I don't usually hear things.' She glanced up quickly to test his mood. He guarded her closely. 'I've checked it out', she said. 'There's nothing to see ... But I hear things. The dog does too. You should see his ears sometimes. And I have to stop him from barking.'

They were silent a moment. Daniel said: 'You mustn't worry, Rosie. I'm not going to mock you. Why do you think I'm reading books like this? Remember the music? I don't know where it came from, but it was certainly here.'

Rosie nodded. 'It's the building, I think', she said, the words echoing about them. 'It gives me the creeps.' She looked about forlornly. Around them the air seemed dense with possibility. The white roof in the afternoon light was a pale yellow. Their voices were hollow. Rosie shivered and rubbed her arms. She swallowed hard and turned her eyes to the corridor. 'There's a man down there in the storeroom.' She bent her head, her voice only a murmur. 'I know it seems crazy. I'm telling the truth though. He talks in German.'

'German?' Daniel said, filled with amazement. He turned his eyes to the corridor. Just now it was dark and gloomy and seemed to go on for longer than the few doors might suggest.

'I know it's German', said Rosie. 'He's talking about a woman. I can't catch the words though.'

Rosie rubbed her eyes. 'Imagine telling them this at the council offices.' She laughed briefly, though without humour. 'I'm handing my notice in soon. This place is haunted.'

'Perhaps it is', Daniel said quietly. Rosie he saw was certain of what she'd heard. He did not doubt her. 'Do you want to look?' he asked. 'I mean with me?'

'You mean in the storeroom, now?' gasped Rosie. She clasped her hands together.

Daniel nodded his head. He would like to see what the storeroom was like and what was in it. So far as the music went, only Rosie, Jeremy and Lydia knew about that, though they had not heard it. He wished someone else had heard it too. It was hard to consider it real when no-one else had heard it though there were others there.

'There's nothing to find', said Rosie. 'I've looked before.' Her long thin fingers worked together nervously. 'But even after I've looked, sometimes, I can still hear him. He paces about and mumbles. Sometimes it's as if he's angry. He shouts out.' She pulled dog hairs from her jersey. 'Anyway, I shan't be here for long. I'm going to New Zealand.'

Daniel went to the edge of the corridor and looked down. The passage was dark and gloomy. A dull mist hovered about it, grey and dreary. He turned to her. 'How many times have you heard him?' he asked, swept up in it all and gripped by what she had told him.

'Four or five times', said Rosie thoughtfully. 'There's no particular pattern.'

'Go get the key', he said, confident and determined. 'Let's take a look.'

Rosie went for the key and they walked down. As they were going she said, 'I'm sorry if I offended you before. About the music I mean. Laughing and that.'

'I don't remember', he said, standing beside the door. 'Anyway, that's not important now.' If the ghosts were really appearing, then somehow he would find out why. Through the agency of science, or some other discipline he did not know of yet, the knowledge would make itself known. The facts would be there as all facts were till found.

'Listen', she whispered. She touched his arm anxiously. 'Can you hear him?'

A deep voice came from the storeroom, almost as if it spoke from the heart of the earth. A voice, Daniel thought, that was filled with yearning and pain. A voice that stunned him to hear, and it came as Rosie had said, in German. Translating it into English, Daniel heard: *'Why must we part, my love! I need you now! Why can't we be together?'* The rest of the words drifted as if in a timeless void. It seemed the voice existed now, in his own time, yet somewhere else also, as if locked out of time itself forever. Daniel felt cold with awe. His mind raced on and came to a block as always. 'Open the door', he said. Rosie inserted the key. What dark world might he enter now, he wondered. What would he find.

As they went in, the small room flooded with thin blue light; the almost turquoise light he knew so well. It expanded slowly, covering the old books and the broken furniture. He stopped cautiously. It seemed a man was appearing before him, focusing as if he were being painted, the flesh filling out, the features filling with power. Daniel could feel his tension and anxiousness. Even his pain. He could scarcely bear the suffering, and for a moment leant on the wall silently. Rosie stood firm beside him. Daniel felt he might be the man himself, and he fought to keep a hold on himself, his senses reeling. He saw now, that the man sat at a table working. The image was blurred, though the room had changed. It was neat and clean, and the desks and books had gone. He sat by the window writing urgently at an old oak desk. He turned slowly, as if aware of their presence, and though his features were vague, it seemed he gazed enquiringly, a crop of dark black hair falling across his eyes, which were dark and intense. As he moved in closer, Daniel found that the man disappeared into shadow, just as if he had never been. He tried to speak, but again, his voice would not come. He stared at the old oak desk as it slowly vanished, the broken furniture coming back into focus, the old books just as they were before, piled on the floor.

Rosie beside him seemed suddenly warm and human. They were both thoughtful. His throat felt dry, though his hands were sweating.

'It doesn't make sense', said Rosie, as they walked back. Her voice was calm and controlled. Daniel took a deep breath.

'Not to us', he said slowly and gravely. 'There must be a reason though, for all of it.' Daniel sighed frustratedly. 'Whoever he was, he is trying to tell us something. We have to find out what it is.'

Rosie stopped and turned. 'You mean you saw somebody?' Her face was pale. Daniel froze beside her, the strength draining out of him. 'You mean you didn't?' he whispered. Rosie's face was blank. She shook her head. 'But Rosie, you were there, with me. Surely you ...' He gazed at the dog by Rosie's desk. Daniel could hardly believe that throughout it all the dog had remained asleep.

'I knew it', she whispered, her tone weak and fearful. 'I knew there was somebody there. Who did you see?'

The sound of voices came to them from beneath the window. Ordinary human voices. People were walking on the path by the river, talking and laughing. Daniel frowned. He didn't want to worry her now unduly. If the ghost was there, then he must have been there before. Perhaps he had always been there. Maybe there were energies that were manifest at certain times, when the time was right, like now. Somehow, he decided though, this was personal. It was about him. 'I'm not sure', he said, slowly. 'Don't let it worry you, Rosie. It was probably just my imagination.' He touched her hand. 'Nothing is going to harm you.' He knew he was right. He gazed down the corridor again. He hadn't felt at all disturbed or afraid. Whatever the energies were he knew them to be benign. He had understood that much at least. The door of the storeroom seemed quite normal now. But who had the man been addressing, and why was he in such pain? Daniel wondered how he would fit it all together. It was all connected, he knew, but he'd have to find out how. Was it possible, he asked himself, that feelings might be caught in time, feelings that went on and on for all eternity?

Rosie made some coffee and sat down beside him. For a while they were silent. Just then they caught sight of a middle-aged man in the newspaper section. He raised his eyes and smiled.

'Ah, there you are', he said. 'Good afternoon. I thought there was no-one here.' He straightened his tie and nodded thoughtfully, looking them over. 'The place seemed empty. Anyway, I helped myself.' Daniel and Rosie watched as he leaned back, adjusting his cuff links, then buttoning up his suit jacket. He picked up his raincoat and slipped it on.

'I don't want to throw you out', said Rosie. 'It's just that I'm closing. I normally leave at five.'

He stood up, tall and thin, the bones of his face sharp and determined. 'Oh, that doesn't matter, my dear. I can come tomorrow', he said.

'You're very welcome', said Rosie, still preoccupied.

He went to the top of the stairs, and for a moment, looked back. Rosie said, 'Did you find what you wanted?'

His eyes filled up with sadness. 'Wanted?' he said, gazing down at the floor. 'Oh, I shall never find what I want, my dear. None of us ever do that.'

'If you come again then you must let me help you.'

'Yes, I will', he said smiling gently. 'Thank you.' He glanced at his watch. 'The nights are so dark', he said. 'Oh, such a blanket of darkness.' His voice trembled with sorrow. Turning to Rosie, he said: 'You see, I must keep on looking. All the time, I must look.'

'I understand', said Rosie. But she didn't. She didn't understand anything now and stood confused as she watched him go down the stairs. Daniel watched too. He did not know his face. But he knew the voice. Oh yes, he knew the voice.

THE DARK STAR

Throughout the next day, Daniel felt numb with thought. As he looked from the window, the trees in the garden, naked of leaf in the grip of winter, seemed stark and still and longing for sun. He too felt cold and alone. And where was Lydia? He decided to phone her again. Come what may, he would tell her about it all: the ghost from the river, the ghosts at Cliff House, the ghost in the library. And also he would tell her about Miranda. That sequinned wilful mermaid she had seen in his arms at Cliff House. He could not put an end to Miranda pursuing him and unless he told Lydia what had happened in London he knew he would lose her. He felt instinctively he had not lost her yet. She had not withdrawn from him. If she had, he'd have felt it.

But the thought of telling her about Miranda depressed him. His life was haunted from both worlds. Miranda wanted more and more from him. His father, always sympathetic, had endless patience with her, sitting for hours listening to her sufferings. But they were the sorry tales of a child. Miranda would not grow up. It was a refusal. The world of adults frightened her with its coldness. She could not get in, she said, in her strange and pleading way, as if he and his father might put it all right at once. But Daniel had often helped her. Probably more than he ought. Now, to his dismay, he saw the fruits of his error. For she followed him everywhere.

He had met Miranda at a party in London, given by Robert, a colleague at the university. They were working on a project together. But Robert worked slowly and Daniel found it galling sometimes waiting for his results. You had to move quickly, he told him, in the research business. You could guarantee that what you discovered was being discovered by somebody else at exactly the same time. Robert, Daniel felt, suffered from the lack of a sense of urgency. The world could dream on casually. He did not care. But he annoyed Daniel because he had a brilliant mind and did not use it. His wonderful ideas went nowhere. The research was published, however, but Daniel had done the major part of the work himself. Robert was smart. But he'd never have won a Nobel Prize. Or any other prize for that matter. He wasted his best time and energies on all-night parties he gave for his friends in his London flat. The trouble with Robert's parties though was they were open house. Anyone could come. And a lot of the people were strangers. Sometimes the house was packed so tight you could hardly move.

At the time of this particular party, Daniel was thirty, and felt strangely old. It was quite irrational, even ridiculous, but happened to men sometimes of his age, he decided. Robert's parties were in some way a chance to be carefree and for a brief while to be young again.

Miranda arrived in the early hours of the morning. Small and delicate and strangely incongruous with the two big fellows who'd brought her, she looked like a child. The men wandered away, leaving her on her own. She squeezed in next to him on the sofa, though it already held four people. 'What's your name? she asked him, snuggling up close to him in a warm and familiar way. Above the loud music her thin voice fell on him like the sound of a bird. Her skin had a faint blue tinge and looked like porcelain. Her long white hair flowed about like a river. He thought her frail and vulnerable. He told her his name. 'And you?' he asked smiling. She seemed to be falling asleep.

'Miranda', she said softly, clinging on to him, her eyes closed and her voice drifting away. The skin, he saw, on her fingers, was thin and translucent like that on the stems of harebells. Her lashes flickered like white little lights on the edges of her eyes. The eyes of a bird, he thought, sharp and glistening. 'Can I get you a drink?' he asked. She wanted a gin and tonic. Thinking he might have another beer, he eased himself from the small space, noting as he looked at her that she seemed to be already drunk. The men, he remembered, had had to support her when bringing her in. Perhaps he shouldn't have offered to get her a drink after all. He pulled himself away from her and stood up. Still she kept her eyes closed leaning her head on the back of the sofa. Her eyelids flicked a moment. 'Where are you going after?' he asked, thinking as he said it, it sounded as if he might be wanting to sleep with her. Her slender body looked frail as a sheet of ice. Her white lashes lifted slowly. 'I'm sorry', he said, 'I didn't ...'

She eyed him with a look he could scarcely read. He glanced downwards thoughtful. He wouldn't have spent the night with her anyway. She didn't look more than fourteen. Just then, he wouldn't have spent the night with anyone. He was far too bruised over Bridget. 'I was meaning', he went on, 'that you'd better look after yourself. You've been drinking too much.' He glanced about; the two men were watching him.

'I shall drink as much as I like', she said crossly, tossing her hair and frowning. Now he felt strangely responsible for her. He didn't like the men who had brought her and wasn't sure what to do. He certainly wasn't taking her home to his flat, and if he took her back to wherever she lived, now, he might have the men to contend with. He tried to think quickly. No solution came to him. Perhaps if he got her a soft drink and sat with her for a while, she might sober up. Then he could reason with her. The men she had come with were thugs and, Daniel felt, were taking advantage of her. It angered him to see it.

'People are always ordering me about', she said, her voice thin and weak. 'But nobody really cares. Not really.'

One of the men came over, laughing loudly and throwing his weight about, which Daniel saw was quite considerable. He looked like a body builder. He stood before them, his huge knees bulging out of his jeans which were torn and soiled. Hitching them up, he poured beer out of a can down his throat and rubbed his mouth with the back of his hand. 'Having a moment with Mandy are we?' he said in a gruff voice. He laughed hoarsely.

'Don't you call me that!' she cried angrily, suddenly alert. 'I hate that name. And why don't you go away!' She turned to

Daniel. 'He thinks he owns me. They both do. Why do they do it?'

The other was dancing now with a tall girl in a leopard-skin dress. 'Better not let Hal see you', the man, sniffed. 'Nobody touches his Mandy.'

'We're having a talk', said Miranda. 'I can talk to whoever I want. Why don't you leave me alone.' She turned to Daniel gazing at him with shy eyes. Daniel wanted to go. The air felt suddenly cold. He glanced again at Hal, delivering kisses on the tall girl's neck. He was obviously blind drunk. Daniel moved to the door. The girl stood up quickly. 'You can't just leave me!' she cried. 'You must tell them to go away. I can't get rid of them.'

The man in front of them laughed hoarsely again. He poured more beer down his throat. It fell down his clothing. He took Miranda's arm and kissed her hard on the mouth. 'See you later', he said.

Hal was coming across. Daniel took a deep breath. A waif of a creature, the girl was in tears. Wondering how he might rescue her from Robert's vile party, and risk the thugs following him, he tried to think of a plan. She clung to his arm. 'Take me with you!' she cried. 'I'm ill. I don't want to go with them. Don't let them get me again.' The man was almost with them, joining the other who waited. Grabbing Miranda's arm, Daniel drew her into the crowd and they ran through the door.

'I shall die!' she screamed, running alongside him in her high-heeled silver shoes. The sequins on her dress flashed beneath the street lamps as they fled. The thugs were almost upon them. Finding an alley, through which a dim lamp lent a steely glow, they hid. Fifty yards away his car gleamed in the lamplight, but he dared not risk it. 'Don't let them get me!' she cried, trembling and clinging to him. 'I don't care if you kill them. It's what they deserve. You can stab them to death if you like. Both of them.'

The hideous possibility struck him, making him even more concerned to stay totally still and completely silent until they had passed. The men were almost with them. 'Down here!' one of them called in a sodden voice. 'Round this corner!'

Enclosed in darkness, the girl leaning against his chest, Daniel pressed himself to the wall. 'Hush!' he said. 'Not a sound!'

'This way!' one of them shouted. They were close on him now. Within seconds he heard their voices again. They advanced on him in a pincer-like movement. 'Got you, you bastard!' one of them snarled, grabbing the front of his jacket and pulling him into his chest. 'Trying to steal our Mandy were you? We'll see about that.'

Daniel felt a rush of adrenalin pierce him. Immediately, like a flash of lightning, his muscles alerted. Finding a strength he had not known in years, he threw the man across the alley. Diving on him again, and pressing him on to the wall, he thrust his fist in his stomach, delivering a punch that would burst a rock. Next, sticking his knee in the man's groin, his teeth clenched viciously, he brought him down to the ground moaning.

He turned then on the other, finding him moving in towards him. The man was waving a knife. Its sharp blade flashed like an evil grin. Daniel surveyed it quickly. Its handle was long. He might push the man to one side and wrench it away, even if he must bleed for it. He thrust himself forward, threw out his foot, and sent him flying against the wall. Next he got hold of the blade with his bare hands, a surge of pain entering him as it sliced his flesh. He wrestled hard for the handle, grasping it hard. The other man lay on the floor. He was still moaning.

'Okay, okay', gasped Daniel breathlessly. 'Come on then. Is this what you want?' He brandished the knife. The injured man on the ground got up and ran off. Now it was Hal.

His eyes were glaring. His teeth were bared. He came at Daniel fast, thrusting his fist in his face and cracking his head on the wall. He pulled on the knife, but Daniel clung to it like the edge of a precipice. The man was trying to twist it, so it would enter Daniel's ribs. With a last great feat of strength, Daniel turned it quickly, finding it resting then in the cushion of the man's heart. Where it stayed, the thick warm ooze of his substance flooding through Daniel's fingers. Soon he was still.

Sitting in the silence, covered in blood in the damp alley, Daniel wondered what to do next. Miranda crept out of the darkness, bending over him. Her moth breath quivered on the wall.

'Did you kill him?' she asked, her voice trembling. She started to cry. For a short while all he heard was Miranda's weeping and traffic droning on the main road. He put his head in his hands. He might have sobbed, and yet he rejoiced that he was still alive. But what had he done? He took his hands from his face. He dared not look. Moving his eyes sideways, slowly he made out the shape of the man on the floor. A twisted shape, blood surging out of him, running away down the alley. So much blood. He glanced about. What if somebody found them now? The police. He would have to tell the police. He tried to think quickly. No, it wasn't a murder. It had all been self-defence. The knife was theirs. They'd threatened to kill him. But where was the man's companion now? Where had he gone? What would he say and would he return?

'What are you going to do?' Miranda whispered, shivering with cold.

He continued momentarily to contemplate the terrible thing that had happened. His hands were shaking and bloody. His limbs felt torn. A strange metallic smell came from the alley. The smell of blood. Daniel knew he would never forget it. He glanced at his clothes. Were all his buttons secure? Was there anything there in the alley they could identify him with? He searched about with his eyes. Already he was planning to run from the scene.

'Look', he said, rising. 'Come with me. I must think.' She had stopped weeping now. Removing her shoes and holding them in her hands, she ran beside him. The street was empty. Most of the lights in the houses were out. They stumbled over a dead cat killed on the road. Getting into his car, they drove to his flat, where Miranda stayed in his bed. Daniel slept on the sofa, wretched and sick with fear. He'd have to report it soon. Why not now? Why was he waiting like this?

Exhausted he slept, finding the girl lying beside him at daybreak, her arms round his neck. He could scarcely pull them away. 'Please don't leave me', she said, opening her eyes. 'Don't make me go.'

And so it began; the long march of agony. After that came the trials. The newspaper reports. The accusations. The testimonies. Robert did him little justice and couldn't even remember that Daniel was only a moderate drinker. For some time it broke him. He could not work. He wondered if he would ever work again. He thought he might never surface. All the time Miranda came to his flat, sitting and making drinks and leaning against his arm. Her mother had left them, she said, when Miranda was small. That much he identified with. Her father had brought her up alone. Or at least had tried to. It seemed, though, that whatever the man did, he did it wrong. Finally, she'd found her way into bad company. Daniel had seen that her arms were blistered and sore, and that she had taken drugs. Not now, she said. The men had done it. Now she was clean.

He dared not turn her away when she came to him. He didn't know where she lived, or how she was living. He hoped, he told her, she would keep off the drugs and be careful who she made friends with. Finally, after all the trials, he was cleared, and thought he might try to live again, returning to Knaresborough to do some work at Leeds. That was when he met Lydia.

Gazing now in the mirror, it seemed as though his spirit had drifted away. So many things had been happening. His mind was bursting with thoughts. He might have been in a separate world from everyone else, he felt so alienated. He needed to take a bath and change into some clean clothes. He hadn't shaved for days and his eyes looked glazed. He needed to shake himself up. More than that, he would have to see Lydia soon.

One of the books he had taken out of the library reported that heightened states of consciousness like this were fertile ground for spirits, and through it they might make themselves known. It was hard to believe what he knew. He wondered how he'd explain it all to Lydia without sounding foolish. He could hardly hold on to the thoughts, they raced so fast. He went to the phone and rang her number at Anderson Terrace.

'She isn't here', said Jeremy. 'She's gone to Alderley Edge. She said she was bringing some books. Find her a Greek restaurant. That'll do it.'

And Daniel did find her a Greek restaurant. One he knew in Harrogate. And they went there that evening. The food and wine were good, and they talked vigorously. She told him all that had happened that day with Sara and James, and how at first it had seemed like a betrayal, but now, she said, was more like a kind of deliverance. The little boy was beautiful. She was glad of him. In truth, he was like a little redeemer, a little Christ-child.

He still hadn't mentioned the ghosts. Nor had he said a word about Miranda. He didn't know where to begin. They had used up so much emotion, and it seemed again, it was the wrong time. He took her hand. He would tell her tomorrow. He could always tell her tomorrow. 'Lydia, darling', he said. 'I know there are things you're wondering about, but I'm glad you trust me. It means a lot that you'll let me take time. I shall tell you everything soon. I promise.' He bent his head and held her hand tightly.

That night they went to Alderley Edge and made love for the first time. How had he lived without her? Now he knew her every contour as well as her mind. And yet he still held secrets from her, fast in his heart. It pained him to think of them.

'How could we do it', she laughed playfully, 'here in this bed?' He kissed her shoulders. 'It was wonderful', he murmured. In his mind he heard again her soft moans as he'd entered her, her cries of pleasure. 'Turn to me', he said. She had never been able to meet his eyes before when they'd spoken of James. 'What matters now is us. You and me.' And he found her mouth, kissing her again deeply.

The next morning they emptied the dresser to take it to Anderson Terrace, removing things that belonged to James and putting them into boxes. Drawing it from the wall, Lydia saw that a small envelope had fallen down by the skirting board. She picked it up curiously. It appeared to be sealed, though it held no name or address. Opening it she drew out what seemed like a letter, and started to read it. As she did, she turned to Daniel, her eyes wide with amusement. This was the letter that James had talked about, the one he had stolen from Bonn. Lydia told him how James had taken it from the old woman's sewing box, and how he had claimed it was sent by Beethoven from England. The words, they saw, were in fine handwriting though the paper was old and quite fragile. Daniel took it. He knew the hand instantly. He fixed his eyes on the words, translating them slowly. *'Still the intrigues surround me. I am trying to be discreet. No-one apart from Broadwood knows I am here. I shall stay with him for two more weeks. He is making astounding progress with the piano. It lightens my heart. He tells me he has some relatives in Yorkshire and would like me to visit them. They live in the town of Knaresborough. A place, I believe, of immense beauty. I shall go there to rest my head. And perhaps I shall write some music!'*

Some of the paper had been torn off and half of the letter was missing. Daniel stood engrossed, reading it through another time before folding it up carefully. 'He'll probably come to look for it', said Lydia. 'He'll know he's lost it.'

'Well he won't find it', said Daniel thoughtfully, turning it in his fingers. 'I shall keep it with me'. He had recognised the handwriting immediately. It was unmistakeable. If this was Beethoven's letter, then the one in the attic was his too. He glanced about. How could they keep it safe? For the time being he put it into his inside pocket. Gradually something was coming together. Little by little a picture was taking shape. In time, he decided, and feeling elated now, it would all make sense.

'Strange', said Lydia, as they drove back into Knaresborough. 'First the music and now the letter...'

Daniel was silent. She asked him about the riding again. Did he want to go? Ought she to still arrange it? A ride in the dales might clear his head, said Daniel. Dropping her off at Anderson Terrace, he told her he'd bring the dresser again, when he next came to the cottage. There were other things more important to do just then. The dresser could stay where it was; snug in the back of his car. The precious letter was snug in his inside pocket.

More than ever, Daniel felt he was now being summoned. He'd developed a kind of energy. An extra-sensory perception. And it was his energy, he now realised, that had brought the ghost from the river, and had invoked her again by the old apothocary shop, and with her husband at Cliff House. From what the man had said, it appeared she had taken a lover. Sometimes Daniel feared the silence might swallow him up. He feared for his mind. How could he hold the two worlds safely apart, whilst seeing, at the same time, how they linked up? For they certainly did. Something had happened at Cliff House long ago. And it wasn't resolved. An energy had been unleashed that could find no peace and was trying to work through him. If he thought about it carefully enough, it might speak for itself.

Here was a letter allegedly sent by the master musician himself. More than that, he was making a visit to Knaresborough. Might he have been to Cliff House too? Daniel felt cold at the thought of it. Beethoven here in his father's house. His mind travelled the still rooms imagining the great man walking there, climbing the stairs, looking perhaps through the tiny kitchen window, watching the water trickling down the cliff face. Daniel's mind throbbed with thoughts. He thought of the ghosts, the man's jealousy and brutality. He thought of the ghost in the library. Could the ghost have been Beethoven? Could it? If that's who it was, then why was he there? And what was he doing?

KENDLETON MANOR

Lydia had booked the riding for one o'clock at the Rowan Tree Trekking Centre. They were looking forward to getting out on the horses. The day was bright and warm for December. Jeremy had been round earlier to take the dresser to Anderson Terrace for Daniel. He'd borrowed a council van from Rosie. Lydia, he said, would arrive soon. 'A grand sight!' he'd laughed. Daniel was almost ready. He turned the last pages of a newspaper then went in the garden to gather some washing from the clothes line. Lydia came through the gate.

'I noticed the treehouse before', she called.

He turned to her. In her riding gear she looked wonderful. Bundling the damp clothes under his arm, he went to her and kissed her. Her manner was bright and cheerful. He hoped they would have a good day. 'Yes', he said, both of them looking into the tree. The tree house was almost hidden now, even by branches. 'I built it with dad years ago. I must have been about nine years old, I think. We stayed in it all night. Mum brought us drinks ...' He smiled quickly and looked away. He gazed at the sky. 'Looks like a beautiful day!'

Going into the kitchen he put on the percolator, then went upstairs for his riding jacket. She laughed as he came back, remarking on how good he looked. She found his watch, which he'd misplaced, on the top of the fridge. It was twelve-fifteen. Finding his keys he locked the door behind them and went for his car in the garage. Lydia's was on the high street waiting.

Soon they were on the road, the car making harsh breathless sounds as it chugged along. 'It'll get us there', he laughed. The car was an old Beetle his father had handed down. 'It's a faithful old thing', he said. 'It's done many a mile with my family.' They found the quickest route by the Abbey Road.

The centre was a large converted farm surrounded by fields and paddocks in which thirty or so horses grazed.

Looking down from where they were, rows of small cottages dotted the hillside, with copses of trees breaking the long smooth undulations of land. The hills were stark in places. The long hot summer had parched the earth, though here and there sheep were attempting to graze. The hills, Daniel thought, had never been so bare. The red grouse, prevalent there, normally living on shoots from the heather and berries, would find it hard the following year to nest and feed. Stepping out of the car, in the distance they saw the old abbey and the reservoirs. The water was very low. The trekking centre had once been Rileys Farm, and had been with the family for three generations. In 1970, Anthea Green, who Daniel had known since childhood, had taken it over, making it into a trekking centre. Lydia did not normally come this far to ride. There were centres nearer to home. At Rowan Tree though, away from the traffic, the air was fresh and clean. Daniel had been there often. He had been with his father and sometimes with friends.

As they arrived, Anthea saw them from out of the window. She came out, standing waiting, her long blonde hair flying about in the breeze. She tied it into a scarf. 'It's good to see you!' she cried, greeting them warmly and in high spirits. 'I thought you'd gone abroad', she said in a rich Yorkshire accent. She offered her hand. Both of them shook it. Daniel introduced Lydia. Lydia gazed about at the horses, grazing leisurely. Daniel told Anthea where he'd been working and put on his leather gloves. He screwed his eyes at the sky. The sun was bright though the air was cold on the top of the hill. 'I saw your book in London', she said. 'I liked the cover.' 'Good', laughed Daniel. 'And I hope you'll like what I've written inside as well.'

The air was crisp and dry. Daniel remembered the last time he'd been at Rowan Tree. He had come when he was fourteen with his father who, though no rider, had given it a go. But he hadn't enjoyed it. It was too nerve racking, he said. He'd rather play golf when he had the time, or sail on Aunt Rachel's boat in Wales. Daniel recalled how after his mother's death, for years his father had tried to make himself a new life.

There were girlfriends. Dithering gentle creatures, fluttering through the rooms at Cliff House, blinks of quivering light in his father's bedroom, drops of water, losing themselves in the sea of life. Yes, the man had tried. Though he'd never found another woman to love. That was when he had started to drink. 'Love can do outrageous things to the human soul', he'd said. 'Outrageous things.'

Daniel breathed the fresh air, watching Lydia gazing down the hills and tying her hair in a band. Outlined against the sky, with the wind on her cheeks, she looked beautiful. A horse in the next field made a whinneying sound, then raced, fast as the wind across the paddock causing restlessness in the others. 'They haven't been out much lately', said Anthea. 'It's a wonderful day for the time of year.' A young boy brought them horses and fitted them bridles. One of the horses snorted loudly, throwing its chestnut head back hard. Its thick mane danced, settling along its neck softly. Lydia mounted her horse, its muscles flexing beneath her. Having got on to his own, Daniel drew up beside her. Their eyes surveyed the valley. It seemed to go on for ever. Lydia's horse snorted again, uncertain, as she exercised it along the cobbles its hooves clopping loudly. 'There's something wrong', she said quietly. She looked for Anthea, attending to the broken wheel on a tractor and talking now to the boy. Coming across, Anthea said: 'You're out of practise. She's restless that's all. Remember to trot before you gallop.' The boy watched, hands in his pockets. 'Come on then!' said Anthea, 'Don't just stand there looking. There's work to be done inside.' He turned and followed.

As they moved out of the centre, Lydia and Daniel stopped to look down the hillside again. It was lit with an orange light. The last embers of autumn scented the air. 'There's the Forest of Knaresborough!' Lydia cried, pointing. 'And that's where mum is now. The manor there, can you see it? That's where she works.' As he gazed ahead, he found the manor, almost lost in the distance. 'She wants us to pay her a visit', said Lyda. 'Do you think we've time?' The horizon seemed far away. The sun was high. He put his hand to his eyes, shielding them from the bright light, then looked at his watch. 'It would probably take half an hour ... Come on, let's do it', he said.

Arriving at the manor gates, they dismounted quickly, finding an attendant and asking if they might water the horses somewhere. He found them a trough where the horses drank and were tethered. The gardens, they saw, were also quite parched. In sixty years at Kendleton, the attendant said he had never known the earth so dry. They were talking to Duncan, a friend of Lydia's mother. And a friend of Howard's too. Duncan had worked with Howard's father, he said, before his death. He had known the family well. 'Your mother's down there in the restaurant', he said, 'if you want to find her.' He pointed. 'You can leave the horses with me.'

As they entered, the restaurant had started to empty. Wearing a white cap and apron, Lydia's mother looked up. She was filling a plate with cakes. Her eyes went first to Lydia, and then Daniel. Her features betrayed no feeling. 'I was wondering if you'd make it', she said, observing Daniel now with a steely eye. 'Duncan has tethered the horses', said Lydia. She moved in closer to Daniel. 'Pleased to meet you', he said to her mother, stepping forward and offering his hand. Lydia's mother took it and smiled, though her eyes regarded him cautiously. Glancing about, he said: 'I haven't been here in ages.'

Dating back to the fifteenth century, Kendleton Manor had been restored a number of times, but always tastefully. The walls of the restaurant held portraits of ancestors. The lord, who now owned it, was often seen with the visitors eating or wandering about. He lived in rooms at the back. The floor, Daniel saw, was laid in strange mosaic tiles that might have been Turkish. As he gazed about he realised how little he knew about Kendleton, though the place was close to his home. He and his father had often talked about how far apart the rich and poor had been in the past, how Knaresborough's poor houses had been flooded with beggarly people, whilst others lived in luxury. Lydia and Daniel had coffee and cakes, and talked about how dry the hills had become and how Lydia's horse had been playing up on the way.

'You mustn't be going back late', her mother warned, getting up from the table where she had joined them. 'Do you want to look round?' She guided them through to the main hall, all the time commenting on the paintings and ornaments. The manor, she said, had belonged at first to the Wentworth family, then later in 1586 to the Eddlestons. Finally it had gone to Sir Christopher Rotherham, who had married Charlotte, the daughter of the second marquis of Evermond. All but one of their portraits hung in the main hall. Lady Chàrlotte's, she said, her favourite, hung at the top of the stairs on account of its rich colour and spectacular likeness. Daniel and Lydia went to see it.

They were standing now, looking into a lifesize portrait, that almost filled the whole of the wall at the top of the stairway. They stood silent. Daniel was lost for words. He could not take his eyes from the image. Eliza didn't know what had caused him to stare at the picture so suddenly, and felt embarrassed. Lydia too was concerned.

'What is it?' she asked, seeing him so engrossed.

He took her arm and drew her close. 'The dress', he whispered. 'Look at the dress! There's something I have to tell you.'

Eliza had moved on, towards one of the bedrooms. People were walking behind them.

'It's almost real', said Lydia.

'It's far more real than you think', Daniel whispered. He wanted to tell her more, but he couldn't yet. He must get it all in order and then he would have a tale that might have some credence. A glimmer perhaps of sanity. For as it was, Daniel thought his mind was fragmented. He was hanging on to the separate bits until he could make a whole.

Lady Charlotte appeared to be in her thirties. She was wearing a red silk dress with a full skirt. Even in oil the silk was dazzling with light. The artist had caught it perfectly. Her hair was fair, and pinned up. Around her neck she wore a pearl necklace. That too glistened. Tiny ringlets clustered around her face. As Daniel looked at the picture, he knew he had found what he wanted. The dress was here, at Kendleton

Manor! He knew its colour and texture, the rustle of the fine silk. The dress had life. A life he knew and had seen. It had only been for a moment on the stairway. But yes, he had seen the dress before, on somebody else.

Lydia's mother returned to them. Daniel forced words. They seemed to be far away from his thoughts, but he forced them. He forced a smile and another handshake. The afternoon light was fading. But another piece of the puzzle had revealed itself and he needed to think. They went for the horses and headed towards the moor.

A HARE

As they galloped across the moor, the sky was becoming a dull grey. Lydia slowed her horse. A violet and yellow light descended through the grey clouds, the last of the daylight lapping the cliffs. Apart from the sound of the horse's hooves the valley was silent. The tangled crisp grass beneath them offered up a warm damp evening scent that was more like May than December. Stopping, they could just make out the fold of the gulley they'd have to reach. Tatters of sun streamed down through the clouds merging with purple shadows.

The horses were moving slowly. 'You're very quiet', he said, aware that he had also been preoccupied since seeing the portrait. 'What are you thinking?' he asked. For most of the afternoon she had reserved herself. 'Lydia', he said, beginning slowly and faltering, 'I've so much to tell you.' He lifted his eyes and gazed ahead. 'The time has never been right. I can't seem to find the moment.' Save for a brief smile that day, he felt she had distanced herself. A nightbird cried a peculiar jarring lament. 'I must tell you about Miranda', he said. 'I shall tell you now.'

'Miranda', she said, repeating the name slowly. 'Miranda.' She turned to him, her features bathed in purple light. 'What does she mean to you?' she asked, searching his face.

Anger rose in him.

'Mean to me?' He started as if he were stung. He looked at the sky and drew in a deep breath. 'Miranda! Miranda!' he cried frustratedly. 'What shall I do with you?' And he startled her horse which whinneyed and raised its front legs momentarily. 'She's just a girl', he said, as the horse settled. 'Seventeen, eighteen maybe. Almost a child.' She glanced at him sideways. He stroked the neck of his horse.

'Why was she there at the house?' asked Lydia. Her voice was bold though its edge was pained. He was silent, struggling for words. She faced him. 'Tell me', she said firmly.

He sighed. 'It's not what you think. She follows me about. You see it's ...' He covered his face with his hand and sighed. 'She finds me, you see. Airports, railway stations, wherever I happen to be, Miranda will find me.' He talked quickly. It sounded as if he was lying, he knew that. He paused, breathing hard, breathing in the scent of the moor. He said quietly. 'She needs me.'

'I see', said Lydia softly. Her features hardened. She looked away. They were silent a while, moving slowly. He could tell by the way she bent her head that she suffered. Even the night as it closed in might have hurt her then. 'I met her at someone's party', he said. 'A couple of thugs had brought her. They were senseless with drink. I doubt if they had a brain between them.' His tone was angry. He hated it; the old familiar tale. It still battered and bruised him, even to tell it.

Lydia listened, her profile strong in the fading light. In his mind he saw her frown. 'She was so frightened. The men were brutes. I ... ' He could not continue. For some minutes they trotted their horses quietly. He carried on. 'I dragged her away. I couldn't just leave her. I did it on impulse, you see. I suppose it was like a sort of rescue. Or that's what I thought.' He laughed briefly, caustically. He could not find the words. The weary, weary words. They would not come. The strong moon lit the moor. 'I didn't sleep with her, Lydia, if that's what you think. I had no intention. I just felt sorry for her. She was so small and defenceless. She'd been taking drugs. The men had made her an addict. I took her home and she slept in my bed. I was downstairs on the sofa. I thought, you know, I thought if she got through the night she could go home after. But she hadn't a home to go to.' He sighed hard. 'I never knew where she lived. I don't know now.' Lydia turned to him and smiled softly. It seemed she had freed her spirit. But he still hadn't told her it all. Not even half. 'But I've seen her father lately ...' he went on thoughtfully. 'He's very close. There was someone in Rosie's library, reading the newspapers. I saw him recently locally. I didn't know what her father looked like, but I'd heard his voice. He would phone me you see and ask if I knew where she was. I didn't of course. He'd scour the papers for accidents, that sort of thing. Then he'd phone up the hospitals, asking if some poor girl had been taken in. The man was distraught. He still is.'

'Do you think he's living in Knaresborough?' Lydia asked.

'He's probably lodging somewhere, looking for her. That's what he does. He travels the country looking.'

'And where do you think she's gone?' Lydia frowned.

'I haven't a clue', he said, still frustrated. 'She comes to see us. She often arrives on the doorstep and wants advice. Sometimes she talks to dad. Then she just disappears. She never says where she's going.'

'Are you hungry?' Lydia asked suddenly. He laughed, 'I certainly am, are you?' Apart from the cakes at the manor, they hadn't eaten that day. 'I've some wonderful bread and fresh Edam at home', he said. Soon they were off down the hillside, thundering over the moor.

Then suddenly Lydia's horse reared and screeched, not like a horse, but almost like a human in distress, twisting on its hind legs, so that Lydia clung frantically as it snorted and jerked. Lydia held tighter while Daniel reached for its reins, finally grasping them whilst clutching his own at the same time with his free hand. 'Hold on!' he yelled. 'We should never have brought her out! I knew it! There now, easy, easy!' He could see the thin reins cutting into Lydia's gloves. It was no good. Straining and tense, the horse threw her violently over its head, and with a dull thud, she hit the ground. As Daniel dismounted, Lydia's horse left them, galloping down the hillside. Holding the reins of his own so it did not escape, he knelt down beside her. She was very pale. 'My back!' she said wincing. 'It hurts.' 'Take my arm', he said, lifting her gently. She pressed her fingers into her spine. 'It's the muscle I think.' 'Can you stand up?' he asked. She leaned on him. Her ankle was hurting too. She moved it around in small circles. It seemed alright. Daniel glanced about, frowning. 'Damn it!' he said. 'We've lost the horse.' Now it was darker than ever. 'Blasted hare! Did you see it?' She shook her head. He drew her close and kissed her brow, breathing the earthworn scent of fern and heather that came from her hair. Her skin tasted salty. 'Can you climb on my horse?' he asked, helping her up. They would have to ride back together.

'Experienced riders, eh?' laughed Anthea Green as they entered the centre. It was almost midnight. Daniel saw that Lydia's horse grazed now peacefully with the others. Forced to go slowly, they'd ridden through the darkness thankful of moonlight and the mild weather. Anthea relieved them of the horse and they went through the farmhouse door, into the kitchen.

'You shouldn't have let us take her', Daniel chided when she came back. 'The horse wasn't fit.'

Anthea sighed, her eyes wide with surprise. 'You can't blame the horse for bad riding', she said defensively. 'You ought to have been more careful.' She stared at them. Lydia and Daniel were both dishevelled and covered with debris.

'A hare came into our path', Daniel said. 'But the horse was jittery. Right from the start it was nervous. You must have known it was wounded. The scar hadn't healed.' He wrung his hands.

'The hills are full of hares', Anthea said imperiously, putting her hands in the pockets of her dressing gown. She gazed at Lydia, watching her removing her boot and wincing. Daniel helped her. The ankle was bruised and swollen, though it was only a sprain.

'I think I'll survive, she said. She was tired and pale and her hair held traces of heather and fern.

'The horse has been back for ages', said Anthea, glancing outside.

'I'm more concerned about Lydia, now', said Daniel coolly. 'She might have broken her back out there.'

Lydia sat by a large oak table. Anthea's husband, who limped, came in and out, piling logs on the fire. A dog came through, vicous and growling. Anthea dragged it away and returned quickly. 'I'll make you a drink', she said. 'And we'd like a bath, too', said Daniel, reckoning they were owed it. He was fuming. Anthea must have seen the wound on the horse. She must have known. Earlier, as they were riding back, Daniel had noticed it. He hadn't wanted to worry Lydia, but he saw it had scarcely healed. He hadn't been sure how severe it was in the darkness, and recalled how people had said that the horses at Rowan Tree Centre were often uncared for. There was talk of Anthea leaving them out in the bitter cold. Anthea Green was large and loud. Arguing with her, Daniel knew, was a waste of time. Daniel's father said she'd changed when her husband had had his accident. He'd fallen out of the hayloft one autumn, fourteen years ago, and they'd called him out. The man was in agony. He'd damaged his spine and was on his back for a year. Anthea had pushed him about in a wheelchair for two years at first and done everything for him. Now he could get about, after a fashion. Somehow though, they had both lost interest in the centre. Watching her now, Daniel saw that Anthea was tired and weary. She had lost her guiding star.

'If you go down there', she began, pointing to a corridor off the side of the lounge. 'There are two bathrooms. I'll get you some supper.'

The fire burned fiercely. The man did not communicate or raise his face. Daniel supported Lydia to the bathroom. After that they had cake and coffee, then made their way home in the car.

It was hard to tell how long they'd been sleeping when Daniel's father came in. It had to have been at least four hours. Daniel and Lydia opened their eyes, finding him in the doorway, silhouetted in the dim light from the stairs. Holding the door with a large veined hand he looked frail and thin. Daniel saw he was smartly dressed in a grey suit, wearing it with a white shirt and a grey tie. It wasn't like him to be so neatly dressed for work. Daniel learned he was going to a meeting about excess paperwork in the Health Service. As he talked, he saw that his father had grown quite bald. Such hair as he had was long and prematurely white, curling behind his ears.

'Dad?' said Daniel, yawning. 'Are you okay?' Lydia sat up, the bedclothes beneath her chin. Daniel turned to her. 'This is Lydia', he said, smiling. 'You haven't met her before, have you? Lydia, this is my father. Lydia's doing research on castles. Her mother lives at Anderson Terrace on the river.'

Daniel's father came forward and sat on the bed, calm and slow like an old bird finished with flight. 'Well then, Lydia', he said, his voice tired and shaky. 'So how are you?'

Under the bedclothes, Daniel slipped his arm round her waist. She was soft and warm. 'We'll come and talk in a minute', he said, 'and have something to eat.' He wanted his father to look at Lydia's ankle. 'Lydia got thrown from her horse', he said. 'That Anthea Green neglects those horses, you know. The one she gave Lydia was edgy.' He told him about the hare and how the horse had thrown Lydia over its head. His father listened carefully, all the time frowning. He rubbed his face and yawned. 'Are you alright?' Daniel asked him again.

'Not so bad, not so bad', he said. 'I shall have to be off in a minute. There's a pot of tea on the table.

'We won't be long', said Daniel. His father went out and closed the door behind him.

VISITORS

After Daniel's father had cared for Lydia's ankle she got in her car. Daniel opened the gate and saw her out. The snow so often forecast over the last few weeks had finally started to fall. Lydia headed the car back down the hill. The sprain was only minor, the doctor had said. It had almost healed. As she drove away from the house, Daniel walked back slowly into the kitchen. The painting he'd seen at Kendleton Manor played on his mind. It lay like a sign. There hadn't been time to talk to Lydia about it. Her accident had prevented him speaking his thoughts. But his thoughts were moving swiftly. Was the dress on Lady Charlotte really the one he had seen on the ghost? Or was it a copy? He made a drink and went to the lounge, stopping a moment by the door and hoping he'd find the lounge he knew and not the other. Heaving a sigh of relief as he sat down, he rested his head on the back of the sofa and closed his eyes. His mind wandered, trying to tie the pieces of fact and fiction together, the pieces of truth and imagination, the pieces of revelation and reality. As he did so, he heard the sound of a carriage drawing up at the front of the house in the gravel. Rising, he went to the window to look, his eyes searching the garden and finding it bathed in the pale blue light he had come to know. It hovered like thin mist. In it butterflies fluttered, beating their wings in the warm air and alighting on flowers, for it was summer again. And as his eyes wandered over the strange scene he caught sight of a coach on the path at the foot of the rockery. For what seemed like several minutes, nothing appeared to be happening. He went to the porch and opened the door, entering the garden. Reaching the edge of the light the strong scent of roses came to him. All around him roses grew, some of them tall and touching the windows. He had never seen roses like that before at Cliff House, nor the other varieties of flowers that he now saw growing about him.

Inside the light now, he felt safe and unthreatened. And though it was dimly outlined, he saw a carriage and coachman, waiting on the pathway, the heads of the horses wandering in the blue light, rattling their harnesses. And a man leapt out, slamming the door and hurrying up the rockery towards him. He was stockily built and of medium height. His head was bent. He went past quickly, purposeful and determined. Daniel turned. A woman was at the porch waiting to greet him. They embraced warmly and murmured to each other. For a moment the woman looked back in the house fearfully, then they sped down the rockery together, passing Daniel, who watched in awe. As they climbed in the coach, the air filled with the crunching sound of the carriage wheels on the gravel as it moved off, going towards the main road. Daniel stood perplexed. He had not seen the faces clearly, yet ideas were flooding his mind. Taking his handkerchief from his pocket, he wiped his brow and neck and sat down. He was quite oblivious to someone else who was standing across the road, and observing him carefully. The man came forward.

About his own height, Daniel saw he was strong and broad with blonde hair falling about his shoulders almost girl-like. He looked like an ancient wanderer, Daniel thought, or another phantasm even.

'I'm looking for Lydia', he said, coming across. His voice was thick with hostility. 'Do you know where she is?'

The coach, Daniel saw, had reached the main road, fading inside the blue light. He gazed at James curiously. Whilst he did not know who he was, he divined it quickly. So here is part of the dream, he thought. For until now, James also had seemed like a ghost. His features were filled with rage.

Daniel had expected this. He hadn't known when it would happen, but sooner or later he knew they would have to meet. Daniel faced him calmly. 'Why don't you phone the house', he said coldly. 'You know her number.' James stood firm before him. He had moved inside the gate and was looking up at the house, searching it with his eyes. 'I have phoned already', he said quietly and casually. 'No-one is answering.'

He turned his eyes on Daniel again, looking him over coolly. 'Have you got her in there?'

'What do you think I am?' said Daniel gazing downwards and looking for marks of the carriage. 'I'm not her jailer.'

James nodded slowly, biting his lip. 'Will you tell her I'm here.' He regarded the house with an icy stare. 'I'd like you to tell her now.'

Daniel listened incredulously. 'Why don't you just go home', he said contemptuously. His palms were sweating and his mind dizzy from what he had just seen. He turned away. James cames closer, putting his hand on his shoulder. 'Nobody turns their back on me', he said through his teeth. 'I think we have things to discuss.'

Daniel turned, feigning surprise. 'I have nothing to say to you', he frowned. 'And you'd better shove off. Or I might remove you myself.'

'What do you think you're playing at?' James said, his voice thick with emotion. Smouldering with anger, he moved up the rockery following Daniel. The path was wet with rain. Daniel turned and faced him. 'Whatever it is', Daniel said, clearing his throat. 'The winning hand is mine. Lydia has left you.'

They were silent a while, guarding each other closely. 'Is it a pastime of yours', James said hatefully, 'seducing women? Do you pounce on them when their boyfriends have gone away.'

Daniel was silent smiling.

'You haven't heard the last of this', whispered James.

'Ah', said Daniel slowly. 'But you, my friend, have. You have heard the last of it all.' Their eyes locked tight and final. James hunched his shoulders. 'Are you in love with her?' he asked wretchedly.

Daniel did not flinch. 'Yes', he said. 'I am.'

James gazed at him, lost and confused. Daniel saw that the words had caused him immense pain. He looked astonished. 'Well', he sighed, throwing his hands out limply. 'That makes two of us.' Daniel watched him walk down the rockery and out of the gate.

Inside the house, he sat at the table thinking, wondering who had come for the woman in the coach and taken her off. He tried to imagine where they might have been going and why. Still he could not put it together. He wanted to know that Lydia was safe and hoped she would have no trouble from James if he went to Alderley Edge. She had gone to collect some things. He paced the floor. He could not relax. But Lydia was stronger now. He need not worry. They had started to build a new life and the structure was strong. He thought about the letter from Bonn. Obviously James was unaware that they had it. It was safe with the other now in a leather attaché case Daniel kept in the lounge. The writing was a perfect match with the other. From time to time he had taken them out to read them. But he didn't know what to do with them. He was waiting for something to happen. He believed now, implicitly, that something would guide him. He'd surrendered himself to the ghosts and must await their bidding.

TEMPEST

Lydia brushed snow from the boot of her car before lifting the lid and removing boxes of books and small items she had brought to Anderson Terrace. Through the window she saw that her mother was getting ready for Christmas. Cards were hung round the room on pieces of string. A Christmas tree stood in a corner, which she had begun to decorate. Lydia put the boxes down by the door. Her mother opened it. 'Can you bring them in later', she said anxiously. 'What's the matter?' asked Lydia, glancing inside. The house seemed still and brooding. Still in her housecoat, her mother looked tired and depressed. 'I don't want them going upstairs', she said. 'Not just now. I'm sorry, Lydia'. She rubbed her eyes tiredly.

Removing her coat and scarf, Lydia sat down. The boxes were still outside. It was snowing again. The cardboard would soon be soggy. 'Aren't you well?' asked Lydia. Her mother's mood was sombre. Eliza shrugged, looking out of the window. 'Old habits die hard', she sighed. Her voice was weak. Lydia turned to the tree. 'It's good that you've bought a real one', she said fondly. 'You know how I like them. Doesn't the pine smell lovely.' Lydia got up and went closer. It was a large tree. Jeremy must have brought it from the village. The decorations flashed and glittered in the morning sunlight. The room felt cold. 'Do you want me to light the fire?' asked Lydia. 'Jeremy was going to do it', Eliza said limply. 'He's back in the annexe.'

The boxes were heavy, lifting them had left a dull ache in her arms. She stretched them above her head. Dismantling her old life, though, had been easier than she'd thought. And her work was developing well. Two good publishers wanted to see it soon. Discovering her interest, the locals had dug out old photographs and documents, sending them round to Anderson Terrace. She had so much information she hardly knew what to do with it. Her mother, she thought, as she sat in the chair, looked like someone from one the sepia photographs Rosie had sent; a stiff Victorian lady, her features still and sad. Lydia shivered. The wretch was back. It was there in her eyes. Her mother rose. 'I think I shall take a bath', she said. 'And put on some decent clothes. You can light the fire if you want.'

'My boxes?' said Lydia 'They're out on the path. Can I bring them in?' The snow was falling heavily. The dresser she'd brought from Alderley Edge was by the wall, her papers and photographs organised now in the drawers. 'I shan't bring anything else', she said. 'Well, not for a while.' Lydia had had enough of the house for now. Her mother was silent a moment, stood on the stairs. An undercurrent of tension filled the small room. 'I was going to iron a shirt for Jeremy', she said. Lydia saw it was strung across a chair. 'He's got an interview at the country park today.' Jeremy couldn't iron shirts very well. He always managed to scorch them. Sometimes he burnt them through. 'I can do that if you like', Lydia offered. She went for the boxes outside and brought them in, putting them on the carpet and closing the door.

'A woman's life is easily ruined', Eliza mumbled. 'You think that love will pull you through, but it doesn't.' Lydia saw she was tearful. Someone was coming downstairs.

'So why are you whimpering now?' Ian Ralphson grunted, coming in and finding a cigarette. 'You're always whimpering, woman.' Lydia closed her eyes and opened them slowly. Her father was unshaven. His shirt was torn and his jeans were muddy. Most of the time he worked as a labourer, hiding his earnings while still collecting benefits. People would come to the house sometimes looking for him, and her mother would stay in the kitchen.

'Does this house have such a thing as a box of matches?' he grunted, sticking a cigarette in the side of his mouth. He searched about. Finding some in the hearth, he lit up. 'Well then, our Lydia', he said, smoking deeply. 'What are you up to?'

Lydia did not answer. She pushed the boxes against the wall, out of his way. 'I'm doing research', said Lydia. 'I'm looking at castles.' A stab of regret entered her as she told him. Whatever she did he diminished it. His words could shatter the whole of her dreams in seconds. Her mother, stood on the stairs, trembling slightly. Her father went about picking things up and gazing at them, making himself familiar again with the house. 'Looking at castles, eh.' He took tobacco from his bottom lip with his fingers. 'So what do they pay you for looking at castles then?' He slumped down in an easy chair and blew out smoke.

'I don't get paid, it's research', said Lydia, meekly. 'They gave me a grant. I'm writing a book.'

'Are you, then', he said, raising his eyebrows. 'And who do you think will buy it?'

'I don't know', said Lydia with sudden awkwardness. 'Whoever wants it of course.'

'Sounds like a risky business', he laughed. He turned to her mother. 'Risky business, Eliza, what do you think?'

'I think it's fine', Eliza said assertively. She was sat on the stairs.

'Something's wrong with my snakes', said Jeremy, coming in from the annexe. ''The heat's gone off and they're cold.' He did not look at his father. He did not address him. 'Have you any ideas?' he said to Lydia. A radiator warmed the snakes with a thermostatic control. It functioned from the gas supply. But the roads were up outside and the men were working. The gas had been off all day.

'Why don't you take the electric fire from my bedroom', said Lydia. 'I'm warm in there, it's next to the boiler.' An immersion heater meant they could have a bath, but without a fire, the house was chilly.

'Looks like you've moved in proper', her father said, rubbing his nose. He spilled ash on the carpet. Her mother sat silently watching. 'Nobody ever told me.'

Lydia did not speak. It seemed her father had mastery of the cottage. Even the rooms seemed to tremble whenever he came. They were suddenly back in the sickening place where they could not breathe and where everything was in darkness. 'I thought you were living at Alderley Edge with James?' her father said. Eliza listened. 'She was', she murmured. 'But not now. Lydia's left him.'

'Left him, has she. Well', said Ian Ralphson laughing.

'It's as simple as that', said Lydia, beneath her breath. 'We're selling the house.'

'And you think you can stay with us, do you?' he said, raising his voice. He sneered contemptuously, addressing her mother. 'I can't be having her here, Eliza. — Anyway, why has she left him? She shouldn't be leaving him now, after all this time.'

'I should do what you do, should I?' Lydia murmured, wanting to flee. Anywhere else would be better than where she was. She could feel herself draining away.

'Cocky eh?' he said, stubbing his cigarette into the hearth. He lit another.

'I'll get that electric fire', said Jeremy going upstairs. Bringing it down he went to the annexe and came back, concerned about what was happening. They all felt stunned. The man's presence had deadened their minds. Her mother came down the stairs again and went to the hearth. She riddled the grate which was filled with ash from the previous day. It would have to be cleaned out. She looked as if she'd been crying. Lydia got out the iron. She'd iron Jeremy's shirt, and after that she would light a fire, she said.

'So where's this interview then?' asked Ian Ralphson, resting his feet on the coffee table. 'In Altrincham', said Eliza. Her husband gave a long low groan. 'The lad can speak for himself!' he cried. 'For God's sake, woman!'

'They want a deputy warden', replied Jeremy. 'I hope I can do it.' 'Of course you can', said Lydia, carefully running the iron over the gleaming white cuffs. 'You know you're the man. Who else could they get who would show the interest that you do? Or offer the dedication?' They were silent a while. Eliza stood by the window looking out at the snow. Jeremy was thoughtful. 'So you're here for Christmas then?' said Lydia, glancing up at her father.

Her father's forehead tightened. 'You know it all, our Lydia, don't you. Coming here as soon as I've turned my back. Organising Jeremy. Getting your mother all worked up like this. "Here for Christmas, are you?" Did you hear her, Eliza. Cheek of it eh?'

Lydia breathed in quickly, catching her breath. It was still there, the panic. The pain that filled the lack of love. How could she get away? She wanted Daniel now. She needed him more than ever. Suddenly she'd found herself a pathetic child again, alarmed that so few words from her father could still reduce her to tears. 'You always upset us! You think you can come whenever you like, and do what you want!' she cried.

'And I can', he said boldly. 'It's my house, girl, not yours.'

'Why do you think it's yours?' Lydia protested. 'It's mum pays the mortgage. She's bought the furniture too. Nothing belongs to you.' Lydia lowered her voice. 'Not even this family now.' She glanced at her mother. Eliza looked wearier than ever. A misery had caught her up, and stronger for waiting. The wretchedness was alive in her eyes.

Lydia reached for her coat and turned to her father. 'You make me ill', she whispered. 'You think you can bully your way through everything.' She faced her mother, appalled at the loss of strength she'd so recently found. How easily it had slipped away. 'I don't know how you put up with it', she said. 'Year after year. Shall I tell you what's going to happen? In a couple of days he'll be bored. He always is. And how will he entertain himself then? I'll tell you ...'

Her mother stood rigid before her, her hand at her mouth. Her father listened angrily. 'Lydia, please', her mother murmured. 'Not at Christmas.'

'I'm going', said Lydia. She didn't know where, but she had to get out of the house.

'Right then, Lydia', said Eliza. 'You start the bother then just go off on your own. Nice performance that.'

'Oh', cried, Lydia. 'Why do you always side with him? What are you frightened of? Do you know what it's done to me, all this? Do you know what it's done to Jeremy? You call him a husband, mum. He's not. He's never here. He's never been there for Jeremy. He's never been there for you. He's never been there for me!' She turned to him, her voice strained with pain. Her eyes were moist. 'Have you any idea how I've loved you? How I've thought of you, wondering where you might be, thinking you might be ill, thinking you might be alone ...'

144

Ian Ralphson stared at her indifferently. He smoked hard.

'You don't, do you? You don't understand about love, you see, people like you never do.' Her mother looked at her anxiously. She came forward, touching her arm and trying to comfort her. Lydia continued. 'And it's just as well you don't, because the love I had has gone. It's gone, dad. It's dead, and it's you who killed it!' She sat down sobbing. 'It's a terrible loss', she cried. 'You don't know what a loss it is.'

Ian Ralphson wiped his nose with the back of his hand. 'Who do you think you are ...' he shouted, his tone furious. 'Talking to me like this? Why I'll ...'

'What?' cried Lydia. 'What will you do?' She braced herself and stood before him. 'Tell me, what you will do?'

'Same old Lydia. Same old fiery Lydia!' he laughed.

Jeremy sat bent over, covering his head with his arms.

'Now then, Ian', said Eliza. 'We can do without all this. Our Lydia's got some problems.'

'Problems?' cried Lydia. 'I've got problems alright. You are my problems. Both of you. I've had enough. I don't know how you can do it, mum. How can you let him come back like this, again and again, ill-using you, ill-using all of us? Can't you see what it does? Someone must pick up the pieces.' Lydia's voice was thin and weak. 'Me, mum. It's me who's picking them up. And Jeremy. Have you any idea how tired we are?'

'Come on Lydia', Jeremy said slowly, rising and frowning. 'Calm yourself down. You shouldn't be getting like this.'

Eliza sat biting her nails, her eyes wide open, her face white with terror. Lydia took hold of her hand, but she snatched it away. 'Oh, Lydia', she said. 'I'd never have thought you'd have turned like this. These terrible words. You can't really mean them.'

'I do, I do', said Lydia, quietening now and trying hard to recover herself. 'And what's more, you must make your choice. It's him or me.' She turned to her father. 'Mum's doing fine. She enjoys her work at the manor and she doesn't need you to keep turning up and spoiling things. You must give her some peace.'

Her father's eyes were filled with rage. They were silent a while.

'Our Lydia's right', said Eliza finally. 'I think you should go.'

He rounded on her surprised, laughing and pointing at Lydia. 'You're not taking notice of her are you?'

Eliza braced herself. 'No, I'm not', she said slowly, facing him. 'I'm taking notice of "me".' Her tone was firm, her features tense with purpose.

'What?' he said aghast, his eyes widening. He steadied himself, drawing hard on the cigarette and blowing smoke at the ceiling. He was losing his hold. 'See where it gets you all this', he snarled.

'I'll not let you bully me', Eliza said, gritting her teeth. 'Not any more.' Standing before him, her hair flying madly about, her face wild as a tiger's, her mother, Lydia thought, looked proud and strong. She pointed towards the door.

Ian Ralphson rocked backwards and forwards, biting his lip, his eyes narrowing angrily. 'I shall do what I want. I'm staying here. And nobody's going to budge me.'

Sustaining her nerve, Eliza said: 'I've asked you to go. I'm not going to ask you again. Now there's the door.'

Lydia watched in awe.

'I'm going nowhere', he said stubbornly, his voice hardening. 'It's my house and no-one will throw me out of it!' He kicked the boxes Lydia had brought and the things spilled out. 'This is Miss High and Mighty this is. It's always her that causes the bother.'

Eliza bent down, putting things back in the boxes. 'These are our Lydia's belongings. It's not for you to knock them about.' She handed Lydia a box. 'Better put this in your room', she said quietly. Lydia went upstairs and came down again. Her mother picked up another. To her horror Lydia saw that her father had grabbed her mother's wrist. Jeremy got up quickly.

'That's enough, I think', he said, his voice cold and strange. 'Enough, dad, eh? My mother's said what she wants. Now why don't you listen?'

In the silence that followed it seemed that something had died. His father turned on him jeering. 'What? Come on. I'll not have a kid chastising me. Don't start it, lad.'

'I'm sorry, dad', said Jeremy quietly. 'We want you out. Okay?' Jeremy's voice was firm and steady. His eyes just then might well have been the cobra's own. He put his hand on his father's arm. 'Take your hand off my mum, alright?' His tone was sharp, his head firmly thrown back. 'Leave hold of my mum, and I'll let you go', he whispered.

'Well it's come to summat, this', gasped Ian Ralphson. He wiped his mouth on the back of his hand and laughed. He shook his head. 'Are you threatening me lad?' Knitting his brows he curled his lip.

With piercing sadness Jeremy looked in his eyes, 'I suppose I am. Let go of my mum, or you'll feel my fist.'

A shiver ran up Lydia's spine as she watched. 'Jeremy, don't!' cried Eliza, tugging her wrist from her husband's hold. 'Right', said Jeremy wrenching his mother away, and punching his father's nose so that he fell backwards. Rising slowly, Ian Ralphson grunted, mopping the blood from his face. 'If you're after a fight my boy, then that's what you'll get!' And he came at Jeremy wildly. Jeremy waited, pressing his mother away with the flat of his hand. As his father advanced, he grabbed his arm again, and twisted it up his back. 'You'll break it, lad!' his father shouted, writhing in pain. For a moment or two, Jeremy held him fast. And Lydia saw that beads of sweat were on his brow, running to meet the moistness that appeared in his eyes. Releasing his hold, and an edge to his voice that was hard as steel, he whispered. 'Come on, dad. Just get your things, and go.'

His father stood bewildered, breathing heavily. A series of wheezes left his throat. His head was bent. He raised it to meet a solid wall of resolve. Shuffling towards the stairs, he turned and looked back.

'Enough's enough, dad. See.' said Jeremy, his voice shaking. 'Next time you'll have the law to deal with an' all.'

Ian Ralphson packed his things and left.

THE MEETING

Eliza talked about going to live with Howard on Abbey Hill. It was no surprise to Lydia or Jeremy. What their mother had hidden from herself she could not hide from them. As she brought holly in from the garden, a wonderful musty fragrance flooded the room. 'See how red the berries are this year!' she cried. A law unto itself, the tree bore berries as and when it wanted. This year they were copious. 'Wouldn't you like to meet Howard?' she asked tentatively, putting the holly on the window ledge in a vase of water. She did not turn. Lydia noted how happy she was. Freed from the weight of what had been her own and her mother's captive lives she too felt glad. She noticed also that Jeremy, coming to terms with Rosie's imminent leaving, and enjoying the thoughts of his new job, was also content. She hoped life might be taking a turn for the better now for all of them.

Her mother wandered the house, looking at things strangely as if seeing them for the first time. She and Howard were the same age. He'd been widowed for eight years. His wife had died in a car accident while they were away on holiday. Helen had died instantly. A poor driver, he'd often told her not to go out in the car alone, especially in mist. Their daughter, Beatrice, was training to be a vet and was seventeen.

At first Eliza had thought him shy and withdrawn. Rarely chatty, he often came in for his midday meal, then left. He'd rather be with his trees and flowers. Howard was chief gardener at Kendleton, and due to the long hot summer had found it a frenzied year. A lot of the plants had died. One day, when she was serving lunch, she'd made him laugh by giving him the wrong meal. But Eliza had been embarrassed. After that he'd apologised and they'd talked together for some time. Eventually he'd invited her to eat with him by the window, looking out on the lawns. There the light streamed in and the lush

148

hydrangeas lent their scent. Last year, needing generous watering, she'd cared for them, and had also fed his seedlings. When December arrived, she'd moved the cyclamens and primulas to warmer spots for the winter. Gradually they'd developed a friendship. But Eliza had been afraid. The threat of Ian had never been far from her mind.

But now it had gone. And she knew in her heart it had gone for good. And her new life surged in her now, as if every window in her being were opened to sunshine. Small things gave her joy as they'd done in childhood. Even the making of a pot of tea held beauty. And she knew that the little fates could come with their sadnesses, and another day would send them down the hill of time. How strange it was that in the past two weeks she'd written four letters to Ian. Letters she'd never sent. Even a month ago she couldn't have written them. They were words of finality. Words that announced the private war with herself and her soul was over.

But imagination's loves were not the whole of her story. Passion had stirred in her, rattling her blood and dragging her spirit through her bones with a new vigour. She wanted Howard. She'd found herself like a girl again. She wanted him. And she'd have him. Somehow Lydia's strength and what she had done had translated itself to her.

Winter pulled its cold weight through the season, whistling its songs, blowing its essences through the rooms of the cottage. Her mother had gone to Howard's. Jeremy had gone to a friend's in Altrincham, and would be out all night. Lydia moved the photos Rosie had sent around her manuscript, still not sure where to put them. Snow fell fast by the window in thick flakes, when she heard a knock on the door, not like a human knock, but more like the sound of a bird pecking against a tree.

Opening it, she found a young girl wearing silver shoes and a sequinned dress. She was trembling with cold. Glancing about, she spoke to Lydia, her voice thin and melodic. 'My name's Miranda', she said. 'I need to see you.' Lydia knew her immediately. Miranda's eyes moved fast to the warm fire, the Christmas tree flashing with ornaments, the cards swinging in the rush of air she had brought.

Lydia stood still for a moment, taken aback, watching the heavy snowflakes cavorting around the long white hair, fluttering about the girl as if she were brought on an elfin wind. 'Of course', she whispered, opening the door wider and letting her through. The girl stepped in, glancing behind her furtively as if being pursued. She moved, fast as a breeze, finding her way to the fire, her blue skin flickering. Crouching, she took off her shoes, and Lydia saw that her toe-nails were painted with bright red varnish. She rubbed her feet silently.

'I hope you don't mind my coming', she said softly. She glanced at Lydia sideways. The white hair streamed down her back, almost silver. She turned to look at Lydia with an almost unearthly face, her long white lashes flickering, the firelight dancing about her. 'I've something to tell you.' She gazed at the ceiling then closed her eyes, warming her neck by the fire and stroking it. Lydia moved in closer and sat down, watching her, listening carefully. 'He's keeping things from you', the girl whispered. 'That's what he does.'

Lydia frowned. 'Who do you mean?' she asked softly, disturbed and confused. What did Miranda know that had not been revealed? What could be so important that she needed to come to her now, on this bitter evening?

'Daniel', the girl said quickly, though with perfect assurance. 'He hasn't told you.'

Lydia pressed her lips tightly together, afraid to speak. Miranda warmed her hands in the heat of the fire. She sang softly, a strange little song. Whatever her next words were, Lydia did not want them. Even if they were true, she'd rather not hear them now. She put her hands to her face, hoping Miranda would disappear before her. Hoping she might be dreaming, she sighed hard and looked at Miranda again. The girl was still there, her face solemn and childlike her great blue eyes staring into the fire. Outside the snow stuck onto the window, holding them in a film of white light.

'You can't marry him', said Miranda, facing Lydia with sudden daring, her cheeks colouring quickly. By the blazing logs she was like an ethereal presence. It was almost as if her delicate bones were about to break. She shivered, clutching her knees and rocking pensively. 'He's marrying me in the spring. He ought to have said.' She stretched her arms, thin little splinters of light, high in the air. The firelight grew nervous about her. 'He doesn't know how to tell you', she said, lowering her voice.

Lydia was on the fine edge of despair. But wasn't it all just nonsense? Her thoughts raced. There were certainly things he hadn't told her about. They'd been in his eyes on the hills. If she hadn't been thrown from her horse, he might have revealed them. Perhaps the accident had aroused his sympathy. She looked at the girl. She was very lovely. And she knew there had been a bond. She'd seen it when they were dancing together at the house. A cold fear seized her. She dared not think. She must hide. But where? She stood up, watching the snow as it flew past the window, her insecurities flooding back, sweeping away her strength. She bent her head.

'Will you make me some food?' the girl asked, glancing at her and stroking her arms. 'You can make me some scrambled eggs, if you want.' Again she sang. Lydia went to the kitchen. Miranda called through, 'I like them fluffy. Don't make them hard, will you.'

Stirring the eggs, Lydia glanced at her, hunched by the fire, her pale blue skin like the skin on a lake, her red lips like they had tasted blood. She poured milk in a high tumbler. She turned the scrambled eggs out on to plate. Putting it all on a tray, she went in to her.

The girl ate quickly, thrusting the food in her mouth and drinking the milk rapidly. 'I knew him before', she said, her cheeks bulging with food. 'I know him better than you do.'

Lydia sat back watching her eat, listening as she finished the eggs, her thin fingers holding the plate before her, gazing at it as though it contained her image. Quietly and slowly, Miranda said: 'Has he told you about the killing?' She glanced at Lydia. 'He's done a murder, you know.' She spoke in a low voice, as if it were hard to tell. 'The blood ... The blood ... You should have seen it. A terrible thing ...'

The words entered Lydia's mind, slowly and painfully. She felt them like cruel blows. Could it be true? Had he really committed a murder? Was that what he had been hiding from her? Was this the reason her mother had been so hesitant at first? How could they all keep secrets from her like this; James and Sara, her mother, and now Daniel.

'So much blood ...' Miranda moaned, handing the plate to Lydia. 'I can't forget it.'

Lydia could hear the kitchen clock ticking. The room felt suddenly hot. She wanted to open the door to get some air. She went to the kitchen to drink some water then came back.

Miranda continued. 'All that fighting and shouting ... Daniel was trying to protect me, you see.'

Lydia took a deep breath. At least she knew some of it then. Miranda said: 'They made me tell it again and again. So many times.' She shook her head, her eyes wide with terror, telling the tale in quick bursts. She told how the men had chased them, how Daniel had fought them off in the alley. And trembling as she said it, she told how she'd heard the sounds of a struggle. The sounds of the killing. 'They asked us so many questions. We had to keep going to court'. Her eyes were earnest. 'I didn't see it properly. They were in the darkness. All I could hear was the fighting. Then Hal screamed out. That was when Daniel stabbed him. Then he was dead.'

Lydia held her breath. She could not speak. Daniel had hidden all this? As she spoke, Miranda's words stabbed her too with their force. They were silent a while. 'I hated Hal', Miranda whispered. She sang softly again. Turning to Lydia she said: 'Do you think you could run me a bath?'

Lydia went upstairs. Her life had shuddered back to a halt. She didn't know how she would move it on again now, or if she could find the strength.

LOSS

Hearing what had happened at Alderley Edge with James and Sara, Daniel felt worse than ever at having kept secrets from Lydia. He knew now, painfully, the danger of doing so. Lydia must know everything. And soon. There was, though, much to do. Trying to make sense of the hauntings, he had fallen behind with his work. Also he could scarcely leave his father for more than a few minutes. His illness devoured him. And something else was bothering Daniel: where was Lydia? Whenever he'd phoned the house there were vague excuses for where she had gone. Once again she'd grown distant. Jeremy too seemed remote. Something was wrong. Confused and hurt, he'd thought he might go to Anderson Terrace to see what was happening, but after thinking it through had changed his mind. For it occurred to him that Lydia might have changed her mind too. About him, that was. What if someone had told her something? The thought chilled him. His painful secret twisted about like a knife itself inside him. He had come to depend on her love; without it he felt cold as ice. Once or twice he had been to the boathouse, finding Jeremy cool and reserved, not even stopping his work to talk to him.

He was fighting too with his father. Though he was in serious pain, he'd shown little respect for the nurse, grumbling at her and sending her off miserable and indignant. He would not stay in bed and instead wandered the house all night, drinking whisky and sleeping by day instead. He'd refused his injections and medicine, and in the end had brought Daniel to reproach him cruelly. Also the death of the child tormented him daily.

During this time, what his father had called his 'conversations' with Daniel's mother seemed to have ceased. He had become weak, as though on a kind of journey, using up all his energies in trying to die. Aunt Rachel phoned again and again. Daniel said he could cope. She'd always been there for them before, this time he would try to manage alone. And he did feel alone. For the first time since they had met, he felt the loss of Lydia's spirit. All around him the air was icy and vacant.

But Aunt Rachel was always there at the other end of a phone. Together they thought they might pull his father through. It was a tug of war, for he resisted all help. Aunt Rachel said to have patience. To understand. Daniel tried. There were, though parts, of his father he could never have understood. Parts that were insufferable. Those were the parts where he neglected himself as though he were of little worth. But his father's relationship with his sister was a shade and colour of its own. They had always been close. It was she who had first introduced his parents in Wales.

Born in Wiltshire, his mother had moved to Wales, where she had met his aunt at an art exhibition. Aunt Rachel had a passion for watercolours and Daniel's mother had shown considerable talent. Invited to come for a holiday on her farm, she had met his father, and there they had fallen in love. But Daniel's father had paid a price for that, he said. Passion, he'd told Daniel gravely, was doomed in their family. A jealous fate had claimed it. They were all cursed.

And Daniel had been disturbed by that. Even into his adult life he had often thought of it, sometimes on falling asleep, sometimes on waking. He had been afraid to care too much for women. And in a way it suited him. Love had consumed his father. And somehow strangely the boy in him thought it had killed his mother too.

But love had found him now, and it would not let him go. It had happened. And since Lydia was now avoiding him, he panicked, thinking she was trying to flee, and he felt like a vile monster chasing her, for that's what he was. He was mad with dread that she'd leave him. For he knew she loved him. She had said so and he'd seen it in her eyes. More than that, he'd abandoned himself to it. The thought of losing her made him feel like a fragile craft on a hostile sea.

And he had little patience for his father, thinking him masochistic. After several days of his writhing and moaning, he'd put on the radio, ignoring him. Though it didn't last long, for he feared he might need him urgently and was constantly up and down stairs listening by the door and wringing his hands. He shuddered at the thought of his father's abandonment, and went about the house moody, staring in mirrors and spilling drinks. It pained him to think of Lydia and the loss of what they had had.

Just then his father cried out — a thin inhuman cry, winding itself through the rooms and finding him in the kitchen. 'Daniel! Daniel! Come to me quickly!'

Entering his bedroom, Daniel found him almost sat up, his eyes staring widely. 'Over here', he said urgently. 'Here, hold my hand!'

The thin bones locked in his own.

For a moment his father was silent, his eyes closed. His hand was moist and warm. Opening his lids slowly, Daniel thought he had a strange unearthly countenance. His glassy eyes held Daniel's gaze. 'You've been good to me, son. You know that.'

And for a moment he was silent again, as if sleeping, his white hair thin and unruly about his pallid face. 'I know how you feel about London. But you mustn't let it destroy you. It was all in self-defence.' His eyes opened slowly, as if searching. 'What else could you do?' He rested a while, then spoke again. 'You mustn't be so hard on yourself, my boy.' Again he rested. After a while his voice returned, his eyes still closed. 'I thought I could heal the sick. I have tried to save lives. And you have done the same. You have saved your own.' And he lapsed into silence again. Daniel could hear the wind beating against the shutters downstairs. His father's room was small and claustrophobic and without windows. He didn't know why he'd chosen to sleep there. A little stuffy room at the back of the house. The only place, he had said, where he could find some peace. He was mumbling again now, struggling for words. 'If there's something you can do for me ...' Daniel fixed his gaze on his father, listening carefully. His father's breath came in quick gasps. His own palms were sweating. 'You can end the shame!' The man's voice trembled, as though it were filled with tears. Daniel looked downwards hard at thought. The shame was a battle. He knew that. And one he had made entirely his own. His father looked up wearily. 'End the shame, Daniel. Do it for me!'

Daniel nodded slowly, gazing down at him. His throat was dry. Watching his father now, he saw that he was close to death, and it plagued him that he'd wronged him by his lack of sympathy. This was his father's choice. He had hurried to death, embracing it with open arms. He had suffered about the child too. His brooding was his worst enemy and Daniel had often tried to wrench it from him, though it was such a potent force, his father would not let it go. Now he had fallen lame on it and it showed itself for the leech it was. It had sucked his blood.

'You can't tell me about guilt', his father whispered, his lips dry and swollen. 'I know about harbouring guilt, my son. And no doubt you have learned it from me. But you haven't done anything wrong. They cleared you, remember.'

'I'd like to think so', Daniel sighed heavily. 'Or I'll burn in the fires of hell.' He attempted a weak smile.

His father shook his head with a burst of excited energy. 'Hell! What do you mean, hell? There is no hell. Oh no. Only the searching for lost love. That's the agony, son. For all love lives. Somewhere it lives!' His voice rose as he spoke and Daniel feared for his strength. 'We have to be our own inquisitor, Daniel. We can't look to God to slap our wrists.' He coughed hard, a rattling sound like stones being moved by a hidden power in the depths of the sea. Beneath the bedclothes he seemed without substance, as if he had gone already. Daniel breathed in deeply, filling his lungs with the stale air of the tiny room. What could he do for his father now at this final hour?

'I always felt', his father laboured, his spirit bright in the last fires of his eyes. 'About your mother, you know ... that I ought to have looked after her more. I ought to have kept the house more warm. Sometimes it's cold in ...' Daniel stroked his father's brow. It was smooth and damp. 'Your mother is in the light', his father rasped, feverish now. 'She comes to me, just as she was. Soon we shall be the in the light together, and all the joys that we knew together will be there with us. Just as it was before, so it shall be again.'

They were silent a while. Daniel looked at his father's face. How could he want go like that? How could he leave him so coldly, so indifferently? For that's how it seemed. And just for a moment he felt vexed with his mother, dismissing the thought quickly for it hurt him to think it. He could not help though, whispering, 'But you're leaving me, father. You're leaving *me*.' He bent his head, ashamed that he could give such life to anger at a time like this.

'I know, Daniel', his father said eventually, clearing his throat. 'I know all that. And you mustn't blame me. I have to be with your mother. My spirit aches.' He tightened his hold, drawing Daniel closer, his breath sour on his cheek, his voice like a thin echo. 'You see, in our family, there are great passions. Passions that grow from radiances the firmanents never dreamed!' He breathed in quickly, a rush of something in his throat that seemed like death. 'Next door!' he cried. 'Go next door and get me more pillows!'

Daniel went next door and returned, finding his father trying to hoist himself up. Lifting the warm frail bones, he arranged the pillows behind him. His skin shone tightly across his bones. Suddenly he coughed again, hard and vicious. 'Quick! Quick! Get me the bowl!'

Daniel drew a small white bowl from beneath the bed in which his father spat in the mornings. That day there had been some blood.

'It's time, I think', he whispered, gasping. And he shook his head, coughing and moaning, clutching the bowl beneath his chin and spitting into it. A tremor ran through his body as he lurched into a quick spasm, his eyes rolling. Daniel held him with an iron nerve.

'Daniel! Daniel!' he cried, gripping the bowl with the last of his strength. 'Be with me now!'

'Don't fight it, dad!' cried Daniel, his eyes brimming with tears. 'Gently now. Go gently ...'

A trickle of white fluid came from his nostrils. 'Here, give me your hand, son. And he snatched it, putting it to his mouth. 'I love you, Daniel. I love you.'

'And I love you too, dad', Daniel whispered, close against him. 'You're going to mother now. I love you both!'

Then suddenly it was over.

A peculiar stillness filled the room. And Daniel pressed his cheek to his father's face. It was warm and moist. He lowered his father's head and closed his eyelids. After that he knelt for some time before going to reach for the phone.

HOWARD

Howard Falkingham wasn't exactly handsome, though he was tall and dark and definitely distinctive. Catching his profile in the greenhouse window, his straight back still, his long nose poised against the light, he looked like an old rook. He was forty-eight years old with the easy heart of a man much younger. Due, he told himself now, to Eliza Ralphson. Till recently he had thought himself middle-aged and done for. But growing older was not so hard, he'd discovered, provided you found the right woman. And things were looking up. Now she'd packed that Thief of Bagdad husband off, he was closing in. And fast. All things come to those who wait, he told himself, as he climbed from his car at Anderson Terrace. He had never forced himself on Eliza. No-one could ever say that. All his moves had been carefully measured. He was past his best, perhaps, but he could still blow fire.

The cottage, he saw, was small and clean and white. Fresh, compared to his own rambling house near the abbey. But it wouldn't take long for her to sort it out. She'd her own ideas for brightening up his cheerless rooms.

Because he took care of the manor grounds, Howard would often neglect his own garden. Sometimes in the college vacations, when Beatrice came home, she would turn the soil and plant some flowers, but she wasn't too keen on gardening. She was prospering, though, on her course, and succeeding too, there was plenty of work for vets in Yorkshire. But she wanted a job in the south she said, for a change. She'd be back though, Howard had told her. There was nowhere nicer than Yorkshire. When she came home, sometimes, she'd come to the manor for afternoon tea with him and Eliza.

The appearance of the Kendleton gardens owed much to Howard's inventive genius. A skilled gardener, he'd followed his father, and grandfather too before that. They had all worked at Kendleton and knew the place like the back of their hand. His father had said he knew every nook and cranny. Between the two of them, they'd created the beauty that Kendleton gardens were noted for. And his grandfather had made it a hobby to learn about Kendleton's history. Telling Eliza all this, Howard thought, had fired her interest, and watching her tour the house and gardens with groups of people had made him proud.

Much of the present glory, though, was due to his own judicious planning. In early days, forced to take orders from others, he'd planted flowers and shrubs where he'd never have put them himself. But he'd bowed to the dictates of others quietly and with sincerity, making the best of things and offering his own ideas when he could, knowing that in time his skills would be recognised.

And they were. Howard was chief gardener by the age of thirty, making all the decisions then about Kendleton Park. The grounds were enormous, with a wild and romantic as well as sublime aspect. Now they were graceful and beautiful with careful clumps of trees around the lake on which wildfowl nested. He'd surrounded the old remains of the first hall, hidden inside the old park and dating back to the fifteenth century, with various colours of rhododendron, making it a special feature. Around the manor were long herbaceous borders and small walled gardens where visitors could sit and rest. His special love was the Japanese garden, flooded each summer with tourists. Howard Falkingham liked both natural and formal beauty, and the gardens reflected his tastes.

Eliza had started to work at Kendleton two years ago as manager of the restuarant. Howard admired the speed with which she could serve a meal. When people had been touring the house and the gardens, they wanted a hot drink and something to eat. Eliza understood all that. She knew how to manage the girls at the back of the counter too. Once or twice, at first, he'd praised Eliza on how she looked after the restaurant. Especially the kitchen, always filled as it was with wholesome food and drink. She had looked at him under her eyelids like a young girl.

After that it was easy. A good-looking woman, he'd seen she was lonely. In fact ridiculously lonely. Though hard to find, her laughter when she let it go flew high above the trees. It lay within her like a flock of captured birds. Sometimes, in autumn, the leaves shining and fluttering, he would think of her laughter and vow to release at least one bird each day.

Of course, Eliza knew none of this. And as he neared the door of her house, he realised that he hadn't told her he loved her either. Those were words for younger men, he thought. And yet he did love her. Especially now, since she'd come to him with every bird in her body flying. Oh, yes, he loved her now. And he'd help her get rid of that husband of hers as well. At least he called himself a husband. But he wasn't a husband as Howard Falkingham knew it. He knew what a woman needed. He knew what he had to give. And he wanted her to have it. Now as he knocked on the door, something leapt inside him as he waited outside, wondering what new world he entered and what new life it would offer.

'Howard', she said, opening the door and smiling. The house welcomed him. 'So what's going on?' he said, removing his coat and hanging it on the door. Jeremy, she said, was out at the boathouse working. Lydia had gone to see a friend of hers — or more than a friend perhaps — a young lecturer, whose father had died recently. Harold smiled. He saw she was looking well and brimming with happiness. Sitting quietly he drank his sherry and listened to what she said. A wholesome smell of cooking came from the kitchen. He rested his head on the back of the chair. Life was rich. Life was good. Life was fine.

A BUNCH OF WOODLAND FLOWERS

It was four o'clock. Daniel rested his head on the table top. The sound of a hammer coming down again and again disturbed his sleep: Guilty! Guilty! Guilty! He shivered. Someone was at the back door knocking. He opened his eyes and blinked hard, trying to think who it might be. Aunt Rachel had gone out shopping and had her own key. The heavy sodden feeling came back to him again. His father had gone for ever. Perhaps it was the woman from church coming for some of his clothes. He stretched his arms and went to answer.

Lydia made a sorry figure standing before him. Her eyes, normally bright and filled with energy, were dull as his own. Behind her the garden was silent and grey. Apart from the occasional drone of a car it seemed like the high street was empty.

She gazed at him, her face confused, her features tight and anxious. She was waiting for him to speak. The moments went by, almost suspended in pain. 'We have to talk', she said in a weak voice that he wouldn't normally have known. It seemed she was drained of her normal strength. As she looked at him, he hoped she didn't see how surprised he was that she'd come, or how much it hurt him to see her. 'What do you want?' he asked coldly. He rubbed his neck and screwed up his face, watching her in the growing dusk.

Lydia put out her hand, but he stepped back. She didn't dare to think just then about what she'd done. The way she'd abandoned him in his grief. The terrible way she'd neglected him. All she wanted now was to see him. To see that he still survived. And to tell him she hoped he was happy. All week she'd watched the cars, coming and going, the cortège leaving the house, the sombre faces of people from Knaresborough who'd loved his father. The night air whispered about her with what seemed like anxious regret. Something was drifting away. She needed to catch it quickly. Her voice came damp on the air. 'Go on then. Tell me how wicked I am if you want. I know it's true. I'm selfish.' She covered her face with her hands. She spoke through her fingers, her voice muffled slightly. 'But I've scarcely been able to breathe for thinking about you. I felt so excluded. I wanted to ...'

The early sound of an owl came from the darkness, wavering mournfully. Daniel braced himself and looked at her properly, daring to see her again. Daring to take in what she had once meant to him. He could feel her remorse, a tangled mass in the air that he could not reach. He retained his composure. He did not know why she'd done it, leaving him like that, just when he'd needed her most. He took a deep breath, hardening himself against her. Against their love. He would not bend an inch. She had hurt him too much. She had taunted him, he felt, deliberately, just like women did. Just like Bridget had done. After all he'd thought and allowed himself to feel, she had let him down.

'Let me come in', she pleaded. He saw she shivered slightly. The air was cold. He wondered what she'd been doing, if she'd gone back with James after all, and if she wanted to tell him. He could not take that now. Not now. She went on, 'I ought to have told you ... I was far too proud. I'd been hurt before, and I ...'

Daniel frowned and put his hand to his forehead. Haven't we all been hurt before? he thought. Did she think she had a monopoly on pain? He felt so exhausted. 'I've been trying to phone you', he said, his voice shaky. 'You've been avoiding me though. No-one would tell me a thing. Not even Jeremy.'

Lydia looked at her feet, at the glistening pebbles. She saw he was wearing shoes, a thing he didn't normally do in the house. He was also wearing a black suit. There had probably been a lot of people to see. He was still in mourning.

'I needed you, Lydia', he murmured. His voice shuddered like the wind in the trees behind her.

'I'm so sorry', she whispered. 'I ought to have come. But the least hint of ...'

'Of what?' he urged, suddenly serious and looking at her. 'What do you mean? Aggression? Anger? *Murder* ...'

'Betrayal', she said, calmly and finally, as if she had said the very last word she would ever say in her life. His eyes flashed in the darkness. Lydia saw there was anger there as well as confusion.

He searched her face. 'I haven't betrayed you', he said, his voice faltering. 'I know there are things I haven't told you about, but Lydia, it is hardly betrayal. I'd never betray you ever.' The words shivered between them. Behind him the small kitchen, where they had sat so often talking, seemed dark and empty. Even the water scurrying down the cliff face sang a different song. Lydia felt like a stranger. She stood waiting, waiting for forgiveness, waiting for understanding. He must come to her now, she could go no further.

Daniel's eyelids were heavy. He was short of sleep. His voice laboured. 'It doesn't surprise me, of course.' He could not look at her now she knew it all. Well, almost all. That was, all of the wordly things that made him afraid. The ghostly manifestations he had lately come to witness had somehow subsided. 'I ought to have told you before. Anyway, there it is. So now you can say what you think, and then I must work. I have things to do.'

'It seems', Lydia said softly, 'there are things we both have to do. Things we must talk about.' She smiled softly, trying to meet his eyes. And for a moment she did. They were eager and fearful. He dragged them away.

'Listen', he said, watching the night sky, his eyes darting from star to star. 'I'm glad you've come round. But you needn't apologise. You haven't done anything wrong. You owe me nothing. You never did.' He rubbed his mouth with the back of his hand. The sound of footsteps came from the high street, passing the gate, then drifting into the night.

'Is that what you think?' she said, looking amazed, her long hair suddenly brushing her face in the slight breeze. 'Do you think I've come to apologise?' He stood very still and silent. She could see he was in suspense. 'I've come because I'm ashamed.'

Daniel leaned on the wall. He closed his eyes. He could not count the times he had sat, willing her to come to him, watching the phone, pacing the floor, unable to do his work, unable to think. He had gone through hell and back. He would not do it again. Now he had nothing to give. He had nothing left. Though still he wanted her. The garden, it seemed, throbbed with her presence. She filled the air. She filled his mind. He breathed her in. 'I don't know what I can do for you', he said quietly. It seemed there were no more words. His throat was dry and his brain was burning with sadness. He glanced at her, a hard stare in his eyes, steeling himself again. She'd ignored his letters, his pleadings, his miserable phone calls. Thinking she no longer wanted him, he'd decided to go abroad again and had made some enquiries. He'd told himself she was part of his past, that she wasn't the Lydia he'd known. Or at least thought he'd known. But he knew that pasts were not so easily done with.

He was weary now though. Right at the end of his tether. Sitting with Aunt Rachel at his father's funeral, seeing the heartless coffin that carried his father away, he'd been reminded again of his mother, and felt the loss just as he'd done as a child. Now he was in his armour again. He was in his steel. He couldn't believe he'd lost his father and felt sick at the thought of it.

'I was at the back of the church', said Lydia, into the darkness. After, when they'd gone outside, she had seen Miranda, standing beneath the trees. Sunk so low in his pain, Daniel had been oblivious to those around him. Miranda had hidden, though Lydia had found her weeping.

'I lied to you!' she'd cried. Lydia had wondered how she survived; the sequinned dress she wore was torn, and her silver shoes were dirty. She seemed lost and wild with a fearful power, like a spark of reckless lightning. She'd spoken quickly and jerkily. 'When I came to your house and told you things about Daniel and me ... Well, it wasn't true. I made it up. We're not getting married at all. It's you he loves, not me ... But what I said about Hal was true. I wasn't lying then. Daniel killed him. That was the truth, he did!' She'd opened her huge wide eyes and stared at Lydia with frightening directness. 'But it wasn't a murder', she'd cried distressfully. 'They said it was self-defence. That's why they let him free! Oh, I wish I didn't tell lies. Will you help me not to?' Lydia had stayed with her a while, watching the mourners. Looking behind her, she saw that Miranda had gone.

'You must let me explain', said Lydia, as everything tumbled back in her mind. If only he'd let her into the kitchen, where they could talk properly, telling each other everything, to finally reach that state of peace and love they so urgently needed. Would she never enter his house again, let alone his heart? 'I thought you didn't want me', she said.

He gasped. 'You thought I didn't want you? Have you any idea how I've hoped and prayed you would come to me?'

She went on, talking over him, telling him how there were things she'd been told that had made her question him. How she hadn't trusted her heart, and felt ashamed. He listened quietly, his head bent before her, almost afraid of her words. He could hear her voice, her frantic need of him, her desperation.

'I've wanted so much to hold you, to comfort you, to be with you', she said. She broke off, starting to cry. 'Daniel, I've been so miserable ...'

He paced the cobbles, his eyes searching the heavens again. 'I'm very familiar with misery, Lydia', he said. His voice was unsteady, he hated to hear her weeping. He glanced at her, watching her suffering, hearing her sobbing quietly. 'I feel so guilty', she murmured. 'I've been so wrong.'

'What is there to be guilty about?' he said. He spoke more tenderly now. These were words he had asked himself again and again. Apart from the sound of her softening sobs there was only silence. 'Look, come on in', he said, indicating the doorway and letting her pass. 'Go and sit down.' As she went by he stretched his arms on the wall, pressing his face to the cold stone. He went to join her. 'Have you been busy?' he asked, standing before her.

'Hardly', she said. 'I couldn't think. I've done nothing useful at all.'

'Me neither', he said, seeing her eyes glistening and worried. She looked as if she had lost sleep. His own listlessness was a burden too. He could not shake it off.

Lydia gazed about, becoming familiar again with his home. She saw that there were flowers in jugs on surfaces and decided the neighbours must have brought them. Cards were arranged wherever they'd lodge. Down at her feet, she saw the floor was piled with boxes and crates containing his father's things. They were mainly books and medical equipment.

'I'm going to give them away', Daniel said, seeing where she was looking. He squatted down and took a book from a box, leafing through it. 'Books like this are expensive.' He clapped it shut and placed it back in the box. 'Well then, anyway ...' he said. Standing up, he was silent a while. That something was different between them now was obvious. They were almost like strangers.

Lydia felt lost for words. 'Talk to me please', she begged. 'Don't be silent like this.'

'What do you want me to say?' he said, his forehead tightening defiantly. He would not say the words she wanted. The words that would heal. He did not trust them.

'Shall I never find you again?' she asked, despairingly.

'Do you want to?' he murmured, getting down by the books again and reading their titles, moving them from box to box pensively.

'How long is this to go on?' she cried. She knew they would have to talk about Miranda. Better to do it now, thought Lydia. She spoke quickly, as if trying to get it over. 'She came to see me. I was quite surprised. It was snowing. She seemed so cold ...' He listened, lifting his eyes. 'Who?' he asked, though Lydia thought he must have known who she spoke of. 'Miranda — she came to Anderson Terrace.' Daniel moistened his lips and stood up, leaning against the sink. He nodded his head slowly. 'Did she now. And what did she tell you?' His tone was angry.

Lydia sighed and continued, 'So many things, Daniel. Absurd things really.' She searched her mind exhaustedly for something that would not hurt or upset him. It seemed impossible. 'I don't know why I believed her. Jeremy was out all night. She stayed in his bed. She left at dawn.'

'What did she tell you?' he asked firmly, guarding Lydia carefully. If a pin had dropped ten miles away he'd have heard it then. 'Tell me.' He did not care what Miranda had said. All that mattered now was how Lydia judged him. He prayed for deliverance.

'You were in a fight', Lydia faltered. 'And someone was killed.'

'She told you that?' He turned away quickly and bit his lip. He frowned. 'Yes, that's right', He spoke slowly. 'She told you the truth. And I did the killing, too. Did she tell you that? You want no truck with murderers do you?'

Lydia went to him quickly, trying to hold him to her. He pulled away. 'You're not a murderer Daniel. It was self-defence. Miranda told me. You're walking free. Don't you see? That means you're innocent. Can't you accept it?'

'Can you?' he asked, turning on her. 'I mean really?' He paced the floor agitated. 'There were those who didn't. There are those who don't.'

'Including yourself', she said quietly, her skin tingling with feeling. She was at the heart of it now. Right where he needed to clear his soul of its terrible burden. He trembled before her, covering his face with his hands.

But something had ravaged his guilt. Something had torn it apart. As he searched his mind he could see his father's face. He could hear his words. And Lydia's words as she spoke them now ... He had nearly lost her through this! You must end the guilt! He told himself. You must end the shame! The words raged on in his mind. 'I intended to tell you before', he moaned. 'But Lydia, I couldn't.'

'You couldn't. Exactly', she said. 'And you didn't.' They were silent a moment. Lydia said, 'Can you imagine what it was like for me when Miranda told me? Having to hear it from her?'

'I thought I'd lose you', he said, going to sit at the table, relief flooding his veins that at last she knew. He breathed in deeply, filling his lungs with strength. 'You were ignorant of it all. The whole wretched business.' He threw back his head.

'Oh, how I liked it, Lydia. How happy I was that you didn't know. I wanted to keep it away from you, just a little bit longer.' His voice rose again. 'And can you blame me for that?' His hands were clasped, his knuckles white with tension, his eyes pleading. He clapped his hands on the table and stood up, 'Damn you, Lydia! You were faithless! You did not trust me!'

Lydia trembled slightly. She was grappling with him now at the heart of his pain. 'She said you loved her.' Lydia's voice was scarcely audible. The words as she uttered them seemed unreal. It was almost as if Miranda had cast a spell. 'It seems so stupid now.'

His mouth fell open. 'Well', he laughed, his eyes wide and incredulous. 'For pity's sake, Lydia, somebody has to love the girl ... Oh, come on. Was she trying to say we were lovers?'

'She said you were going to be married.'

He clapped his hand to his brow, shaking his head. 'What will you tell me next?'

She went to him, putting her arm round his shoulder.

'And you thought it was true?' he whispered. He did not move her hand, though he looked at her strangely. 'I still love you', she said softly. He took her into his arms, holding her tightly against him. 'What must you think of me?' he said, his lips on her hair.

She met his eyes. 'I think you are kind and good. I love your talk of stars and galaxies. And I love you, too. I've always loved you.' Her eyes were moist. She looked away. 'That's why I brought the flowers ...'

He frowned, smiling playfully. 'Flowers? When did you bring me flowers?' He glanced round the kitchen.

'No, not those sort', she whispered smiling now and embarrassed. 'They were out of the woods. It was ages ago ...' She laughed and sighed. 'It was when my aunt was ill. You came with your father, remember. I told you about it. I picked some flowers from the woods and brought them here. I put them at the foot of the rockery. You wouldn't have seen ...'

'Oh but I did', he said, holding her shoulders and smiling, his eyes thoughtful. 'I remember the day. And I have the flowers right here.'

He took her hand and led her into the lounge, removing a book from the bookcase, and finding a page. There were the flowers, neat and tiny, purple and brown and gold, pressed to the page almost as if they were painted on.

'All that time ...' she said, flooding with warmth and the memory of it.

'Oh, Lydia', he said. 'Let me hold you. I've been so unhappy without you. Your skin is cold.' Silently, they held each other a while. 'What have we done to each other, my darling?' he whispered. And they went upstairs and made love. They might have been the only people in the entire world.

GORDON

Lydia had left next morning. Aunt Rachel had phoned to say she'd met a friend in Harrogate and wouldn't be home till midnight. She had to return to Wales that week and must see as many friends, she said, as she could. Daniel opened a book and tried to return to his work. It was hard to believe that Lydia now knew everything. Even about the ghosts. All the time he had thought she might dismiss him, say that he wasn't well and his father's illness had preyed on his mind, tell him perhaps he ought to see a psychiatrist. He had half-expected her laughter too. But no, she had listened to all of it, hearing him out to the end, and treating it all with a kind of respectful awe which he had not discovered in himself. His own thoughts had been much more scientific. To find an explanation in science for what had been happening would certainly have calmed things. But his mind wouldn't have it. The supernatural events had really happened, and he had to find out why. Now that things were better between him and Lydia, they'd talked about how they might find a pattern together for what had occurred. It suited her historical tendencies too; she had even been enthused, telling Daniel how her mother had feared the house, how people had seen the woman's ghost banging hard on the door. They had talked till quite late, when Aunt Rachel's taxi drew up outside. 'She must not know about this', Daniel had urged. But for them there was no forgetting. Lydia was with him now. They would strive together to find out what the ghosts needed, and how they could help them.

The morning sunlight streamed through the trees and into the kitchen. Aunt Rachel, he found, was up and out already. She had so much energy. He was sorry she had to go back to the farm alone. She wasn't a woman to be on her own, he thought. And he wondered now if she'd sell the farm and move somewhere else. It's a devilish thing when a woman writes off all men due to one foul blow, he thought. If he could say his aunt had a fault, then that was it. Whenever she came to see them, Raymond, one of his father's colleagues, would ask her out. But she always refused. Then he would find excuses to come round and talk to her, but nothing had ever developed. 'Banging his head on a brick wall', his father had said. Which was just how Daniel saw it. His aunt had built a brick wall round herself that no-one could ever break through. 'I shall never allow myself to love again', she'd said joylessly. And it seemed she meant it.

He began to wonder, though, if the ghosts had gone for good. And he found it hard to believe he had really seen them. For it seemed that since his father's death the ghosts were missing. Neither had there been any word from Rosie. It seemed that all had silenced there too. But he couldn't get back to his work. His mind was racing with thoughts and he found it hard to concentrate. Research was all about breaking boundaries and finding things out; things you could write about precisely and sensibly. His mind was searching now in an unknown world for which there was no vocabulary and no real basis for enquiry. He was without direction. The fact that the ghost in the storeroom might be Beethoven had filled Lydia with awe. She had not mocked him and Daniel was thankful for that, though they were both disturbed. Lydia wondered about the dress on the portrait and how the woman in the house had come to be wearing it. How was the manor involved with the ghosts? they asked themselves. Whatever had been revealing itself before, had come to a halt. All he could do was wait. Tomorrow, though, he must find the nerve to look at his father's clothes and sort them out.

He accomplished it in short spells, putting the clothes in piles along the bed, dividing them into shirts, pullovers and trousers. Lydia had gone to Alderley Edge to show round some viewers. So far there had only been two sets of people, neither of whom had wanted to buy it. Since she was his father's executor, and there were things to attend to, Aunt Rachel was staying a few more days. Daniel's head was throbbing again and despite taking pain killers it had scarcely eased. Going for a brisk walk in the fresh air, he met Rosie. She was going for lunch with Jeremy at the boathouse.

'Do you remember the man in the library?' she said, her voice loud and forceful. She didn't intend he would think her foolish about the storeroom. 'The one who was reading the papers', she added quickly. As she spoke he was filled with apprehension. Miranda's father! Rosie strode on, straight backed, tall, her arms folded. 'He came again today.'

'Did he talk to you?' They were walking quickly. It seemed like Rosie was rushing. 'He tried to, but I can't say I understand him. He's very eccentric. Harmless I think, but eccentric. He was talking about accidents. Were there any I knew of lately, involving a girl. I can't say I know of any.' She glanced at Daniel sideways. 'You seemed to recognise him.'

'Did I?' said Daniel, laughing briefly. His head had begun to throb again. It was worse than ever.

'Pin stripes and cuff links today', Rosie droned. 'What do you think he does?'

'I haven't a clue', said Daniel. It was true, he hadn't. But where was Miranda now? What if she went to Anderson Terrace again to see Lydia? Where did she live and how was she coping? Would it just go on and on, Miranda wandering about, and her father forever searching? For a brief moment he imagined himself in Australia, Miranda having pursued him there, her father taking a plane. Rosie watched him curiously. She always watched him curiously now. He felt like a kind of devil. As if he should wear a holy cross as protection. 'Did he stay there long?' asked Daniel. Rosie adjusted her gloves. She was almost running beside him.

'Half an hour, I should say', she said breathlessly, stopping a moment to face him. Daniel drew up abruptly. 'He seems quite sad.' Daniel wanted to ask her more. About the music. About the storeroom. About the sounds ... But he didn't. He searched for something to say that would change the subject. They walked on quickly. 'He's really desperate', she murmured, embarrassed now at her strength of feeling. 'You don't often see them like that. Men, I mean. Not so frantic as that. I wish I could help him.' Her voice trailed off thoughtfully.

Daniel sighed. Miranda's father was far too busy trying to help Miranda. But Daniel had done all he could. He'd sent her for counselling. She'd been in psychiatric care for six months once. It hadn't done any good. Sometimes when she'd come to his flat, he hadn't known what to do. Threatening to kill herself if he phoned her father, he'd felt useless, sitting for hours and trying to help her through. It seemed, though, she was lost in a world of her own. A place of utter hopelessness that she couldn't get out of.

'Where are you going?' asked Rosie. From the look on her face, she seemed suspicious.

'Nowhere special', he said casually. 'I need a walk.'

'He told me he'd lost his daughter', Rosie continued, still involved in their conversation. 'She's run away, that's why he's searching the papers. He asked me to keep a record of any accidents, that sort of thing. Can you imagine?'

Daniel could imagine. He certainly could. He shrugged awkwardly. As they came up to the boathouse, Jeremy called to them and waved.

'Yes, a funny bloke', said Rosie. 'I sent him to Bessie's tea-shop up on the high street. If anything happens round here, they'll certainly know up there.'

The story, Daniel saw, had captured Rosie's imagination. He smiled at the thought. Jeremy listened whilst going about his work. 'She's only small, and not very well, he said. Her hair is long and white, like a child's apparently. We have to keep looking out.' Rosie was glancing about and frowning. Daniel stood by. 'He's been round here', said Jeremy, drying some dishes and stacking them on to a shelf. 'I made him a pot of tea. I didn't say, but I think it was her who stayed at our house with Lydia. It sounds like her. She'd gone first light.' They went outside for a while. All three were silent.

'I'm going to New Zealand', said Rosie, out of the blue.

'Is that so? Well, when are you going?' asked Daniel.

Rosie's lips moved nervously, 'As soon as I can, I suppose. I've applied for a job.'

Jeremy shrugged. 'It's a bitter wind on the river.' He gazed at the sky. 'I think it might snow again.'

'Library work?' asked Daniel. Rosie stood with her hands in her pockets frowning. She looked preoccupied.

'What? Oh, no.' She drew her scarf round her neck. Her face looked cold. Her red hair shone like fire. Jeremy kicked at stones, picking one up and sending it over the water, spinning along as it went in a fine spray.

'I'm going to get something to eat', he said.

'Wait for me', said Rosie, hurrying after him.

Watching them as they went inside the café, Daniel turned and walked back. Reaching the stone steps he saw his aunt, talking with a man. As he approached he saw that the man was Miranda's father.

'I shall certainly keep my eyes open', she said, her voice loud in the still air. 'You must try not to worry'. Seeing Daniel she called out. 'Daniel! Have you seen a girl with long white hair? She looks like a child, but her father tells me she's seventeen.' Daniel joined them. 'This is her father', said Aunt Rachel, introducing them. 'We met in Bessie's tea-shop. The poor girl seems to be missing.'

'How do you do?' said Daniel, offering his hand.

The man frowned sadly. 'I blame myself, you see', he said, shaking Daniel's hand and addressing Aunt Rachel. 'She doesn't mean to do it, you know. She hates being bad. And she isn't really. It's just that ...' He smiled thoughtfully. 'She was always such a beautiful girl before.' He stood for a moment, his eyes moving between Daniel and Aunt Rachel. 'I'm sorry to bother you', he said to Aunt Rachel finally. 'I shouldn't have told you all that.' He took a clean white handkerchief out of his jacket pocket and wiped his brow. His silver cufflinks glistened. 'It's just that she's my only child, and I've failed her. We do, you see. We fail our children so often.'

Daniel's aunt listened enrapt, stood by the wall. She said, meekly. 'I can see you have quite a job on. If I can help you, you must let me know. I'm up at the house on the cliff. You can always call. I'll be here for a couple of days.'

'She needed her mother', the man said, his voice fragmenting around them. 'She went away when Miranda was small. I suppose it is all she knows, this running away.' He braced himself and sighed. 'She's seventeen now, but she doesn't grow up, you see. She won't.'

Aunt Rachel was fixed to the spot as if she were rooted. The man's hand moved around his jaw, backwards and forwards thoughtfully. He frowned. The wind made a rustling sound around their legs. Aunt Rachel held her small red hat tight on her head. 'How could she leave her like that?' she whispered. 'I could never have done it myself. Never.'

'I'm sure you couldn't', he said kindly. 'Do you have children then?'

It had started to snow, though only lightly. Daniel pulled up his collar. Snowflakes fell on Aunt Rachel's hat and melted. Her face was resolute, though in it Daniel saw a softness he liked. It seemed that Miranda's father had touched a nerve in her.

'Children?' She brushed her hands down her skirt, emotional now. 'Oh, no. I have never been married.' Her purple jacket, nipped at the waist, was far too thin for the hostile weather.

Miranda's father smiled. 'I can scarcely believe it's true. A woman like you?'

She laughed nervously. 'Well.'

He threw out his hands in a little hopeless movement. 'Anyway', he continued, preparing to go. 'Thank you. You've been more than kind.' He looked at the house on the cliff, then back at Aunt Rachel, holding her gaze for a moment before leaving.

Daniel looked at his watch. All of them were wet from the snow. Miranda's father though, Daniel saw, had been courting his aunt ardently. And, he hoped, once they were back at the house, she would come to her senses and find herself some dry clothing and didn't catch cold.

MORE DISCOVERIES

Sorting his father's clothes was hard to bear. It seemed his essence lingered in their very fibres. Having lived with him over the past six months, Daniel had grown to know him again, and would like to have known him more. But it was not to be. The distinct smell of spring met him as he opened the window that morning.

Due to return to Wales shortly, Aunt Rachel had been going out a lot, though he didn't know where. Wherever she went, she was always eager to go, and he hadn't asked any questions. Something had lit her life again. And he thought he knew what it was. She was seeing Miranda's father. Daniel was glad of that just then for it helped her cope with her grief. There was still a lot of work to be done before any of them could surface. His father's clothes must be sorted out ...

Daniel shook out a black bin-bag and opened it. As he piled in the clothes, trying to forget they had once been part of his father's life, the filmy plastic clung to his fingers. What a terrible thing it is, a black bin-bag, he thought, securing it with a tight knot. And he wondered for a moment what people ever did without them. They were almost like black holes for the sad detritus of humanity. That afternoon, some-one would come from the church again to take things away. Who, he wondered, would walk out in his father's clothes? Somewhere in his mind, he could hear his father laughing. Or see him winking. He'd rarely laughed. Most of his humour was dry. He'd have thought the whole scenario very funny.

Lifting another suitcase down from the wardrobe, Daniel opened it. A dank and musty smell pervaded the room. The last time his father had used it was when he had gone to Rome with a colleague for a holiday. He'd returned refreshed, but the mood hadn't stayed with him long. He had little will to pull himself out of his misery. And little strength.

Daniel folded his shirts. Had they fitted him, he'd have worn them. They were good strong cotton. Similarly, he liked the sweaters his father chose. They were beautifully knitted in soft warm wool but they too were the wrong size. He couldn't believe his father had gone for ever. Always expecting his key in the lock, the weight of his absence pressed on his mind each day.

Towards his death, there had been no signs of the ghosts. And swallowed up in his private grief, had they appeared, Daniel would probably have ignored them. He gazed round the room. It seemed somehow windblown. He could almost feel the bewildered leaves of memory falling about him; careless, inventive, sacred and profane. What must his father have thought in that airless, windowless, room. Might things have been different with a window? Might there have been more joy in his soul had there been a window to let in the light? Was it possible that something as simple as that could alter the course of your life? He shook his head.

Taking his father's grey suit from the back of the bedroom door, he emptied the pockets. In them was a fountain pen and a box of licorice imps. Old-fashioned now, he doubted anyone would want it, though it was finely tailored. Lost in thought, he opened an inside pocket, finding a silver brooch in the shape of a rose and a snuff box holding a key. He took it out. The key was tiny. Very small in his fingers. What did it fit?

Turning his thoughts to the brooch, he saw that it had a clasp on the side, and as he worked it, it sprung apart on a tiny sepia image. Though it was faded, he saw that the face of a woman looked out at him. With immense care he observed it. His breathing caught in his throat. For again, it was her. He was looking again at the ghost. And as he stared at her, a peculiar stillness hung about him, as though he were with a presence. And a feeling entered him, like a fervent longing. Why had his father never spoken of her, or shown him the picture? Who could she be? It did not look like his mother. It did not look like his father. But in it, he saw with a rare and magical shiver, that the photograph had a look of himself. Her eyes held a wild and fearless gaze he had sometimes seen in his own. The fullness of the bottom lip was the same. He was filled with excitement. Footsteps arriving in the hall announced Aunt Rachel.

'Daniel', she called upstairs. 'I brought some milk. Didn't you say that Lydia was coming today?'

'This evening', he shouted, still preoccupied and dragging himself from his dream. He went downstairs. Aunt Rachel was filling the fridge. He took two mugs from the cupboard and prepared the coffee percolator. Over his shoulder, he said: 'I've discovered a brooch. I'd like you to see it.'

He turned, finding her watching him strangely. Observing her face, he thought his aunt had the type of beauty that bloomed at once if charged with passion. Her features, he saw, were dancing now with her soul.

'I met him again today', she said, removing her coat. She sat by the table. 'He still can't find his daughter.'

Daniel sat down beside her. 'I doubt if he ever will', he said slowly, and still thoughtful. 'She'd rather stay missing.'

Aunt Rachel's mood was serious.

Daniel stared at the floor, cleared of the boxes now. 'I know her, you see ...' he said awkwardly. Breathing in deeply, he told her. After all, it would have to be done, Miranda might just turn up. And in any case, he had done with the business in London. 'You remember the fight ...' he said, trying as hard as he could to sound tranquil. Aunt Rachel closed her eyes. Daniel knew, it hurt her. 'I know it's a painful memory. But don't be bothered for me. I can cope with it now. I've put it behind me.'

'I'm glad about that', she said tenderly, glancing at him, then away quickly. He could see it had been a burden.

'There's Lydia to think of', he said, his voice strong and filled with determination. 'The girl, though, that you're talking about is Miranda.'

'You mean Miranda's his daughter?' said Aunt Rachel, looking at him as if what he had said were impossible. She blinked hard. He knew she was thinking quickly. His aunt was going through too many thoughts at once. She put her hands to her cheeks and left them there for a moment. 'And this is how it has left her?' she said, murmuring into the silence. 'She is driving herself insane, and her father too no doubt.' Putting her hands flat on the table, she said firmly. 'She has to be found. Someone must help this little creature to learn some sense.'

'I'm sorry', said Daniel, surprised at his aunt's intensity and resolve. Something new was growing in her. It wasn't true that people stayed always the same. People could change. People could grow and develop. It thrilled him to hear her. Though his heart felt heavy at the thought of Miranda. He had found it a stressful business.

'I shall talk to Gordon about it', his aunt sighed. 'He didn't tell me this. But anyway, we have formed a plan.' She bit her lip thoughtfully. 'We shall comb the length and breadth of the land between us. Not an inch shall we miss. And when we find her we shall make her happy.' She glanced at Daniel, returning then to contemplate her fingers. 'Oh we will, we will. We know we can do it.'

Daniel watched and listened. Suddenly it all seemed wonderfully simple. As though a holiness might fold around Miranda now and heal. His aunt talked on.

'It's such an ordeal for him, you know. He can't possibly manage alone. The girl needs a mother. I thought, you see ...' She glanced at Daniel again, looking to see if what she was saying was alright. He held her gaze firmly, his face stern and certain. 'I thought they might live on the farm with me. He's used to life in the country, they were there for some years when the girl was small. She likes to ride horses too.' She smiled, gazing at Daniel with a look that pierced him to see. 'I could give her so much love', she said softly. 'So much love.'

He pursed his lips. 'She's almost eighteen, Aunt Rachel', he said, pacing about, thoughtful. A splendid plan indeed. But only a plan. 'She's a woman now. That is, if she'd grow up.' He sat down again, pouring coffee. 'There are other things she needs. Things you can't give her. Things her father can't give her either.' He looked at his aunt steadily. 'You know what I mean.' He kept his eyes on her face, then sighed. 'It's medical help she needs, most at the moment. She's so confused, and whenever she can't cope, she resorts to drugs. You should see her arms. They're a terrible mess. My father was often angry when he saw them.' Daniel's throat was dry. And as he spoke, the words seemed cold and harsh. As cold and harsh as they were. His aunt sat quietly listening. 'The pity is in the need', she whispered. 'It's all in the need.'

Daniel felt they were coming now to the end of their conversation. As he passed her the sugar, he noted her clean bright skin, her refreshing wholesomeness. Aunt Rachel was short and pretty, with large bones. Her hands were strong and she had immense vigor. When he'd phoned about his father's death, she'd driven from Wales in the early hours of the morning and had taken care of it all. She'd also got back on her feet, quicker than he had. He was grateful for that. He wasn't doing so well himself. His limbs, it seemed, were an encumbrance to him. He moved about like a lumbering giant, resting by turns on the chairs, the lounge, the sofa, the stairs. So much was happening in his head he had scarcely room to think. He'd neglected his work, and at that moment didn't think it mattered. The worst neglect of all. He'd a very important paper to write for a spring journal, but he didn't think he could do it. All the time he wanted Lydia, occupied now at Alderley Edge. Why didn't someone buy the house? They could drop the price. He wanted it over and done with. He wanted her there with him at Cliff House.

Aunt Rachel sipped at her coffee. Her eyes were thoughtful. Bringing the brooch from his trouser pocket, Daniel sprung the clasp and showed her the picture. 'It was in dad's suit. I found it this morning. I thought you might know her.'

Aunt Rachel observed the photograph carefully, shaking her head. She looked at the image and then at Daniel by turns. 'She's a look of you, I think.'

He smiled. 'I thought so myself, but I haven't a clue who she is. Surely you know?' He guarded her with uncertainty. Was she keeping something from him. Somewhere in the depths of his soul, he wanted the ghost to be part of him. And he knew that she was. 'Do you have any photos yourself?' he asked.

She laughed briefly, almost caustically. 'No, not now. I did, but I tore them up.' He saw that his words had vexed her. It did not fit with her newly growing identity. Also, he noted, tears had formed in her eyes. He did not want her to cry and it bothered him that he'd upset her. 'It doesn't matter', he said. 'I was only wondering.' He knew, though, why she'd destroyed her pictures. But he couldn't believe she had none at all. There must have been something somewhere.

'I'm not proud of it', she murmured regretably. 'But you know how it was at the time. It was like a vendetta.' She frowned, nervous and anxious. 'It's an awful thing to have done. It was pure destructiveness.' She sighed. 'But you know how I was jilted by Geoffrey' — she spoke his name so easily now — 'Well, because he was a photographer, the photos were like a malevolent force, so I ripped them to pieces'. She searched his eyes, then covered her face with her hands. 'Wasn't I stupid. All of them! The whole of the family photographs!'

After she had said these things, she sobbed quietly. Daniel sat waiting. What could he say? The words had caused her a lot of pain for she wept profusely, weeping, Daniel thought, the tears she needed to cry. Tears of sadness. Tears of sorrow. And now perhaps, with what she had found with Miranda's father, tears of joy. What did it matter about the photos. After all they were only photos.

'Oh, your father was so good about it', she said, finally drying her tears with her hanky. 'He was so understanding. You see, they were entrusted to me, and I broke the trust.' The light above her head filled her face with a soft warm glow. Having cried her heart back in, she looked refreshed. 'That's how selfish I am', she whispered. 'At the right crossroads, I too am a wilful child.'

He held her hand across the table. 'The past is often painful', he said. Seeing her now for the first time as adult to adult and talking about the past, he felt suddenly older. It was almost as if his father's voice spoke from within him. 'We humans are peculiar creatures. Sometimes we insist on pain as if some God-forsaken law demands it. No-one will hurt you now.' He bent his head and sighed deeply, recalling the

182

weight of the task ahead. 'But you see', he continued, 'there are things I need to know.' Taking a last look at the image, he closed the brooch and put it back in his pocket. He would place it in the attaché case with the letters later. If he kept all his findings together, something might surface to help him. The ghosts would remain a secret between himself and Lydia. They would do what had to be done.

Aunt Rachel got up, still disconcerted. Her face damp and shining from weeping, she wandered the room, drying some dishes and putting them back in the cupboard with easy precision. He moved towards her, placing his arm round her shoulder. Beneath his hand he felt her warm to him. He remembered how it had been with Geoffrey. How he hated him all those years ago for what he had done. Returning to boarding school, he'd hoped that someone would make her happy, someone who didn't take photographs, someone who'd take the clear bright promise of now, right in his hands, and give it the kiss of life. He'd have carted Geoffrey right to the nearest cliff and thrown him over the edge had he come within a foot of him, though he'd never seen him again.

Aunt Rachel said quietly. 'I've always felt bad about that.' She laughed briefly, drawing a quick breath. 'I thought I might stick them together, you know, with cellotape ...'

And he wished she had. Anything now would be better than nothing. He wanted so much to see his ancestors. The urgency forced like a tidal wave inside him. He thought hard. The letter he'd found in the attic and the fragment from Bonn were both in the attaché case. He went for them to a drawer in the lounge to check their contents. Relieved to find they were safe, he slipped the brooch inside and pulled up the zip. Afterwards, going upstairs for the snuff box, he brought down the tiny key, letting her see it. 'I wondered what it might fit', he said. Aunt Rachel frowned. 'A suitcase perhaps?' And something occurred to him: the padlock on the trunk in the attic? Later that evening, he and Lydia would investigate.

THE TRUNK

After the woman from church had been to the house to take what had been his father's belongings, Daniel went to the boathouse. Jeremy told him Miranda's father had been in the library again.

'Rosie can't see the problem', he said casually, his voice muffled beneath a boat he was painting. It rested on a plinth above him. From time to time the paint dripped from his brush on to his green overalls. Drops had got on his face, and Daniel saw it was smeared where he'd wiped them away with his palm. 'She can't understand why he's chasing her. He should let her get on with it.'

Daniel nodded, his lips tightly together. It would have been an anathama for Rosie to have had her father searching for her. It would also have been impossible. Her parents didn't care where she was or what she did. And she knew it.

The day was mild and dry. Jeremy had thought to paint the boats that day while the weather was fine. One of them, a gleaming yellow, nestled at the side of the boathouse. The other was in the process of gaining a bright green glow. Richard gave him pride of choice when it came to painting the boats. He had chosen green and yellow and that's how they stayed.

'It's all gone quiet in there', Jeremy called, his voice vibrating on the underside of the boat. The thin grasses about them, Daniel saw, were also spattered with paint. Jeremy wasn't a tidy worker. Beneath the boat, he wondered how he was doing. The smell of the paint was oppressive. But the boats looked better for paint. In the wintry weather the yellow and dark green colours looked healthy and comforting. Daniel sat on a stone bench. He could hear the sound of ducks flying across the water amplified in the stillness, making their way to the valley. He shaded his eyes with his hand and watched.

184

They flew off into the distance merging with clouds. Jeremy looked out. 'No more ghostly footsteps, eh, or ghostly music!' He laughed loudly. 'What an imagination!'

Daniel started. For a moment he wondered how Jeremy knew of the footsteps, then put things together. Rosie would tell him, of course. She'd have to tell somebody. It certainly wouldn't be Lydia. 'Yes', Daniel said good-humouredly. 'Rosie can tell a fine story. She's missed her way!'

The energies though, did seem to be falling away. He'd felt it himself in the house. The place had lost a presence. It wasn't just his father's death. It was more than that. It was almost as if the ghosts themselves were in waiting.

'Did you like the snakes?' called Jeremy, talking to Daniel's feet.

'Can't say I did', laughed Daniel. 'A little bit risky for me. I think I'll stay with the stars.' Earlier that week, Daniel had seen the snakes in all their glory, slithering round Jeremy's shoulders with awesome familiarity. Lydia's mother had gone upstairs while it happened. 'I can never stand it, myself', she'd cried from the bedroom. 'I'm glad they're going to Cheshire!' Jeremy was moving soon to his new job. To Eliza's relief the snakes were going with him.

Daniel sighed. Life had a way of taking its own course whatever you did. You never knew what might happen. Jeremy hadn't seen the telescope at Cliff House yet and the visit to Jodrell Bank had never transpired. Something had passed them by. It seemed as if Jeremy's interest in stars had been short-lived. Some things were, Daniel reflected. Other things lasted forever.

'I think I put paid to those ghosts', Jeremy laughed, peering out again. His eyes, Daniel thought, looked wonderfully clear and alive. A pleasant day for December, the sun shone like a silver light on the water. The sky was a brilliant blue. From behind him came the sound of children, coming to look at the painting.

'Watch out!' Jeremy called. One of them had decided to climb in a boat, though the paint was still wet. He dragged it back to the boathouse. The children ran off. He poured turpentine on to a rag and cleaned his hands. 'Sorted those ghosts out though', he murmured. 'Rosie kept phoning the council. But nobody came. If they want that stuff from the storeroom, they'll have to go to the tip.'

Daniel froze at the thought. What had been thrown away? What terrible thing had Jeremy done in his innocence? 'So what did you sling?' he asked, trying to sound casual.

Jeremy sniffed. 'Oh, desks and things.'

Daniel thought of the cold bare room and the blue light and what might be there in the silence. 'Have you seen Rosie today?' he asked.

'She's taken a few days off', said Jeremy. 'Someone's come from New Zealand.' He sniffed again and wiped his nose on the back of his hand. 'The library's closed.'

'Closed?' Daniel said, wondering how long it was going to be shut. Jeremy's word seemed final.

Jeremy pointed to Anderson Terrace. 'There's our Lydia.'

Daniel saw she was getting out of her car. He hadn't expected her yet. He walked across.

'Have you managed to sell it?' he asked, approaching her and embracing her.

'It's all so tedious', she moaned. 'But I think we've sealed it now.'

The bells from the church pealed out over the trees. She took some things from the car into the cottage, them came out, closing the door. They watched a throng of children passing, eating ice creams. The scent of raspberry permeated the air.

'Has Aunt Rachel gone home?' asked Lydia. During the last few days, they'd had little time on their own.

'She went at lunch time', he said. 'I got her a taxi. I expect she'll be back soon though. She's made a friend of Miranda's father. She's helping him search.'

They walked to the path, leading to Cliff House, moving past Jeremy's feet again beneath a boat. They could hear the lick of his brush. 'I've made a discovery', said Daniel. He spoke slowly. The morning had been tense with excitement. He was overwhelmed with thoughts.

'Something else?' she asked, turning to him surprised and serious. He could see in her eyes she was captive to what was happening. But he also saw that something worried her too. 'He was on my answerphone', she said morosely, looking down at her feet. 'When I went in the house just then. He's returning to England tomorrow.'

Daniel felt a rush of frustration. James. James. James. Only when they had sold the house would Lydia be free.

'He will want the letter', she said.

'Ah', said Daniel. 'Will he.' His face was pale with emotion. 'You must never tell him we have it.'

'Of course not', she whispered, annoyed he should think she might. 'It's just that he'll know he's lost it. And he's going to ask me. Where have you put it?'

'I've got it safe in the lounge. It's with the other. It's just as important to me ...' He stopped for a moment and turned to her. 'Let me re-phrase it. It's "far more" important to me than it is to him. Don't you think that's better?'

Lydia was silent. The sun came out from the clouds, settling soft on their faces. The air was still. Back at his house they went upstairs, then came down later for drinks and sandwiches. Daniel went to the lounge to fetch the attaché case.

'I wanted to show you this', he murmured, removing it carefully. 'I found it in father's pocket.'

Lydia took it from him, feeling the cold weight of the brooch, heavier than she'd expected in the palm of her hand.

'Open it!' he said urgently. 'Try the clasp! Look!' He watched restlessly as the brooch sprung open again and the woman's face returned to him. 'See. It's her. It's the face of the ghost. See how lovely she is.'

Lydia observed the woman's features. The dark eyes stared from the tiny image, sensual, bold and proud. 'She looks so happy', said Lydia, filled with wonder and eager to know who the woman might be. The eyes of the ghost seemed alive. She had seen the ghost as a sad and wretched creature, but here she was, smiling and beautiful. Who could have taken the picture? 'There is love in her eyes', said Lydia. What tragedy had occurred, she wondered, that had caused her to haunt the house? She examined the brooch, looking to find an engraving, though she found nothing. A silence filled the rooms, like a mournful longing. It seemed they were there with the ghosts, all that time ago, in the very house where they now sat. 'She's a look of you', said Lydia. 'I know', he said. 'I wish I'd talked to my father more. He must have known her.'

'There's something else', said Daniel going to the case. He brought out the snuff box. 'What do you think of this? It was with the brooch.' He took out the key. 'I thought it might fit the padlock on the trunk. No-one has ever looked in there to my knowledge. Perhaps we'll find something.'

His skin felt hot as they climbed the stairs. The play of shadows along the walls did not disturb him now. His mind was open and free. The cool dust of the attic met them, smelling as if they had entered a place that had never been entered before. They stood for a moment, curious. They were on the edge of a revelation. A kind of unveiling would happen. Something, they knew, was about to make itself known.

Lydia saw that Daniel had put the silk shoes back on the trunk, just as before, as if there had been an order he dared not disturb. Might they disturb it now? Was it the time?

Going to the padlock they found it was old and rusty, though the key seemed new. Daniel held it firmly, and forced it into the steel, turning it quickly. The lock was stubborn. He gave it another twist. And then another. Thinking it might break off, he turned it gently for one last time, and the padlock gave suddenly, the key falling out on the floor.

They did not stoop to retrieve it. For the heavy scents of sandalwood and saffron, and what they saw before them, dizzied their senses. They were looking in on a sea of red silk. Shining neat with tiny crocheted roses on the neck and hem, a dress lay before them. They lifted it out, amazed as the endless folds of silk rustled and slid through their fingers. Both of them knew what they held. This was the dress in the portrait at the manor. This was the dress that Daniel had seen on the ghost. Here it was at Cliff House, almost warm to the touch, the silk whispering as if unloading its secrets.

Bringing it out, they saw there was something else beneath. From the bottom of the trunk, Daniel drew out a string of pearls. They were light and cold and felt almost damp. He gave them to Lydia, finding also a brown paper parcel, secured with string. Lydia watched the light from the attic window playing along his hair as he bent to reach it. The paper was stiff and firm and crackling with age. The knots were tight. He looked about for something to cut the string with, but could find nothing. He pulled with his fingers and the knots broke free quickly. Removing the paper he found a small painting. Here was the ghost, again, looking as she had done in the brooch, happy and smiling. The woman was loved without doubt. And the love had been stolen away. Her heart had been wrenched from her, and with it her spirit. It was hard, Daniel thought, as he gazed at her, to relate her image to the woman he'd seen in the river and the sad creature whose ghost lived there at Cliff House, unable to reach beyond it.

The woman, they saw, wore the dress they had just dis-covered, and the painting was almost the same. The same red scarlet. The crocheted roses were perfect. 'It's almost as though these things were hidden', said Lydia curiously, examining them carefully. She ran the pearls through her fingers. They seemed to be new. The painting was skilfully done, the oils carefully mixed for the right skin colouring, the scarlet, after all those years, vivid and bright. Nothing had aged the con-tents in the trunk. Not even time had managed to mar their beauty.

Daniel felt uneasy. Feeling the silk had almost brought the ghost to life. She might have been with them now, in that very room, watching them as they drew her things from the past, afraid and alone. More than that, he felt he had a place in it all. A place of his own. 'The letters', he murmured. 'The brooch, the dress, the painting — it's all connected. The manor too and the music. And the coach that stopped out-side. I couldn't see who the man was. But I think I know. It's the music, you see. The music's the key.' He felt a rush of excitement. He was finding a story. A story that made some sense.

Together, they thought hard. Why had it started? What must they do? There had been a beginning to this. Shouldn't there be an ending too? But where were the ghosts? Neither through sound nor image did they come to them. Daniel felt lost and deserted. Almost as if he had failed.

Together they lay the dress back in the trunk with the pearls just as it was before. Then they looked at the painting together.

'When she came to me from the river ...' Daniel began, his voice shaking slightly, and suddenly loud in the small space, 'she pointed to Rosie's library. Now why do that? It has something to do with the storeroom, Lydia, I'm certain. Beethoven's at the heart of this, I know. He was there in the library. It was he who came in the carriage.' They were silent a moment. 'I suspect he has been in this house.' Daniel's voice was a whisper. 'Perhaps with her. There are no historical records of this. But it's here! Here in her eyes. And I've heard it too in the music!'

He put the painting beneath his arm and they went downstairs. Even the air seemed lighter now about them. It was easier to breathe. The sun streamed in through the kitchen window. The water raced fast down the cliff. The painting would help them find things out. Daniel had an idea.

THE PROPER PAST

Lydia's mother gazed at the painting with interest. Lydia, she said, had no doubt made an incredible find. But how the woman had come to be wearing the red silk dress was any-one's guess. She didn't see how it was possible. Lady Charlotte had never had anything copied, and she usually designed her clothes herself. It was quite a mystery. Neither did Eliza know who it was in the picture. It was no-one she knew from the history. Adjusting her glasses, she peered at it thoughtfully. Lydia saw she had set her mother a riddle. She would not rest till she'd solved it.

Wrapping the painting back in the paper, Lydia decided she'd told her mother enough. Little did she know that this was the ghost who haunted the gardens at Cliff House. The one she had always feared. The smell of baking came from the kitchen. Her mother was baking an apple pie for Howard. Later that day she would take it up to his house.

'Would anyone know her at Kendleton?' Lydia ventured. She saw that her mother was deeply curious. She had gone to one of her early books on the manor, turning the pages mindfully. 'I was trying to find her in here', she said. They went through the pages together, though nothing appeared forthcoming.

Lydia held the parcel against her tightly. Desperation was mounting. 'Why don't you let me take it?' said Eliza. 'I can certainly make some enquiries.' Lydia considered it. But what if her mother lost it. Howard, though, knew a lot about Kendleton's history. Her mother was in the kitchen now taking the pie from the oven. Very soon she would go for the bus, and that would be that.

'Do you want me to take it?' her mother asked as she entered the lounge. It was almost eleven o'clock. 'I can always ask Howard. He might not tell me the truth though', she laughed, 'that's the trouble. Half of the time he doesn't know truth from fiction. If he hasn't an honest tale to tell, then he'll make one up.'

Lydia was restless. It wasn't easy to talk. She might give something away. It was almost Christmas now. The tree was filled with coloured baubles and tinsel. Cards were strung across walls. 'Do you think I could come?' asked Lydia. She'd like to have talked to Howard, and she couldn't part with the painting. 'I haven't seen Howard's house', she said, 'and I'd like a drive in the country. We'd soon be there in the car.'

Her mother put on her lipstick and straightened her hair. 'He'll be very surprised', she smiled. 'Pleasantly so, at that. And I'd rather not wait for the bus.' She went to the kitchen and wrapped the pie before putting it into her bag. Lydia reached for her coat. 'I dare say he'll have some food prepared', said Eliza. 'I generally take the pudding.'

Lydia knew that very soon they'd be living together. The cottage would have to be sold. Everything seemed to be breaking up and reforming. Passing the market place, they made their way to the open country, towards his house. After a while they drew up. Howard was waiting outside.

'Two for the price of one!' he laughed. 'Well, what a surprise.'

'I thought you might like it', Eliza said, climbing out of the car and going to meet him. 'You won't often see our Lydia though. She's come on an errand.'

He scratched his head. 'An errand is it?' he laughed. 'And I thought you'd come to see me.'

'Well it certainly isn't a dull one', Eliza said, hanging her coat in the hall. 'Wait till you hear the story.'

Lydia saw that her mother was happy here. The house contained her. 'Give me your things', she said. Lydia removed her coat and scarf and her mother took them away. She called to Howard in the kitchen: 'Is there food for our Lydia, Howard?'

Howard called back: 'There's some chicken salad. Do you like chicken, Lydia?'

'She's fine with chicken', called Eliza. 'But she's not so fond of tomatoes, don't give her those.'

He came out, finding them seated by the brisk fire. They ate the food on trays. 'Our Beatrice brought me the chicken', Howard said. 'She's just gone out. It's a shame you've missed her.'

Eliza removed the apple pie from her bag. It was still quite warm. She took it into the kitchen. Howard continued to talk, though Lydia's mind was somewhere else. She could scarcely eat for suspense. As her mother talked, Lydia saw that what had been her canary-yellow hair was now giving way to her natural brown. She hadn't seen it in years. Here in Howard's lounge, the ghosts seemed far away, and beyond belief. She counted the minutes, watching each mouthful of food, waiting until the time they had finished eating.

'Shall I pour some wine?' said Howard. The minutes ticked by. 'Whisky?' he said to Eliza.

The fire blazed strongly. He went to the logs, stirring them with a long poker. A photograph of a brass band stood on the mantelpiece. Howard was in the middle.

'You play the trombone?' said Lydia.

'Not so much now', he said, smiling, and nodding towards his case, which lay dusty in the corner. 'I used to though.'

The room had a fresh and airy feel. The carpet was soft and warm. On the sideboard were other pictures. One of Howard with his wife. Another with Beatrice. As they came to the end of their food, Lydia brought out the painting. He watched curiously. The day turned quickly dark and he switched on the light. Such was the mood of December. 'Well, what are we looking at then?' he said, coming to see. As he gazed at the painting, Lydia observed his face. He turned it over, finding some numbers inscribed on the back. 'Twenty-seven', he murmured. Holding the small picture carefully in his fingers, he ran his thumbs down the frame. 'An oak frame finely crafted', he said, 'in tiny leaves and flowers'. It was beautifully made. The joints at the corners were well concealed. Lydia noted that as he looked at the image, his face seemed lit with knowledge. 'Do you see the slide at the side of her head?' he said, pointing to the black rose hairslide holding her hair. 'They were popular then. Men would buy them as gifts.

Usually for lovers.' He winked at Eliza. 'There are copies up at the manor. We must take a look.'

Lydia saw there was sympathy in his look, and sadness too. 'Where did you get it?' he asked.

'It belongs to a friend', said Lydia. 'It's been in his attic for years. We've only just found it.'

'Do you know who she is? asked Eliza, catching his eyes. 'You must say if you do. That's what Lydia's come for.'

He shook his head. The high spirits he'd first had, somehow seemed to have left him. 'I don't know the face', he frowned, handing it back to Lydia. 'But I know the dress.' He glanced at Eliza. 'Anyone working at Kendleton knows that dress.' He took their plates in the kitchen and came back. Eliza and Lydia were silent.

'It's disturbed you', said Lydia. 'Why don't you say what you know?' The talking had moved to a greater tension now. 'The painting's old', said Lydia entreating him. 'Nothing you say can hurt this woman now.'

They sipped their drinks. 'I can tell you this ...' he said, thinking it over, his voice thin and strained. 'Oh, I don't know if I should ...'

'But you must', said Eliza. 'It isn't fair. You can't keep secrets from me.'

'It's only a story of course', Howard began, speaking slowly at first. 'My father would tell it often. He wasn't a man to tell stories much, but it hurt the heart.' He hesitated, Lydia thought in fear. She urged him on.

'The girl was married, they say. But she fell in love with another. And a passionate love at that. It would know no pace but its own.' He spoke fervently, his voice trembling slightly. The clock ticked loudly beside them. 'It happened one spring. The river was fast and the trees were thick with green. The sun was urgent. And the lovers were drawn together. Nothing could keep them apart. But they say that the husband knew ...'

Howard's eyes stared at space as he spoke. 'It was all such a terrible waste', he murmured. 'A terrible waste. My mother would weep.'

Lydia gave him a searching look. 'Are we talking about the woman here? The one in the painting?'

'It has to be her', said Howard. The story was hurrying now. 'She's wearing the dress. She's the only one who'd have had it. She was treated special, you see. Just like a daughter. She was rarely apart from Lady Charlotte. They'd work for the church, you see, visiting the poor and the sick. Not a bitter word was spoken of Lady Charlotte. There were some who called her a saint.'

Lydia exulted now in what she heard. The mystery was fast unravelling. She gathered it in. What a story it was. The room was like a kind of sanctuary now. A sacred place where pain might finally heal.

Howard went for his pipe, lighting it and smoking pensively. 'Ah, the girl, poor soul. A terrible time she had. Her husband would make her suffer. A vicious bully he was. She should never have wed him really. But the man was rich, and the girl was poor. He brought her out of the poor house. She had no choice.' Howard stopped and shook his head.

'Do go on', said Lydia.

Howard looked up at the ceiling. 'There's something I'm trying to remember ... She was all but a pauper then. There were lots of paupers in Knaresborough. The lady became her friend. That's how she'd get the dress. Everyone knew what her marriage was like. She was nought but a child.' Howard went to the window and opened it. The air in the house was heavy. 'Anyway, he had money. He knew how to make it too. He built a house on top of the cliff in Knaresborough. He'd have kept her a prisoner in it, if it wasn't for Lady Charlotte. Just like a prisoner she was. Lady Charlotte went to the house and took her clothes and linens, but he didn't like it.'

Lydia was breathing fast, trying to hold the whole of the story safe in her mind, to take it back intact. A tragedy lay at the heart of this. A deeper tragedy still. Did Howard know what it was?

'I believe that's her in the painting', he said, running his tongue round his lips. 'I'm almost certain.' He stood by the window, a dark shadow talking into the garden. The thin trees fluttered. There was something else he needed to say, though his voice was troubled. 'She was better than him. A different spirit, she was ...'

Lydia's eyes rested again on the image. The ghost in the river. The ghost at the house. Where did this woman fit in?

'The Lady was quite a painter', said Howard, turning. 'Her pictures were given a number, and she always initialled them. Look in the right-hand corner there, you'll find it.' He sat down pouring drinks.

Lydia saw that fearing he'd said too much, he seemed to have stopped. There were so many pieces missing, she hoped he'd continue. He put his glasses back in their case. Lydia traced a C and a W where he'd said, though she hadn't seen it before. The letters were almost illegible.

'And then the musician arrived', said Howard sighing. His tone was grave. He had finally come to the heart of his tale.

Lydia thrilled at the word. 'Musician?' she repeated. The girl's lover had been a musician? Now the darkness was lifting. The scattered pieces of information were finally coming together.

'He was staying in London. Lady Charlotte invited him up to Knaresborough. My father said it was instant. They couldn't help falling in love.' He handed over the drinks. Lydia looked at her mother. Eliza sat silent. She had never been so entranced. Howard went on. 'The husband loathed her for that. Lady Charlotte had ruined his marriage, he said.'

Now Lydia felt that she knew the woman at last. The doors of time were opening up and letting her in.

'A tricky business, though', Howard continued. 'Her husband was threatening to shoot them. All three of them at once, they say. The musician was proud and bold. Fearless he was. Backwards and forwards he went. Nothing would stop him.'

'And what did the husband do?' Eliza asked, flushed from the whisky as much as the story. 'Did he finally kill them?'

'No, not that. But he certainly tried. He quietened them down. A few shots here and a few shots there. I know of a tree in the wood ... She was frightened then. She feared for her lover's life. Her husband was mad, they say, a real demon. They reckon he broke her spirit.'

Lydia wrapped the painting back in the paper and tied the string. Now she was with the tragedy. She had reached its place.

'He'd quietened her down alright', Howard said, filling his pipe and lighting it up again. 'But the girl was having a child. And it wasn't her husband's either. Everyone knew at the manor, but nobody said. She wanted her husband to think it was his. But something happened. — The musician went back to Germany.'

'Germany'? Lydia said, her heart pounding. Listening to Howard and watching her mother, she wondered what they would think if she'd told them the truth. The real pitiable truth, as she now knew it. Everything Daniel believed was accounted for here, right by Howard's fireside. She felt exhausted. But whatever it was she must hear it now. She wanted to hear it all.

'She pretended the child was her husband's. Though the bully wasn't fooled. Right from the start he knew. He'd throw her outside. All kinds of weather he'd do it. She'd thump on the door from dawn to dusk and from dusk to dawn. The girl was in torment. She wanted the German they say, but she'd asked him to go. Though her husband cared for the boy. He did more than his duty. A wild young whelp of a lad he was at that, and magic on a piano.'

'A boy ...' Lydia said, her voice failing. She concentrated on listening to Howard though her mind was reeling with thoughts. Howard continued. 'She left the child. Some of them said she'd joined her lover in Germany. They searched for a year.'

Lydia shivered, remembering the ghost in the river. The ghost in the house. And the music. The question returned again and again in her mind. *What could they do to help them now after all this time?*

MORE LETTERS

Daniel made a sandwich and a cup of coffee. He glanced at his watch. It was coming up to eight o'clock in the evening. Lydia would soon be arriving. She hadn't phoned him that day and he wondered what she might have discovered. The house seemed wondrously peaceful. He was still having trouble, though, knowing his father would never come back, and expected constantly to find him wandering the house. The loss cut into him deeply and no light gleamed in any window without he did not think of him. Just then Lydia opened the door. He could tell she'd been hurrying.

Her voice came quietly and unhappily, though her eyes were filled with amazement. 'Whatever notions you've had about this painting', she said, removing her coat, 'they'll never match up to the truth! Oh, let me tell you ...' She sat down breathless. She was silent a moment, thinking.

'Come on then', he said, sitting across from her. 'Tell it me slowly.'

For a moment Lydia's eyes wandered the kitchen, towards the tiny window, the cliff face dripping with water, the door, half open, that led to the lounge. Who had walked through that doorway? Who had looked out of the tiny window? Where should she begin? There was too much to say. Too much to feel. Something fluttered against the window. It was cold and windy outside. The small pane rattled. Lydia surveyed the room with a dreamy sadness.

'I went to Howard's with mother', she said finally. 'He told me so many things. I know who the ghost is, Daniel. Everything made such sense.' She took his hands in her own. 'The girl had a lover, you see. And her husband threatened to kill them,' Lydia's voice fell low. 'He had probably thought it through right here in this house. Perhaps he loaded the pistol here where we're sitting.'

'Her husband?' Daniel said frowning.

She held his gaze. 'The man you saw in the lounge.'

'You're saying he wanted to kill them?'

'He'd threatened them with a pistol.'

Lydia told him about the girl, how she had worked at the poor house till her marriage, and then at the manor. 'She became Lady Charlotte's friend.' She told him how she had married young without knowing her husband's nature. Then she told of how the German musician had come to the manor, and how they had fallen in love. 'She was having a child ...' Lydia watched Daniel's face. She knew how the words would affect him. This was all so real for him, as if it were happening now.

'The musician's child?' he said, his eyes flashing. He remembered the scene in the lounge, the very first time he had seen them, how someone had come to take her out in a carriage. It must have been Lady Charlotte. He recalled the carriage arriving at the front of the house, the man hurrying up the steep gardens, the woman embracing him warmly. Most of all he remembered how the woman had been thrown outside in the cold. Was she with child? Beethoven's child? Could it have really happened?

Lydia nodded. 'Those at the manor said nothing. She pretended the child was her husband's, and he connived in it, treating him like his own, and kindly too. I expect he was proud.'

They were silent a moment. 'A boy?' Daniel murmured, finding his voice again, though it was deep and low and, as he spoke, filled with the pangs of injustice. 'I can hardly believe a man like that was kind. And what about the musician?' The words stuck tight in his throat. He had played the piano himself. If it hadn't been for the stars, he might have been a musician instead. 'What did he do?

'They say he left. They didn't know where he'd gone. They thought he'd returned to Germany.'

'Without her? Without his son? No, no, no.' Daniel rose from the chair and paced the floor. 'There has to be some mistake. He wouldn't do that, I know!'

'Times were different then', said Lydia. 'I expect it was quite a scandal. They might have wanted to cover it up.'

'I wouldn't have thought he'd have cared', Daniel said, bending his head and gazing out of the tiny window, watching the water scuttling down the cliff face.

'But what about her?' Lydia said quietly. 'It might have been different for her.'

'But the pain of it all', said Daniel, 'How did she cope? And him, having to leave her, leaving his son ...' And it came to him then, the enormous weight of the suffering, there in his father's house. The endless ache of it. The anguish. 'She should have gone to him!' He clapped his fist in the palm of his hand. 'She ought to have taken the child!' If only he could go back in time and save her. But you weren't allowed to go back. That sort of thing didn't happen. Or perhaps it did in a way. He hadn't been able to talk to the ghost, that was true, or get her to know he was there, but somehow a kind of energy seemed to be working things out. Something greater than all of them was busy. If he could think it through and allow himself to be guided, perhaps they might still help them.

'Perhaps she did', Lydia said quietly. 'She disappeared. Nobody knew where she'd gone. They searched for a year.' Lydia sighed. 'They never found her. Perhaps she went to him after all and no-one ever discovered.'

'They probably had their suspicions', said Daniel, his eyes narrowing scornfully. He gazed about. 'If he'd threatened to kill them.'

'You think he murdered her?' Lydia gasped. She caught her breath at the thought.

'God, I hope not', Daniel said, going to Lydia and holding her tightly. They could almost feel the ghosts watching, listening to what they were saying. Lydia saw that his dark eyes stared intently beneath his thick black eyebrows.

'I wonder why lovers must suffer', she said. Her voice was weary. 'Why must it happen, Daniel?'

'It doesn't have to, my love', he said. He kissed her hair. 'It's not going to happen with us.' He sat down thinking. Somehow a truth would reveal itself and lead them. Now they had entered the ghosts' secrets. Whilst others knew of their past, no-one but Daniel and Lydia knew of their pain, or had felt its suffering. Were the ghosts there now? he wondered. Had they always been there? And were there others, living in countless dimensions, inside the blue light, or another light, or even another? Were these the fears you sometimes felt of a sudden? That tread on the stair? That pain in the soul? Could suffering just go on and on and never end? And so it had all started, there at Cliff House, years ago.

Lydia brought the painting out and looked again. 'We must put it back with the dress', she said, 'where it belongs.'

As they climbed the stairs they felt like messengers of hope appointed to a hallowed task. Entering it, the attic seemed strangely bright. Slowly and carefully, thinking the dress might too have gone when they opened the trunk, they lifted the lid. The scents of sandalwood and saffron met them swiftly as the lid clanged hard on the wall, and the sea of red silk sprang to life again before them.

Lydia lifted it out. The folds of silk seemed endless, soft to the touch. Running it through her hands, she stopped her fingers on one of the seams. Something was there! Stitched in the silk, it crackled hard as she touched it. It felt like paper.

The stitches they saw were large and loose, concealing yet another square of cloth holding some pieces of paper. Undoing the stitches, the papers fell out quickly. Unfolding them, Daniel saw they were two letters, penned by the same hand as the others. These were written in English:

'*Beloved, why are you so afraid? Shall I never be able to see my child? You are saying that we must part for ever. It is too cruel! I promise you, my dearest, nothing will harm you. You must come with me to Germany. I need you. And I need my child. Why must that man have my child? You fill your head with trivial concerns. There is no disgrace with us. The only disgrace is the damage we do to our souls ...*'

The second letter they saw was more resigned, and obviously written later:

'*Sweetheart, It is finished! Whenever you hear the music, you will know that each note climbed from my heart! Take it my love.*

It is yours! It is all I can give you now. Perhaps in time you will change your mind and join me. I shall wait for it. I shall long for it. I have to return to Germany now. But take the Concerto! Take it, and remember our love! You will find it beneath the floorboards at the dye-house where we meet. The boards are loose by the desk and are easily lifted. Find it at leisure. Oh, beloved, if I could only kiss you just once more ...'

At the end of each letter a piece had been torn away, as if to hide the identity of the sender.

'A concerto!' said Daniel in awe. 'He wrote her a concerto!' He read the letters again, murmuring the words. 'We are finding our way, Lydia', he said, his eyes filling with hope.

Tomorrow they would go to the archives department. There were maps and plans in the cellars. They would find out where the dye-houses were, and then they would find the concerto.

PLANS AND SKETCHES

The young boy seated before them at the archives department carried on eating his biscuits. Having produced a file for Daniel and Lydia, he had left them to look at it.

'We're getting nowhere', groaned Daniel. The plans were old and worn, and the writing was almost illegible. 'Surely they've more than this.' He glanced about for help. An old man sat at a table writing. Daniel called over.

'Deaf as a post', said the boy. 'You can shout all day.'

'Have you anything else on dye-houses?' Lydia said to the boy, as he filled his mouth with biscuits.

'I'm only here on work experience', he said.

The old man turned. 'What do you want?' he called. His voice was hoarse, like it came from the depths of the cellars.

'We want to know where the dye-houses were', said Lydia. He shook his head and returned to his work. The boy got up and removed another worm-eaten file from a cabinet, handing it over. 'You might find something in that.'

Daniel and Lydia removed the papers carefully, laying them out on the floor. 'They're falling to pieces', she grumbled. She glanced at the boy, imploring him. 'Do you think you could find some more? It's very important.'

'Have we got any more?' he shouted across to the man.

'Any more what?' said the man.

'Any more files', called the boy.

'I don't know', the old man said without turning. 'You must go and look. What do you think you're here for?'

'Everyone's gone on holiday', the boy said sleepily. 'We're just standing in.' He went downstairs to the cellars. The old place hissed and moaned and cared for nothing. After a while he returned. He opened another file, and a damp and musty smell pervaded the room as he lay the papers over the floor as Lydia and Daniel had done.

'Hey!' the old man shouted, hobbling across. 'The boss'll have your guts for garters lad! Walking all over his documents.' He rubbed his eyes and yawned, speaking to Daniel and Lydia. 'What is it that you're after then? Tell me again.'

'We'd like to know where the dye-houses were', said Lydia, scanning the papers. 'I can't find anything here.' The sketches were old and vague and the writing had gone.

'Dye-houses went in the olden days', he yawned. 'I'm afraid I can't help you there.' Daniel and Lydia watched him pushing the documents back in the file. He handed it back to the boy who took it downstairs. They stood for a while despondent. The man frowned thoughtfully, then went to a drawer for a key. 'Mike lad, here', he called. 'Go downstairs again. There's a dark green file in the second drawer in room number ten. Now fetch it me quick.'

'They re-designed them, I think', the man went on. 'They were made into bakeries, florists, that sort of thing.'

The boy came back and gave him the new file. The old man fumbled inside. 'There might be something in here. How far did you want to go back?' He went through the papers, turning them over — 'dye-houses, dye-houses, dye-houses ...'

'A hundred and eighty years', said Lydia.

The boy's mouth gaped. 'There must have been dinosaurs then', he murmured, a mouth full of biscuits.

Lydia was thoughtful. 'Are there any old plans for the libraries?' she asked suddenly.

'Now there's an idea!' cried Daniel, turning to her.

'Libraries in Knaresborough?' The old man scratched his head. 'Now we might have something there ...' He went off searching again, then came back. The time seemed eternal. Taking another folder, Lydia went through it rapidly.

'Here!' she said, pointing. 'I think we've got it, Daniel! There, can you see? It's Rosie's library. The library was once a dye-house!'

Soon they were out of the building, racing towards the river.

THE OTHER CONCERTO

'But what if we can't get in?' said Lydia, stopping as they walked to the library and turning to Daniel. 'Rosie's away.' They had almost reached the boathouse.

'Does anyone else have a key?' Daniel gazed about, looking for Jeremy. They'd seen him earlier that day. He wasn't sure where Rosie had gone, he said. Nobody told him anything now, he grumbled. He'd been pretty miserable. Suddenly there he was, wandering towards them.

'What's going on?' called Daniel.

'Nothing much', he said, casually. Though he didn't look happy. Lydia knew he was missing Rosie. However he tried to forget her, she would always come flooding back. 'Where are you going?' he asked.

Where were they going? Daniel felt the sense of urgency pounding within him. 'Do you have a key for the library?' he asked. Lydia stood by waiting, glancing towards the old building, suddenly quite magnificent now above the water. She thought of what it might hold and her heart pounded. Daniel said, 'Surely Rosie has given you a key for emergencies.'

'Just a minute', Jeremy smiled, standing back and watching them. 'Is looking for books an emergency? I'm presuming that's what you're after?'

Lydia and Daniel gazed at the floor confused. 'I'm sorry', Daniel began, glancing at Lydia. 'It's just that we ...'

'Jeremy', Lydia said, embracing him suddenly. 'It's hard to explain ...'

'Secrets. Secrets. Everyone's having secrets', he moaned. Oh, do as you want', he grumbled. 'Everyone shuts me out. It's all I expect.'

'It isn't like that', said Lydia. 'You'd understand. Really you would if I told you. But I just can't tell you now. You wouldn't believe me, you see.'

'Lydia', he sighed, thrusting his hands in his pockets. 'You're talking in riddles. I'd understand, but I wouldn't believe you? I think if it's something like that, then it's better a secret anyway.' He laughed into the cold air. 'If you want a key to the library, you'd better go get it.'

'Do you have one then?' said Daniel,.

'It's back at the cottage', he said, turning and looking. 'It's on the hook by the fire.'

'Thanks', said Lydia, kissing his cheek. Her face was flushed from hurrying, and the thoughts of what they might find. A purpose burned in her heart of which she could not speak. 'I'll tell you in time', she whispered. 'I promise.'

'It's almost over', said Lydia. The library door, as they pushed it, gave a sharp unearthly creak, as if opening into another world. They shut it quietly behind them, ascending the stairs with a kind of reverence they'd never felt before for the old familiar building. 'All this time they've waited', Lydia whispered. 'Just for us.' She took the storeroom key from the hook in the kitchen and went down the misty corridor with Daniel. Their footsteps echoed as if they were entering a cave. Outside the door, they stopped. A pale blue patch of light appeared by the door, like a thin mist rising, widening and growing till the whole of the door was covered. Daniel inserted the key and turned it. The door swung open slowly. The fragrances of sandalwood and saffron met them, the pale blue mantle of mist surrounding and enclosing them as they entered. 'It's happening', whispered Lydia. 'They are going to find some peace!'

Daniel removed his jacket and rolled up his sleeves, testing the floorboards. He went to those by the desk. Four of the boards were loose. He removed them one by one, till the gaping hole stared at them from the cobwebbed innards.

It was all so easy. His hands perspired and his head ached with the thrill of it. But what would they look for? He didn't know what to expect. He thought he might hear the music again, or Beethoven's ghost might appear to them in the room. He could hardly steady his nerves as he rummaged about in the darkness.

And yes, it was there! Something felt like a parcel. Stretching down with both his hands, he drew it out. At first it seemed like a package of books, though it flexed in his fingers. The contents were wrapped in thick brown paper, secured with string, just as the painting was in the trunk at home.

'Do you think we've found the concerto?' Lydia murmured, hardly daring to speak. She would not touch the package. Her lips were dry with excitement.

They stared at the paper, covered in cobwebs and dust. Their breathing came heavy and strange in the dark damp room. Church bells pealed outside. And for a moment they looked at each other, tense with emotion. Ought they to tamper now with this sacred past? Might it be wrong? The blue light lolled above them, changing to purple, and back to blue by turns, finally resting as turquoise. They struggled and swayed in their thoughts.

'Yes', said Daniel, his voice unusually shaky. 'The concerto is here.'

The paper felt waxed and slippery, and he knew what it held. It was right where the letter had said. But what would it look like? How would it sound?

'Open it now', said Lydia, kneeling to look.

'I hope it's right', he whispered. 'It's got to be right.'

Carefully and methodically he untied the string. As the last of the knots gave way, the paper opened. And there was the music! Page after page of notes. Daniel wiped his hands down his jacket and turned the pages gently. Almost tenderly even. Two hundred pages of beautiful notes in bold black ink. Not a single correction. And no-one had ever heard it. No-one even knew that the music existed.

'A piano concerto', Lydia said breathlessly. 'And it looks so new.'

The paper was crisp and fresh, just as the dress had been, and the painting, as if suspended in time. The turquoise light drifted away, and they sat back thinking.

'What now, Lydia?' said Daniel softly. 'What now?

A FORESAKEN ANGEL

The water glittered. Grasses strained at the dew. The river blubbed at silence. The tunnel of night was finding its end.

'What are you doing in there?' asked Jeremy, pulling in one of the boats. A young girl lay inside, tightly curled up. Over the rubber sheet she had wrapped herself in, her blue eyes peered anxiously. Each day when he arrived, before he did anything else, Jeremy saw that the boats were safely tethered. Sometimes they were filled with leaves. Now and then an odd bird nestled there. He had never found a girl before.

'You'd better get out', he called. He rubbed his face and gazed at the water. He felt as if he were dreaming.

'Leave me alone', the girl said weakly. 'I'm trying to sleep.'

'Not in a boat, you aren't', he said firmly. 'We'll be needing them soon. And anyway, you'll catch your death.'

A yellow sun broke through the sky. He could hear the girl stirring. He knew who she was. There was no mistaking the long white hair. He knew he would have to wrangle for her to come out. 'Are you sick?' he called.

She did not answer, but went down further beneath the sheet. He could see her face. Her skin looked cold. 'You'll have to come out', he called, firmly but gently. What if she wouldn't budge? What would he do? He shook his head and blinked hard. 'Are you going to come out?'

'I probably will in a minute', she murmured.

She emerged slowly, bringing with her a scent of violets and roses, and something like spring. He heard her sigh. A strange little noise like the sound of a reed in the river. 'You're sick', he said slowly. 'I can see it.' It was there in her eyes, he thought. A peculiar sickness he'd felt when his dad was about. He supposed it was a kind of fear. He lay on his back on the wet grass, his face to the sky. It was almost as white as her hair. 'You have to make peace with yourself', he said.

'Don't talk stupid', she said, coming to him.

Along the path, the houses began to appear. Jeremy's neck was hurting. All night he'd slept on his arm, wondering about Rosie. Worried how he would feel when she'd gone for good. Whenever he tried to forget her, she'd sneak back into his head, just like a thief in the night, and steal his composure. Everybody was moving to somewhere else. His mother was going to live with Howard on Abbey Hill, Lydia was going to Australia, and he was going to Cheshire with his snakes. He stood up, waiting.

'I haven't done anything wrong', she said. She might have been a river rodent, such was the thin squeak of her voice. The light trembled, nudging the trees into morning. Jeremy wrapped his arms around himself, guarding against the cold. 'You're not doing anything wrong', he said slowly. 'But can't you see? It's morning now. People are going to be coming.'

She appeared between the shadowy trees, her sequinned dress and her high-heeled shoes, flashing silver.

'Have you been there all night?' he asked, standing.

She looked so frail and alone. She bit her lip and frowned beneath her soft white brows. Her bright light flooded his being. He covered his face for the rawness of his desire.

'I can do what I want', she said. 'Nobody cares about me, so why should I care about them?' She stood by the oak tree, gazing at a dead vole by her feet. 'Does a little creature like that have a spirit?' she asked sadly.

'Who can say', he said, bracing himself. He breathed the morning into his lungs. He flexed his arms.

'You make me sick', she said stiffly. Her face seemed swollen with sleep. She was watching him carefully now, he thought, as if trying to make him out, see what kind of a man he was and figure out if she could trust him. He tried to relax.

'You don't even know me', he smiled, looking away. The water was making an icy music behind her.

'All sorts of people make me sick', she said nonchalantly.

Jeremy screwed up his eyes. The morning light was blinding. She yawned slowly, her small mouth opening white and clean as a kitten's. 'You should be more sparing', he told her, looking downwards and frowning. 'Nobody's perfect. Only the angels are perfect.' Just then she looked like an angel. Perhaps she had left her wings in the boat. 'Where do you live?' he asked.

'It doesn't matter', she said, shrugging her shoulders. 'What's it to you?' Her long thin fingers slid through her hair. She shivered; a thin slice of white light in the icy air.

'You have to live somewhere', he said curiously. 'We all live somewhere.' Which wasn't true, he knew. Everywhere there were homeless people, sleeping in cardboard boxes, or on benches in parks, or in boats like this ... Or anywhere else where the fickle hands of fortune might grant them some measly respite. He'd rather work with animals in a country park.

She glared at him coldly. 'As a matter of fact, I don't live anywhere, really.'

'You mean you're homeless?' He knew she wasn't. Her father would see to that.

'I suppose I am', she said, pursing her lips indifferently. She sat down on the landing bay, trembling with cold.

'You don't have to wander about', he said, tentatively. 'There are places for homeless people.'

'I don't want places, she snapped, turning from him and frowning. 'Why don't you leave me alone?'

'I expect you're hungry', he said, sighing.

'Can you give me some food?' she asked, her blue eyes widening. 'I haven't eaten for ages.'

As he watched her, he thought she might fade away, her limbs were so slender. He glanced towards the café. The shutters were still down. He was way behind with his work. It usually took about fifteen minutes to start up the kitchen. 'I could cook you something hot, if you want', he murmured. 'But you'll have to wait.'

'Can you?' she said, her face suddenly brightening. 'Do you have any cocoa?'

'Drinking chocolate', he said. He made his way to the boathouse kitchen, sending the shutters clapping into the morning. He warmed some milk in a pan, then poured it into a mug, stirring three large spoonfuls of chocolate into it. Watching as she made her way, stumbling on the high-heeled shoes, he thought she might fall. She stood beside him, warming her hands on the mug, taking it to her lips and closing her eyes. Richard would soon be arriving. Then people would start to come. He could make her some bacon and eggs he thought, if he did it quickly.

'Do you always work here?' she asked, glancing about and finding a stool to sit on. She watched him basting the eggs.

'Most of the time. But I'm going to work in a country park. I've got a new job.'

'A country park, what's that?' she said, searching his face. He saw that her cheeks had warmed. Her eyes, previously glazed, were now clearing. Once in the dales he'd seen a white hare. As he watched her, he thought of it.

'It's like a wood, I suppose. A wood of your own, with a lake and animals. You have to take care of them, see.'

'Is that what you like? I mean looking after animals?'

'I think so', Jeremy sighed. Animals, he thought, were easier to manage than people. 'There'll be plenty of work though. The woodland needs a lot of care and attention. There's a river as well. Lots of things live in the river.' He smiled at the food as he put it on to a plate.

'You're very strong', she said, watching him.

He laughed, flexing his muscles, his back towards her. When he brought the eggs and bacon, she ran her finger along the cobra, watching his eyes. He took bread from the cupboard and made her toast, spreading the butter thick. The breeze rushed into her hair. His heart beat fast and the blood pulsed hard in his veins. 'I've a lot to do', he said loudly. 'I can't have you here all day.'

She ate the food quickly and drank the chocolate.

'You were starving', he said, standing beside her. 'You shouldn't be getting like that.'

'I've got no choice', she said, cleaning her plate with the toast. She glanced at him sideways. 'I don't have to pay you, do I?' She drew back quickly.

He waved his hand. 'So long as you're warm.' He swept the floor. Then he stopped for a moment to watch her again. Her eyes were closed. She had turned her face to the sky, the light streaming down, through and beyond her. 'Where are you going?' he asked.

'Going?' she said, turning to him. The daylight might have lost her for its careless hold.

'You have to be going somewhere.'

Her eyes, large and round, he saw, were almost grey.

'Who cares?' she said. She threw out her arms.

'About what?' he asked.

'About me', she said softly, looking down at her fingers. 'Nobody cares about me.'

'Somebody does, somewhere', said Jeremy, frowning curiously. He couldn't decide what to do. She seemed so lost.

'No they don't', she replied quickly. 'I know.'

He shook his head. The sequins flashed on her dress, glinting hard and metallic. She sparkled like fresh ice.

'Do you love somebody?' she asked him.

He gazed at the trees and the river. 'Lots of people.'

'No, I don't mean that', she said. Her tone was urgent. 'Somebody special, I mean. Like people do.'

He looked away. Rosie's red hair burned inside him. He started to sweep again. The cobra surged in his arm.

'I'd like to have someone to love', she said, getting down from the stool and following him about. 'Do you think that's childish?' She frowned hard. 'Anyway, I don't care if it is. It's the way that I feel.'

'No', he said, stopping to look at her again. 'I don't think it's childish at all.'

'You see', she continued, wringing her hands. 'I can't stand it.'

'What?' He leaned on his brush again, her face suddenly alive, as though the universe might hear what she said. The air seemed brittle about her.

'Being like this', she said, covering her face with her hands. 'I can't stand being alone you see, like this.' She worked her fingers together nervously and turned to him. 'Can we live without love? Do you think we can do it?'

He shook his head confounded.

'You see. I can't do it. I've tried to do it. But I can't.' She rubbed her thin arms.

He stood for a moment silent. Into the stillness he said: 'Somebody's searching for you.'

Her red lips trembled. 'Here?'

He nodded slowly, without looking. He'd said it now. She would run away, or she'd ask for her father. She did not speak. It was almost as if she'd gone. He turned to her. She swept her hair behind her shoulders, 'You mean my father?'

Again he nodded.

Climbing back on the stool, she said: 'He's always searching. I wish he wouldn't. He follows me everywhere.'

'He loves you.'

'It's not the same.'

'It's important. All kinds of love are important.'

She stretched her arms above her head and yawned. 'I'm an actress. I have to find work.' She glanced about. 'Do you think I might find some here?'

'What? Acting in Knaresborough? I doubt it.' There was something of an amateur group at the church, but that was all.

The day was beginning to warm. A radiance stirred the water. 'Do you know the time?' she asked.

He looked at his watch. 'It's seven o'clock', he said. The river birds were busy now.

'I shall have to go', she said, her shoulders drooping.

She'd dissolve, he thought, into light. Or sigh away on a shiver of breeze. She wouldn't wander aimlessly through the streets, begging for food, sleeping in doorways, preyed upon by every vampire of the night. Had he believed that, he would never have let her wander up the path towards the main road.

FINAL ADJUSTMENTS

At last the house was sold. Lydia took some papers out of her bag and laid them out on the table. They were in a Harrogate tea-shop. James took a pen from his pocket and scrawled his signature. The child on his lap drew on the menu with a felt tipped pen. Sara smiled casually.

A touching little family, thought Lydia. Philip, Sara said, had painted the house outside that they'd lived in in Harrogate. Now it looked fresh and new. It would probably fetch a better price. He was moving on. Watching James as he played with Michael, Lydia felt something had been released in him. A divinity perhaps. Pain, she now knew, should be avoided at all costs. Wrong relationships were curses. You should tear out their hearts, or else they would tear out yours.

'We're going abroad', said Sara.

Lydia thought she looked stronger now, more beautiful. More the girl she had known at college. And James, she saw, had cut his hair. It made him look older. Lydia did not grieve now for the part of herself that had died with James. A shadowy soul had stretched its limbs and walked away.

'Any more, and we'll go to the car!' James scolded. Michael had drawn on the cloth. 'Children are a ton of work', he said, smiling embarrassed.

'I'm sure', said Lydia. A lion of a boy, he had his father's vigour and could not stay still.

They ate salad and quiche. Afterwards they had ice cream and another pot of tea. 'We're going to live in Vienna', said Sara. 'It's better for James's career. Look!' she cried, taking the pen from the boy's hand. 'See what you've done to your father's shirt!'

'He wants to go home', said James. 'He doesn't like public places.'

'I'm expecting again', said Sara, glancing at James.

Lydia raised her eyebrows.

'July', said Sara smiling. James stood up. It seemed the lunch weighed heavy.

'Come on, darling', he said, addressing Sara and holding the child on his arm. He turned to Lydia. 'It's been good to see you, Lydia. Give my regards to your mother. And Jeremy, of course. I think we can do the rest by post.'

'Wouldn't you like to eat flowers, daddy?' Michael said, running his hand round his father's chin. 'Like gorillas do in the wild?' He stretched down for the flower in a pot on the table, pulling it out and thrusting it into his father's mouth.

'That's artificial!' laughed Sara, putting it back. 'You mustn't give that to daddy.'

'What's *artificial?*' asked Michael. Sara and James looked away.

As she started her car, Lydia breathed a sigh of relief. He hadn't mentioned the letter from Bonn. It was in the case with the others at Daniel's house. Now it held the concerto too. They were all intact.

Drawing up at Anderson Terrace, she found Daniel outside waiting. 'How did it go?' he asked as she climbed from her car.

'There's nobody quite like Sara', Lydia laughed, relating what she had learned. She saw he had brought her roses. Bright red winter roses. She took them from him and kissed him. He stamped his feet on the ground. There was snow in the offing. Dressed in a suit and tie, he was going to Leeds for a university meeting later that day. He moved his neck about uncomfortably, always uneasy in ties. She saw he held the attaché case beneath his arm and remembered she'd asked him to bring it. Once they were in the house, and she'd found a vase for the flowers, he passed it across.

'I wanted to see it again', she whispered, taking it from him carefully. Soft in her hands, the dark brown leather case bulged with its contents, happy it seemed with its cargo. Yesterday there had scarcely been time to look. Once Daniel returned from Leeds later that evening, they'd lay it out on the floor and examine it properly. She placed it on the top of the dresser, then went to make coffee.

'I wish we could hear it!' Daniel called. He had taken the manuscript out of the case and was trying to read the notes, the beautifully written notes that had surged in his mind. He turned the pages. What could they do? he wondered. They'd need a hall and a set of musicians. Then there would be the reporters ...

Lydia came through. Together they gazed at the manuscript. 'Something will happen, I know', she murmured. 'It's all going to fall into place.' The silence around them, it seemed, weighed heavy that evening. They were looking for guidance now, listening at every turn of a corner, every creak of a door.

'It's all the disorder that bothers me', Daniel said. He sighed deeply. 'All the loose ends.'

But they all connect', said Lydia urgently. 'They will all find their place in the harmony. These people, these lovers ...' Lydia talked quickly now, certain of what she was saying. 'Their lives have been so cruelly struck by tragedy. How did he live with that painful secret? How could he write his music? What if she'd died and he didn't know? What if he'd waited and waited?'

'I'm finding it hard to sleep', said Daniel. He went to a chair and sat down. Something was trying to reach him, but he didn't know what it was. All night long the music had raged inside him, bursting his mind. 'I'm trying to understand', he said. 'It's so difficult. How can we get to hear it properly?' She knelt beside him. He stroked her hair. His eyes ran over the olive tones of her skin.

'Deep down', she whispered, 'deep in my heart, I don't think it matters, you see.'

He held her gaze, surprised. 'What do you mean?'

She did not answer immediately. Slowly and steadily, she told him how the solution had finally come to her. 'It doesn't matter, at all. We don't need to hear it like that. Nobody needs to hear it. What matters is that we've found it. That you have found it, Daniel.'

He listened carefully, widening his eyes at the thought of such simplicity. What would they do with it then? Keep it in the attaché case for ever? Hide it away, just as the letters were hidden before, and everything else?

'It's the end of the search', said Lydia. 'We have done all we can. And now you have found the concerto.' Lydia was filled with emotion. 'Don't you see? The manuscript has been found, and "you" have heard the concerto. You have heard it in your mind. Haven't you said so yourself. It plays itself, over and over, just for you! It's you that must hear it, Daniel. It's for you to *feel*.'

'And I do feel it, Lydia. I do.' He put his hands to his face. 'It's like a memory ... a sea ... each wave its own.' He rested his head on the back of the chair and closed his eyes. For a while they were silent.

'It's over', Lydia whispered. 'I think it's ended.'

Daniel shook his head. He knew there was more. What it would be he could not say. But again, they must wait.

RESTING PLACE

Snow fell fast by the window. Daniel had gone to his meeting in Leeds. The evening was heavy and sombre, just as the afternoon had been earlier. All day long Lydia had felt that something would happen. It was almost as if she were being followed, a pace or two behind. The scents of sandalwood and saffron entered the rooms of the cottage, and left them as quickly. Lydia breathed them in and the fragrances impressed themselves on her mind as a searching distant music might that could find no hold. She relaxed herself and tried to put logs on the fire, though her mind abounded with feelings. Someone knocked on the door. Pale and drawn, Miranda stood in her dancing clothes and her silver shoes. She seemed delirious and steadied herself on the doorframe.

'You'd better come in', said Lydia, directing her to the fire. Miranda's fists were clenched. Her hair was matted with snow. Lydia thought her calmer now than she'd been before, though she seemed more humbled and weary. She went to sit by the fire, as she'd done previously, her thin bones falling in. Lydia perceived she had come to the end of her fight. Miranda, it seemed, was fading away. With her eyelids down, she said to Lydia, in what seemed like a different voice: 'I'm going to be better now. I've been trying hard to be bad. I thought it was easier.'

Minutes passed. Nothing particular marked them. It seemed that a gentler spirit possessed Miranda now. One that might heal. The firelight sent a milky shimmer across her skin. 'I'm going to be good', she said. 'I shall find my father and tell him.'

Lydia wanted to draw her close and comfort her. The bright eyes searched her own.

'Do you think I can do it?' she asked. 'I could really try.'

'Of course', said Lydia.

Seeing Miranda like this, determined to change her life, brought fresh hope. She was cold and debilitated, but at least she was still in Knaresborough where her father might find her.

'But I don't like the thoughts', she said, her eyes staring wildly. She put her hands to her eyes and hummed again the same little tune as before. Lydia thought it must have been something from childhood. She began to murmur again. 'Oh, how I hate the dark, and the light. And the dark and the light again. I hate the days! They are so, so long, and I never know what to do with them.'

Lydia drew the curtains on the cold evening.

'Don't', said Miranda, raising her hand quickly. 'You mustn't close me inside.' She went to the window to look out, though the glass was covered in snow. 'Some people', she said, her eyes filling with tears, 'think we can live after death.' She glanced at Lydia. 'But you have to be good for that.' She bent her head. 'I'm not good, you know.'

Lydia's thoughts raced on anxiously. What could she do for Miranda now? This poor lost girl. She could run her a bath. She could feed her. At least there was that.

'My father's here', she whispered. 'Your brother told me. He cooked me some food at the boathouse.' She shook her head in a busy determined way. 'But my father wants me to see the doctor again. I won't. I won't.' She screwed up her eyes, as if she might hide herself away.

Lydia saw the needle marks on her white mysterious skin. The little blisters, barely healed, still raging with pain.

'They write things down, you see', Miranda said. 'They don't let me see. And all the time they are talking.' She gazed at Lydia sadly. 'You wouldn't like it to happen to you, would you?'

Lydia sighed and sat down. Miranda needed help and attention. She needed a place to live, some regular food and decent clothing. Her shoe was broken too. The heel, Lydia saw, was almost off. 'They're only trying to help you', she told her gently.

Miranda was murmuring again. 'I'm searching for something', she said. She removed some grass from between her toes. One of them seemed to be bleeding. 'I just can't find it though. But I keep on looking.'

'What is it that you want?' asked Lydia. The familiar room, with its low ceiling, its thick stone walls, and the firelight darting its normal usual shadows, seemed suddenly quite unearthly. Miranda's world, Lydia knew, was fragmenting about her. The girl was thinner, dirtier now, she was losing herself in her sadness.

'I'm not really sure', she said moodily. 'It's a sort of music, I think. There's a music, you know, that can put things right. Sometimes, if you are very quiet, you can hear it.' She trembled and looked about warily. A little tattered creature lost in the firelight. 'I shall find it though, soon.'

Lydia saw that her eyes had gone to the dresser, and then the concerto, which she and Daniel an hour before had left on the top. 'What have you got?' she asked, going to see.

Lydia's heart beat wildly. Gathering the music quickly, she put it in the attaché case, and then in the drawer, closing it loudly.

'What are you hiding?' Miranda asked suspiciously, narrowing her eyes. 'Why won't you show me?'

'It's nothing important', said Lydia, her cheeks paling. 'It's something I'm writing.'

'Are you writing things about me?' Miranda asked, her eyes flashing.

'No, no, no', said Lydia, her back to the drawer. 'Of course not. I'm writing a book about castles.' She drew some pictures out of the drawer then handed them over. 'These are the things I'm talking about in my writing.'

Miranda pushed them away. 'I don't want to look', she said. 'I don't like castles. And why are you showing me dungeons? Do you want to keep me a prisoner?' Wringing her hands, she glanced at the door anxiously. 'You'd better not lock it.' Her quick little breaths, Lydia thought, tore at her chest.

'Let me run you a bath', said Lydia. 'It will make you feel better.'

Miranda moved close to the fire and loosened a little. The veil of her strength was falling away from her fast. Lydia went upstairs.

Having turned on the water, she went for the clothes she had found for Miranda before, though she had not worn them. This time, Lydia decided, she would; she could not wear her sequinned dress any longer. It was torn and dirty. Also she needed some new shoes. As she went to a cupboard, she heard the door at the front of the house crashing about in the wind. She hurried downstairs to look.

Miranda had gone. The door was open. The baubles on the Christmas tree cavorted about. The cards on the strings swayed madly. Reaching for her coat, she threw it on and rushed outside.

She searched the path by the river. She searched the trees. The boathouse. Even the boats. The light was fading quickly. It was hard to see. She moved on down the paths and between the rocks, slipping about in the snow. Miranda was nowhere in sight.

Presently she met Jeremy sauntering home. Through the snowflakes she called to him: 'Have you seen Miranda? She came to the house and has gone. She looked so sick and feverish. I should never have left her alone.'

He stopped, lifting his head from the deep sleep of his thoughts. 'Miranda? No, she hasn't passed here', he said, suddenly vigilant.

'I ran her a bath', said Lydia. 'I should never have gone upstairs.'

Jeremy ran through the trees.

Walking on, Lydia met Miranda's father, stumbling along in the snow. 'Have you seen my daughter?' he asked. Snowflakes tumbled about him. 'I know she was here earlier. Somebody saw her today. She's hiding somewhere, I know it. She isn't well, you see.'

'She's been with me', said Lydia. 'She came to the cottage.' Lydia's eyes searched the distance. Nothing. They stood by the roadside, longing for Miranda's face to appear. The trees were restless. The wind moaned high in their boughs. 'I went to run her a bath.'

Miranda's father murmured something, shaking his head. 'I really must find her. Oh, I must.' An orange light from the darkening sky coloured the path in an almost yellow glow. He gazed upwards. Snowflakes on the dark lids of his eyes melted down his unhappy face. For a moment he looked, Lydia thought, like an old and twisted tree, his features gnarled and knotted up with pain.

'Oh', he whispered. 'Oh, you shouldn't have left her. This is how she is, you see. You ought to have kept her by you. Why, the child is deranged.' His eyes were wide and bewildered.

'I'm sorry', Lydia said. 'I'm so sorry.'

'Never mind my dear', he said. 'What's done is done.' He patted her back and smiled. 'We'll find her soon. I am quite determined. I'm doing it with a vengeance, see. With a vengeance!' And he raised a fist at the sky.

Lydia had learned from Daniel that this was something Miranda's father did. But the girl's light splintered about him. Even her shadow.

'She might be hiding', he said, glancing about. 'She does it sometimes.' He stood for a moment thinking. 'We must search the trees and crevices. Why, she will crawl into the very cleft of hell if I am not quick!' He bent his head, shaking it slowly, his mouth opening and closing like that of a fish.

'She might be in one of the boats!' called Jeremy running towards them.

'I looked before!' called Lydia.

From the crest of the trees came a terrified cry, 'Help us somebody! Help us! For God's sake somebody come!'

Jeremy turned and ran. Lydia followed, Miranda's father behind. 'Over there!' cried Lydia. 'By the side of the library!'

It seemed that time was slipping away. Sliding out of their grasp. And in it Lydia sensed the echoes of something departing. She hurried with Miranda's father, offering him comfort by holding on to his arm.

'Oh, it's useless!' somebody shrieked. 'What can we do?'

A woman sat on the bank, almost hysterical. 'She's thrown herself in!' She pointed into the river. 'That's where she did it. There! A little girl with long white hair!'

In a grey anorak and wellington boots, the woman stood shivering. Her friend had gone for the phone.

'She's in the river!' cried Lydia, as Jeremy found them. 'She's jumped in there.' Lydia pointed, her eyes searching wildly.

Jeremy's eyes scrutinised the inky water. He was breathless from running. He threw off his jacket quickly. Within seconds the greedy gulp of the river had gathered him in. Miranda's father gazed at the membrane of water, holding his daughter beneath it. He walked about in circles, scratching his head. 'My daughter, my daughter', he chanted. 'I forgive you this terrible deed. You were never taught to hurt yourself, like this. Oh, the world is a wicked place, my pet. Come back, sweet child. Come back. I promise you, you will never suffer again.'

Lydia waited, the cold biting into her. What was Jeremy doing down there? The water was freezing. *Oh, Jeremy, please come up! Come up!*

'What's going on?' asked Daniel running towards them. Having returned from his meeting, he'd come to find them. Lydia grabbed on to his arm, and drew him close. 'Jeremy's in the river', she cried. 'Miranda's thrown herself in. He's gone to rescue her.' A wind was up. Lydia bent to the water, calling into it. 'Jeremy, Jeremy, hurry!'

Daniel stood bewildered. What was happening? Beside him a woman wept. An ambulance was coming, she said. It would soon be with them.

'God help them!' Daniel said. 'The water is foul with cold.'

There wasn't much he could do just then. The evening was darkening. The wind grew worse. He knelt at the water's edge. Jeremy surfaced, then went back. Miranda's father walked about in faster and faster circles.

Suddenly, with a mighty slap, Jeremy's arm reached out, his muscles flexing, his fingers searching the bank. Daniel grasped his hand as his face appeared, his eyes like an animal's at a kill. He sucked on the air, then snatched his hand from Daniel's, going beneath the water again as fast as he came.

Within minutes he surfaced, breathing hard and gasping. Miranda was in the crook of his arm, purple with cold. With the hand that was free he hauled himself out.

A hushed silence fell on them as he dragged her out. All that everyone wanted now was the quickening sound of Miranda's breath in that frenzied air. She lay on the bank. Her father knelt down beside her, taking her hand, her slender body limp and lifeless looking, her lips parted. Her face was serene. It was almost as if a lingering ache had finally left her.

Lydia leaned over her, taking weed from her hair and mouth. No movement stirred in her wraithlike body. Jeremy knelt beside her quickly. He pressed his lips to the thin white mouth, offering himself again and again, pounding the frail chest hard as he dared. Seized with fear, everyone watched. Till Miranda coughed suddenly, like the rasp of a bird.

'Oh, you're a fine boy!' said Miranda's father. 'A very fine boy indeed!'

Miranda spluttered leaves and water and tiny stones from her round white mouth. Fear shrivelled beside them, and slithered away. The pillar of hope stood strong. Miranda fell to coughing again, while Jeremy held her, removing hair from her face and pieces of grit from her eyes. 'What do you think you're doing?' he said, her body loosening. The snow had stopped and the wind had lifted. He laughed briefly, glancing about for the ambulance. 'You've nearly been to the back of beyond.' Still she coughed.

'My poor baby!' her father cried. 'My poor little girl!'

And the ambulance men came then, sliding and slipping about on the snowy bank, reaching her and wrapping her up in a blanket. They lifted her on to a stretcher. Miranda's father followed them up the slope. The women turned and went down the path, making their way to the main road.

But for Jeremy's gasps and grunts, everywhere else was silent. Lydia reached for his jacket, putting it round him. 'She was holding something', Jeremy murmured, shivering. 'Heavy it was. I let it go.' His teeth chattered. Daniel gazed at the water. This was where the ghost had appeared at first. The river flowed on carelessly, its thin echoes lapping against the bank. A world of dark shapes rose and fell, circling and twisting before him. Jeremy stood up slowly, looking towards the path where he would find his way to the cottage. 'It felt like a thin leather case', he murmured. It was all so strange and unreal, he thought as he left them. He was glad he had saved Miranda. The knowledge of it made him tender with hope.

'What?' cried Lydia, suddenly as the words broke through her thoughts. 'Did Jeremy say it felt like a leather case?' . She put her hands to her face. 'Miranda took the attaché case — Daniel, she took the concerto!'

Daniel removed his shoes quickly then threw off his jacket, diving into the water and swimming deeply.

Deep, deep down he went, where the reeds gathered in thick black clumps, and the water was murky and freezing. Small fish slid by his face. He was blind to where he was going, feeling his way, spitting the sweet sour taste of rotting leaves and fronds out of his mouth. A blue dust glowed like a mystical light in the wetness.

And as he swam it seemed that the water drew him on. Deeper and deeper he went, his hands groping and parting the reeds, till his lungs were bursting. He threaded his way through the broken branches of trees and roots, swimming as if for dear life in the thin blue light.

And suddenly he was there. His fingers alighted on something that felt like the case. He grasped the leather. He had found it at last. He had found the concerto! He folded his fingers around it. And as he did so, he found they had touched on something else. Not stone. Not wood. But *bone*. That sacred place where light lands best and finds its heart. His palms embraced the smooth skull, the shoulder blades, the tender curve of the ribs. The attaché case lay in her arms. She held it fast. He dared not budge it now.

Frozen with cold he surfaced, finding Lydia trailing her hands in the water. 'Oh, thank goodness you're there!' she cried. 'Come out! Come out!' Climbing out, he gasped, clutching his chest and choking with pain and cold. She found his jacket. Everyone else had gone. He sat there quivering with cold, the thrill of what he had found surging through him. How dark with secrets the night was. Against the snow his skin was blue and translucent. It was far from easy to tell her what he knew.

'She's in the river', he said, lifting his head slowly and searching her eyes. He stopped for a moment, the awful truth of what he'd discovered raged in his mind. Lydia reached for his hand, sticky with mud and slime. She held his fingers. 'I touched her, Lydia', he whispered. '*I felt her skeleton.*'

For a long moment, the darkness held them in silence. Daniel's voice trembled. 'The attaché case was there in her arms. The concerto was in it.' His sturdy shape in the moonlight, on the river bank, was dense and black with finality. His words were solemn with meaning. Here was an ending. And here too was a beginning. And they clung to each other, knowing that in the quietness around them was a rare and sacred peace.

'The concerto is where it belongs', Lydia murmured.

She gazed at the river, the place that had known the ghost for so many years. The fragrances of sandalwood and saffron came to them again. A thin blue light encircled them, drifting through them, then disappearing along with the scents. And as they found their way to the top of the bank, they imagined the music, dancing on hills and crags, sounding through drystone walls, charging the wind, and winding itself around the stars, cascading through time forever, and finding the limbs of lovers, wherever they are.